L

Marc Rigole
Claude Morneau Langlois

ULYSSES
TRAVEL PUBLICATIONS
Travel better... enjoy more

Editorial *Series Director and Editor:* Claude Morneau; *Project Supervisor:* Pascale Couture.

Research and Composition *Authors:* Marc Rigole, Claude-Victor Langlois.

Production *Design:* Patrick Farei (Atoll Direction); *Proofreading:* Jennifer McMorran, Sarah Kresh; *Translation:* Tracy Kendrick, Danielle Gauthier, Emmy Pahmer, Sarah Kresh; *Cartography:* André Duchesne, Patrick Thivierge (Assistant); *Layout:* Sarah Kresh.

Illustrations *Cover Photo:* Bairro Alto - Joao Paulo (Image Bank); *Interior Photos:* Câmara Municipal de Lisboa, Tibor Bognár, ENATUR, Marc Rigole; *Chapter Headings:* Jennifer McMorran; *Drawings:* Lorette Pierson, Marie-Annick Viatour.

Thanks to SODEC and the Department of Canadian Heritage for their financial support.

Distributors

AUSTRALIA:
Little Hills Press
11/37-43 Alexander St.
Crows Nest NSW 2065
☎ (612) 437-6995
Fax: (612) 438-5762

BELGIUM AND LUXEMBOURG:
Vander
Vrijwilligerlaan 321
B-1150 Brussel
☎ (02) 762 98 04
Fax: (02) 762 06 62

CANADA:
Ulysses Books & Maps
4176 Saint-Denis
Montréal, Québec
H2W 2M5
☎ (514) 843-9882, ext.2232 or
1-800-748-9171
Fax: 514-843-9448
www.ulysse.ca

GERMANY AND AUSTRIA:
Brettschneider
Fernreisebedarf
Feldfirchner Strasse 2
D-85551 Heimstetten
München
☎ 89-99 02 03 30
Fax: 89-99 02 03 31

GREAT BRITAIN AND IRELAND:
World Leisure Marketing
9 Downing Road
West Meadows, Derby
UK DE21 6HA
☎ 1 332 34 33 32
Fax: 1 332 34 04 64

ITALY:
Centro Cartografico del Riccio
Via di Soffiano 164/A
50143 Firenze
☎ (055) 71 33 33
Fax: (055) 71 63 50

NETHERLANDS:
Nilsson & Lamm
Pampuslaan 212-214
1380 AD Weesp (NL)
☎ 0294-465044
Fax: 0294-415054

SCANDINAVIA:
Scanvik
Esplanaden 8B
1263 Copenhagen K
DK
☎ (45) 33.12.77.66
Fax: (45) 33.91.28.82

SPAIN:
Altaïr
Balmes 69
E-08007 Barcelona
☎ 454 29 66
Fax: 451 25 59

SWITZERLAND:
OLF
P.O. Box 1061
CH-1701 Fribourg
☎ (026) 467.51.11
Fax: (026) 467.54.66

U.S.A.:
The Globe Pequot Press
6 Business Park Road
P.O. Box 833
Old Saybrook, CT 06475
☎ 1-800-243-0495
Fax: 1-800-820-2329

Other countries, contact Ulysses Books & Maps (Montréal), Fax: (514) 843-9448
No part of this publication may be reproduced in any form or by any means, including photocopying, without the written permission of the publisher.
© January 1998, Ulysses Travel Publications
All rights reserved. Printed in Canada
ISBN 2-89464-156-7
Canadian Cataloguing in Press see p 8

Para o viajante que chega por mar, Lisboa, vista assim de longe, ergue-se como uma bela visão de sonho, sobressaindo contra o azul vivo do céu, que o sol anima. E as cúpulas, os monumentos, o velho castelo elevam-se acima da massa das casas, como arautos distantes deste delicioso lugar, desta abençoada região

To the traveller who approaches by sea, Lisbon is, even from afar, an idyllic silhouette clearly outlined against the azure sky and gleaming in the golden sunshine. Its domes, its monuments and its ancient castles tower proudly over the houses below, as though heralding the glory of this fabulous city and of this blessed country.

Fernando Pessoa

O que o Turista deve ver
What the Tourist Should See

TABLE OF CONTENTS

PORTRAIT 13	EXPLORING 85
Geography 14	Tour A: The Rossio and
Flora 15	the Baixa 88
Brief History of Lisbon . 16	Tour B: The Castelo and
Economy 24	the Alfama 97
Politics 26	Tour C: Graça and East
Population 27	Lisbon 101
Arts and Culture 29	Tour D: The Chiado and
	the Bairro Alto ... 107
PRACTICAL INFORMATION . 41	Tour E: The Rato and
Entrance Formalities ... 41	Amoreiras 116
Portuguese Embassies,	Tour F: Marquês De Pombal,
Consulates and Tourist	Saldanha and North
Offices Abroad 42	Lisbon 118
Foreign Embassies and	Tour G: Restauradores
Consulates in	and Liberdade ... 123
Portugal 44	Tour H: Santa Catarina
Tourist Information 45	and Cais Do Sodré 127
Excursions and Guided	Tour I: Estrêla and Lapa 130
Tours 46	Tour J: Alcântara, Santo
Getting to Lisbon 47	Amaro and Belém . 133
Getting Around Lisbon . 53	Tour K: Parque Florestal
Getting Around Outside	De Monsanto 143
Lisbon 60	Tour L: Estoril to Cascais 145
Insurance 63	Tour M: Queluz to Sintra 149
Health 64	Tour N: Setúbal and
Safety and Security ... 65	Surroundings 160
Climate 67	Tour O: EXPO 98 165
Packing 69	
Mail 69	OUTDOORS 177
Telecommunications ... 70	Parks and Beaches ... 177
Money and Banking ... 72	Hiking 181
Accommodations 73	Golf 182
Restaurants and Fine	
Food 76	ACCOMMODATIONS 185
Entertainment 77	Tour A: The Rossio and
Shopping 79	the Baixa 185
Holidays 79	Tour B: The Castelo and
Sports Clubs 80	the Alfama 188
Time Zone 81	Tour C: Graça and East
Electricity 81	Lisbon 188
Women Travellers 81	Tour D: The Chiado and
Language 81	the Bairro Alto ... 189
Weights and Measures . 82	Tour E: The Rato and
Police and Emergencies . 83	Amoreiras 190
	Tour F: Marquês De Pombal,
	Saldanha and North
	Lisbon 190

Tour G: Restauradores and Liberdade 194	Tour E: The Rato and Amoreiras 258
Tour H: Santa Catarina and Cais Do Sodré 199	Tour G: Restauradores and Liberdade ... 258
Tour I: Estrêla and Lapa 199	Tour H: Santa Catarina and Cais Do Sodré 258
Tour J: Alcântara, Santo Amaro and Belém . 201	Tour I: Estrêla and Lapa 259
Tour K: Parque Florestal De Monsanto 201	Tour J: Alcântara, Santo Amaro and Belém . 262
Tour L: Estoril to Cascais 201	Tour L: Estoril to Cascais 265
Tour M: Queluz to Sintra 204	Tour M: Queluz to Sintra 265
Tour N: Setúbal and Surroundings 208	Tour N: Setúbal and Surroundings 266
	Cultural Activities 266

RESTAURANTS 211
   Tour A: The Rossio and
     the Baixa 216
   Tour B: The Castelo and
     the Alfama 219
   Tour C: Graça and East
     Lisbon 220
   Tour D: The Chiado and
     the Bairro Alto ... 220
   Tour E: The Rato and
     Amoreiras 228
   Tour F: Marquês De Pombal,
     Saldanha and North
     Lisbon 229
   Tour G: Restauradores
     and Liberdade ... 231
   Tour H: Santa Catarina
     and Cais Do Sodré 234
   Tour I: Estrêla and Lapa 235
   Tour J: Alcântara, Santo
     Amaro and Belém . 238
   Tour K: Parque Florestal
     De Monsanto 241
   Tour L: Estoril to Cascais 242
   Tour M: Queluz to Sintra 244
   Tour N: Setúbal and
     Surroundings 247

ENTERTAINMENT 251
   Tour B: The Castelo and
     the Alfama 251
   Tour D: The Chiado and
     the Bairro Alto ... 252

SHOPPING 269
   Tour A: The Rossio and
     the Baixa 269
   Tour B: The Castelo and
     the Alfama 271
   Tour C: Graça and East
     Lisbon 272
   Tour D: The Chiado and
     the Bairro Alto ... 272
   Tour E: The Rato and
     Amoreiras 275
   Tour F: Marquês De Pombal,
     Saldanha and North
     Lisbon 276
   Tour G: Restauradores
     and Liberdade ... 276
   Tour H: Santa Catarina
     and Cais Do Sodré 277
   Tour I: Estrêla and Lapa 278
   Tour J: Alcântara, Santo
     Amaro and Belém . 278
   Tour L: Estoril to Cascais 279
   Tour M: Queluz to Sintra 279

PRONUNCIATION GUIDE .. 281

PORTUGUESE-ENGLISH
   GLOSSARY 283

INDEX 291

LIST OF MAPS

Cascais	p 148
Great Discoveries of the 15th and 16th Centuries	p 21
Lisbon	p 11
Lisbon and Surroundings	p 146
Location of Suggested Tours	p 87
The Metro	p 57
Portugal	p 10
Sintra	p 155
Tour A: The Rossio and the Baixa	p 89
Tour B: The Castelo and the Alfama	p 99
Tour C: Graça and East Lisbon	p 103
Tour D: The Chiado and the Bairro Alto	p 109
Tour D: Bairro Alto	p 110
Tour E: The Rato and Amoreiras	p 117
Tour F: Marquês de Pombal, Saldanha and North Lisbon	p 121
Tour G: Restauradores and Liberdade	p 125
Tour H: Santa Catarina and Cais do Sodré	p 129
Tour I: Estrêla and Lapa	p 131
Tour J: Alcântara, Santo Amaro and Belém	p 135
Tour J: Belém	p 137
Tour K: Parque Florestal de Monsanto	p 144
Tour O: EXPO 98	p 167
Urban Zones	p 35
Where is Lisbon?	p 9

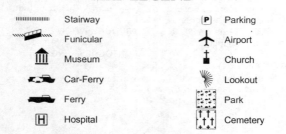

MAP LEGEND

|||||||||||	Stairway	P	Parking
~~	Funicular	✈	Airport
🏛	Museum	✝	Church
🚢	Car-Ferry	☀	Lookout
⛴	Ferry	⬚	Park
H	Hospital	✝✝✝	Cemetery

TABLE OF SYMBOLS

🏛	Ulysses favourite
☎	Telephone number
ᴪ	Fax number
≡	Air conditioning
⊗	Ceiling fan
≈	Pool
ℜ	Restaurant
⊛	Whirlpool
ℝ	Refrigerator
K	Kitchenette
△	Sauna
☺	Exercise room
tv	Colour television
pb	Private bathroom
sb	Shared bathroom
ps	Private shower
½ b	Half-board (lodging + 2 meals)
bkfst	Breakfast

ATTRACTION CLASSIFICATION

★	Interesting
★★	Worth a visit
★★★	Not to be missed

HOTEL CLASSIFICATION

Unless otherwise indicated, the prices in the guide
are for one room in the high season,
double occupancy, including breakfast.

RESTAURANT CLASSIFICATION

$	1600 ESC or less
$$	1600 ESC to 3200 ESC
$$$	3200 ESC to 5000 ESC
$$$$	5000 ESC to 7000 ESC
$$$$$	more than 7000 ESC

Unless otherwise indicated, the prices in the guide are for a
meal for one person, including taxes, but not drinks and tip.

All prices in this guide are in Portuguese escudos.

Help make Ulysses Travel Guides even better!

The information contained in this guide was correct at press time. However, mistakes can slip in, omissions are always possible, places can disappear, etc. The authors and publisher hereby disclaim any liability for loss or damage resulting from omissions or errors.

We value your comments, corrections and suggestions, as they allow us to keep each guide up to date. The best contributions will be rewarded with a free book from Ulysses Travel Publications. All you have to do is write us at the following address and indicate which title you would be interested in receiving (see the list at the end of guide).

**Ulysses Travel Publications
4176 Rue Saint-Denis
Montréal, Québec
Canada H2W 2M5**
www.ulysse.ca
e-mail: guiduly@ulysse.ca

Special Thanks To

José Antonio Preto da Silva (ICEP-Toronto); Maria Helena Mora and Mrs. Barlier (Office du Commerce et du Tourisme du Portugal in Paris); M. Gomes and Maria de Lourdes Braancamp Mancellos (ENATUR); Fernanda Guedes Machado, Lídia Monteiro and Ana Cerreira (ICEP-Lisboa); Maria Paula Vinhais (Carris); Maria do Rosário Taurino (CP); Helena Taborda (Metropolitano); Paula Nascimento, José António dos Santos and Jorge Cruz (Lisboa Turismo); Luís Hespanha (Turismo Costa do Estoril); Maria João Brandão (Palácio Nacional de Sintra); Isabel Sousa, Miguel Silvano and Luís Esgonnière Carneiro (EXPO 98); Catherine Nappert and Yves Drouin; Isabelle Miralles and Patrick Pinzelli; Vicky Cheang. Finally, particular thanks to Judith Lefebvre, Virginie Bonneau and Bruno Salléras for their contributions and support.

Canadian Cataloguing in Publication Data
Rigole, Marc, 1956-
    Lisbon
    (Ulysses travel guides)
    Translation of: Lisbonne
    Includes index.
    ISBN 2-89464-156-7
1. Lisbon (Portugal) - Guidebooks. I. Langlois, Claude-Victor II. Title.
III. Series.
DP757.R5313 1997   914.69'4250444   C97-941449-0

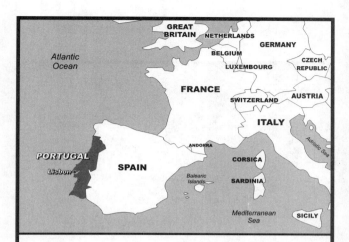

Where is Lisbon?

Portugal
Capital: Lisboa (Lisbon)
Language: Portuguese
Population: 10,800,000 inhab.
Area: 89,000 km²

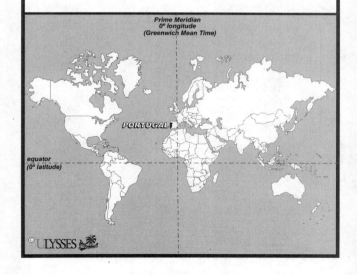

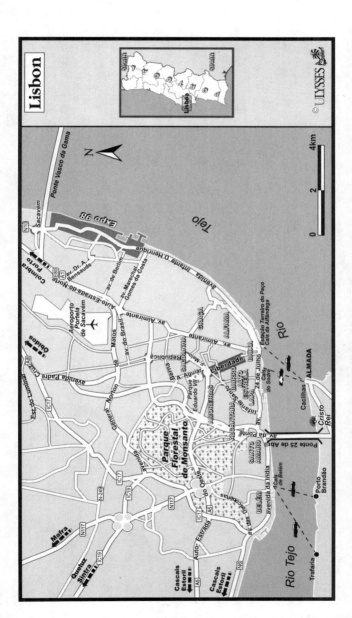

PORTRAIT

Portugal occupies a special place in the history of the Western world. Located at the edge of the known world for thousands of years, it contributed in a dramatic fashion to the widening of that world's horizons, sometimes with the dreadful fear of a wizard's apprentice, like when Catholic expeditions set out to expel demons from the Madeira archipelago, newly discovered by fishermen (1420). Afterward, the country seemed to know no limits, sharing the world with Spain by papal decree and colonizing Brazil, a territory ten times its size! Portugal's unique role in history is reflected all over the country, making a trip here a veritable journey through the ages.

Lisbon (Lisboa), home to nearly 2,000,000 inhabitants, lies at the mouth of the majestic Tagus (Tejo) River, which flows into the Atlantic Ocean. Strolling through the different parts of Lisbon, visitors will discover that this city has many faces — at least as many as it does hills. The Castelo is suffused with Medieval imagery, while the architecture of the Armoreiras shopping centre evokes a futuristic world. The "village" of the Alfama offers a glimpse of what life is like in the confused jumble of a crowded North African medina, while the terrace in Parque Edouardo VII and its view of the Tagus epitomize a "noble" vision of the city. If you thought you'd stumbled upon a quaint artists colony while exploring the little streets of the

Bairro Alto, stop by at night when the nightclubs, bars and restaurants fill up with trend-setters decked out in the latest fashions and styles. Such is present-day Lisbon, swept up, like the rest of the country, by *movida*. Since being designated "European Cultural Capital" for the year 1994, the newly revamped city has been undergoing a major overhaul, and is proudly demonstrating its penchant for innovation. Becoming more and more beautiful by the day, the Daughter of the Tagus is striving to recapture her former glory, to once again be the envy of all of Europe. Lisbon is also gearing up to welcome visitors from around the world when it hosts the 1998 World Fair.

Imagine your dream world: a verdant land with an abundance of vegetation from the four corners of the earth, with a baroque palace, a romantic *quinta*, fashionable beaches, fine golf courses and Lisbon, all close at hand. Well, your dream world is a reality in Costa de Lisboa. In this veritable playground for Lisboans, you can escape the city for a few days of relaxation, or perhaps stay in one of the nearby *pousadas*, in Queluz or Palmela, or at the beach resorts of Cascais or Estoril. And don't miss Sintra and the surrounding area, where hikers can head off on spectacular trails lined with exotic, twisting vegetation. Once in Sintra, why not make the pilgrimage to the end of Europe and head for Cabo de Roca, if only to say you have tread upon at least one of the continent's extremities! Finally, in this history-laden region, don't forget Palmela with its lovely Santiago monastery, now a *pousada*.

GEOGRAPHY

Excluding the islands of Madeira and the Azores, Portugal covers an area of 89,000 square kilometres, and is bordered by Spain to the north and the east, and the Atlantic to the west and the south. To reach the rest of Europe by land, you must pass through Spain. Portugal has always been linked to Europe historically, although it has often cut itself off from the continent; in World War II, for example, it was one of the few countries to remain neutral.

The only thing that sets Portugal apart geographically is its proximity to the ocean. Otherwise, it resembles the rest of the Iberian peninsula, which it shares with Spain due to a combination of historical circumstances and also, perhaps, because of the distinctive character of its inhabitants. The landscape and terrain, however, are more varied here than in Spain and change more often, even over short distances.

No part of this oblong country, which measures 560 kilometres from north to south, lies more than 220 kilometres from the sea. No peak reaches higher than 2000 metres; north of the Tagus (Tejo), the land is fairly hilly, made up mainly of old plateaus that shifted when the Pyrenees and the Alps were formed. There is still some seismic activity here, but nothing comparable to the earthquake that destroyed Lisbon in 1755. Generally speaking, the altitude increases from south to north, the closer you get to Spain. The region south of the Tagus is relatively flat.

There are three major rivers in Portugal: the Tagus, which rises in Spain, (where it is known as the Tajo) and flows past Lisbon; the Douro (pronounced "dooro"), which runs alongside Porto; and the Minho, which marks the northern border between Portugal and Spain.

FLORA

In addition to its varied terrain, Portugal features a diverse range of soils and climates, and therefore a wide assortment of flowers. Long considered the garden of Europe, Portugal is home to more than 2,700 species of plants. It is the world's leading exporter of cork, the outer bark of the famous cork-oak, which can be found throughout the country, especially in the Alentejo, south of the Tagus. A number of species, such as the eucalyptus, have been successfully imported here from Africa and South America. The maritime pine has also been widely planted as part of a major reforestation program, with the result that Portugal is much greener and boasts many more flowers than Spain (another contributing factor is the generally more humid Portuguese climate).

Portugal is often classified as a Mediterranean country, even though its shores are not washed by that sea. As far as its climate, flora and fauna are concerned however, Portugal displays many Mediterranean characteristics.

BRIEF HISTORY OF LISBON

Although both the Phoenicians and the Greeks set up trading posts at the mouth of the Tagus, few traces of these two civilizations remain. To this day, historians disagree about the origin of the name *Olisipo* (sometimes spelled *Alis Ubbo* or *Alissipo*), which was apparently used to designate this area. According to some, it was an early form of the city's present name. Next came the Romans, who invaded the Iberian Peninsula and founded a number of towns here, including Felicitas Julia (named after Julius Caesar), which was built on the site now occupied by the Castelo. The residents of Lisbon thus became Roman citizens. Felicitas Julia never became an important city, however. Toward the 4th century, the barbarian invasions that swept through Europe marked the end of the powerful Roman empire, and by 458 AD, the Visigoths had taken over the city. Thanks to a relatively long period of peace, the Visigoths played an important role in Lisbon's development, most notably, perhaps, by building the city's first large-scale fortifications. Despite these defensive measures, a second invading force, the Moors, managed to take over the city in 716 AD. Lisbon continued to grow and prosper under Muslim rule, and new fortifications were erected (see p 97). Nevertheless, in 1147, when it already had a population of 15,000, the city was conquered one last time (not including the much later Spanish period and a brief French occupation) by Afonso I, with the help of crusaders en route to the Holy Land. The Flemish, Normans, English and many others thus participated in capturing the city. Lisbon was elevated to the rank of capital by Afonso III in 1255, and despite an earthquake in 1344 and a thwarted Spanish attack in 1384 (whose failure can be partially attributed to the fortifications still standing today, built in 1373), it grew rapidly and firmly established its role as a royal city.

Throughout the 15th century, the capital became more and more prosperous as new territories (Madeira, the coasts of Africa, Brazil, etc.) and the route to India were discovered. The support of the rulers of these regions and the ingenuity of Portuguese navigators (new navigation techniques, the invention of the caravel, etc.) enabled Lisbon to become the capital of a vast kingdom. All sorts of palaces, monasteries and churches were erected here, making this one of the most envied cities in Europe, renowned for its Manueline architecture. In 1527, however, Lisbon was hit by the first of a series of catastrophes when the plague wiped out a large portion of its population. In 1531, the city was seriously damaged by an earthquake. Then, around 1569, the plague swept through the region again. Finally, upon losing its last king, the country was invaded by Spain and forced to give up its autonomy.

Starting in 1640, when the country regained its independence, and especially after gold was discovered in Brazil, Lisbon enjoyed a new era of prosperity. Many prestigious buildings, such as the Mosteiro dos Jerónimos, bear witness to this time. Once again, however, these golden days were destined to be short-lived.

November 1, 1755 marked the beginning of the city's decline. On that black day in Lisbon's history, a terrible earthquake destroyed three-quarters of the city in just a few seconds. To make matters worse, the working-class neighbourhoods in those years consisted mainly of wooden houses, so the huge fire that followed the earthquake reduced some areas to ashes, killing large numbers of Lisboans. This catastrophe created such a stir in Europe that Voltaire devoted a chapter to it in *Candide*. In spite of all its misfortune, Lisbon the Proud refused to take its fate lying down. Thanks to the brilliant Marquês de Pombal, it picked itself back up again. The ingenious reconstruction of the Baixa turned the city into one of the most modern capitals in Europe. Regardless of this achievement, however, Lisbon's era of prosperity was clearly over, and the 19th century ushered in a slow period of decline. Portugal's gradual loss of its colonies and international influence was to the benefit of other European powers, leaving the country mired in stagnation for many years.

From the beginning of the 20th century until the establishment of the Salazar regime in 1933, the capital was the scene of numerous revolts and outbreaks of violence, which did little to further its development. The long period of dictatorship that followed ended up stifling the city's dynamic spirit and isolating it from the rest of the world. Portugal did not take part in World War II, and a large portion of its population emigrated to the United States. The enormous statue of Cristo Rei, looking out over the city from atop its ridiculous stilts and opening its arms wide in a protective gesture, is a perfect example of the mawkishness of this era. It was erected as a gesture of thanks for the city's having been spared the great upheavals of the Second World War. Despite the construction of the magnificent Ponte 25 de Abril (formerly known as Ponte Salazar) and a few horrible Stalinist-style buildings, both the city and its population continued to decline. On April 25, 1974, however, tired of the dismal atmosphere hanging over them, the people of Lisbon rediscovered their taste for new ideas and democracy, and Portugal's entry into the European Economic Community in 1986 helped put Lisbon back on a par with the major European capitals.

A Few Important Dates in Portugal's History

- Around 500 BC the Celts invade the Iberian Peninsula. The union of the vanquishers and the vanquished leads to the birth of a new people, known as the Celtiberians.

- Around 150 BC, the Romans have conquered the peoples living along the Tagus. A significant part of present-day Portugal's national character can be traced back to the Romans' lengthy occupation of the country (from the 2nd century BC to the 5th century AD). The Latin language and culture linked Portugal to Europe, while the construction of a road running from north to south, with perpendicular offshoots leading to the coast, seems to have launched the country's development towards the Atlantic. Several important cities are also founded during this period: Lisbon (then known as Felicitas Julia), Évora (Ebora), Coimbra (Conimbriga) and Portus and Cale, located on either side of the Rio Douro. The last two are the source of the name Portucale, which later became Portugal.

- Around the 5th century, the Swabians and the Visigoths assume almost total control of the Iberian territory.

- In 711, the Tāriq Ibn Ziyad the Berber crosses the Strait of Gibraltar and, taking advantage of the weakened position of the Visigoth kingdom, hobbled by internal quarrelling, succeeds in invading the Iberian peninsula.

- In 838, with the help of the House of Burgundy, the crown of Castile is reinstated in Braga and soon after Porto. In 1093, the territory between the Minho and the Mondego is granted to Henry of Burgundy and becomes the county of Portucale.

- In 1139, following a victory against the Muslims in an area known as Ourique, Afonso Henriques (son of Henry of Burgundy) declares himself King Afonso I of Portugal. At this point, his realm covers only the northern part of modern-day Portugal.

- It is not until Afonso III seized Faro (1249) and the Moors were driven out of the Algarve once and for all (1250) that the country takes its present shape.

Henry the Navigator (1394-1460)

Henry the Navigator (or Henrique O Navigador as he is known is Portugal), perhaps the country's most illustrious prince ever, would become the real driving force behind the country's colonial expansion. After settling in Raposeira (Algarve), he built the fortress of Sagres on a peninsula, and proceeded to amass numerous documents on subjects like navigation, astrology and cartography. He thus created a veritable research facility for navigators, referred to by some as the School of Sagres. The studies conducted here prompted a craze for discovery that spread throughout Europe. Such eminent figures as Christopher Columbus, Vasco de Gama and many others obtained all sorts of information here. Although he did not actually take part in any expeditions, Henry surrounded himself with celebrated navigators and scientists in an effort to develop new methods of navigation. As a result, Gil Eanes was able to round Cape Bojador (Western Sahara) and begin exploring the coast of Africa in 1434. Thanks to the prince's exceptional administrative skills, the Portuguese were also able to set up efficient colonial trading posts, thus ensuring their country a predominant role in Africa. Later, improved shipbuilding techniques (the development of a new type of boat known as a caravel) enabled the "masters of the sea" to press on with their explorations, leading to the discovery of new riches and unprecedented territorial expansion.

- Dom Fernando I dies in 1383. His only heir is his daughter Dona Beatriz, wife of the King of Castile. Spain reclaims its sovereignty over Portugal.

- In 1385, the Cortès, an assembly representing the three orders of society (the nobility, the clergy and the bourgeoisie), designates João, Grand Master of Aviz and illegitimate son of Pedro I, as the only legitimate successor to the Crown; he ascends the throne as João I of Portugal. The disgruntled Castilians immediately set out to conquer the territory and take their due, but João I emerges triumphant after the historic battle of Aljubarrota.

- Henry the Navigator, or Henrique O Navigador as he is known is Portugal, is born in 1394.

- Discovery of the Madeira Islands in 1419, the Azores in 1427, Cape Verde in 1445, Guinea in 1446 and São Tome e Príncipe in 1471.

- The Treaty of Tordesillas is signed in 1494. Spain and Portugal must thus limit their power to either side of a line dividing the world into two distinct parts (see map).

- Discovery of the Cape of Good Hope in 1488 and Greenland in 1492.

- With the help of Manuel I, Vasco de Gama, the navigator, discovers the maritime route to India in 1497, while Pedro Alvares Cabral reaches the shores of Brazil in 1500. A great patron of the Arts and Sciences, Manuel I inspires a rich and unique style of architecture proper to Portugal later termed the "Manueline style".

- Sebastião I dies in 1578 during an expedition to Morocco. Once again the Portuguese kingdom returns to the Spanish, the only successors to the crown. Portugal is integrated into the Spanish empire as of 1580.

- In 1640, the Duke of Bragança is brought to power and named King João IV of Portugal. Spain, coping with rivalries from other great powers (mostly France and England) acknowledges Portugal's regained independence in 1668. Though the House of Bragança was one of Portugal's most

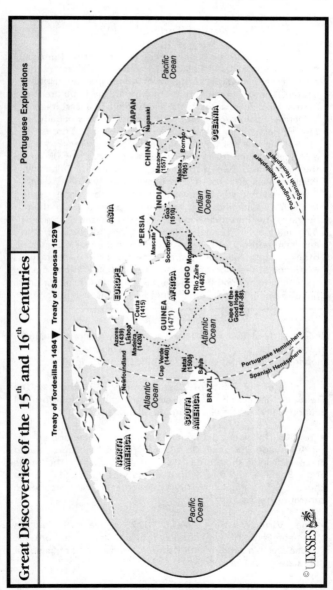

The Treaty of Tordesillas (1494)

It began to irritate the Spanish more and more that Portugal had discovered the African coast and established trading posts there, increasing its sphere of influence to an alarming degree. Then, rubbing salt in the wound, the Pope granted Portugal exclusive rights to its discoveries. To assert its own influence, Spain succeeded, with the help of the papacy, in forcing Portugal to sign a treaty. The Treaty of Tordesillas (1494), endorsed by Pope Alexander VI, required Portugal and Spain to limit their power to either side of a line dividing the world into two distinct parts (see map). Originally, Portugal was entitled to take possession of any new land discovered within 100 leagues west of the Cape Verde Islands. Dissatisfied with the limits imposed upon them, however, the Portuguese managed to extend the distance to 370 leagues. This later enabled them to discover the immense territory of Brazil. According to some, Portuguese officials were already secretly aware of the country's existence at the time of the final negotiations! In any case, the treaty confirmed Portugal's role as a great explorer and gave the country a disproportionate amount of influence.

enduring dynasties (1640-1910), its only historical legacy, according to some, is a series of mediocre, unambitious monarchs with little concern for their country's interests.

- Signing of the Treaty of Westminster in 1654 and then the Treaty of Methuen in 1703, which links England and Portugal economically, to the disadvantage of the latter.

- In 1807, following the French Revolution, Spain and France jointly invade Portugal. Dom João VI and his court flee to Brazil, remaining there until 1821. Portugal is left in the hands of the Spanish, and then with the Treaty of Paris in 1814, the English, who, thanks to trade agreements, take economic control of the country.

- João VI returns from exile in 1822. He leaves behind his oldest son Pedro IV, who not only refuses to return to Portugal, but declares himself Emperor Pedro I of Brazil, and brings about the colony's independence.

- João VI dies in 1826, thus ushering in a long period of instability, during which a power struggle erupts between the late king's two sons (Pedro IV, now Pedro I of Brazil, and Miguel), each of whom symbolizes a different political trend. After a brief return to absolutism under Miguel (1828-1834), Pedro IV manages to seize power with the help of France and England. The period that follows is a mixture of revolts and uprisings, with intervals of relative stability. Although these are fairly dark years, some important progress is made in the realm of human rights, namely the abolition of both the death penalty in 1867 and slavery.

- In the face of growing popularity of republican sentiments, the monarchy launches a terrible campaign of repression, which, along with the monarchist parties' incessant bickering, permanently tarnishes the crown's image. A clumsy armed takeover led by King Carlos I, followed by the institution of a ruthless dictatorship, seals the fate of the monarchy once and for all. On February 1, 1908, the king and the crown prince are assassinated, clearing the way for the Republic.

- Though the king's successor, Manuel II, rapidly restores democracy, the 1910 elections bring the Portuguese Republican Party (P.R.P) to power. On October 5, 1910, the Republic is proclaimed. The country's last king goes into exile in England, dying there in 1932 with no descendants.

- From 1910 to 1926, a rapid succession of no less than 45 governments, two coups d'États (1915 and 1917) and the country's entry into the war in 1916 weaken its political and economic institutions.

- Taking advantage of a coup d'État, General Antonio de Oliveira Salazar joins the military government in 1926. After much political manoeuvring, he becomes prime minister in 1932, and installs a dictatorial regime, which lasts until 1974.

- On April 25, 1974, a number of young officers belonging to the M.F.A. (Armed Forces Movement), a previously unknown movement, rise up under the leadership of Ottelo Saraiva de Carvalho. Backed by the democratic wing of the army, which is in favour of change, they take over all strategic locations in the capital. The dictatorship falls within a few hours. Immediately afterward, a junta is placed in power, with the promise that free elections will be held and all political prisoners released. Tired of so many years of stagnation, the people joyfully welcome the soldiers of democracy in the streets of Lisbon. Thousands turn out to show their support, offering the men carnations as a symbolic gesture. A carnation in the barrel of a gun remains to this day the most striking image of this day of revolution, which later comes to be known as the Flower Revolution.

- On January 1, 1986, Portugal officially joins the European Economic Community.

- On August 1988, a terrible fire ravages the historic neighbourhood of Chiado, in Lisbon.

- The escudo is introduced into the European Monetary System in April, 1992.

- In 1994, to celebrate the 600th anniversary of the birth of Henry the Navigator, Lisbon is named European Cultural Capital. The same year, the General Assembly of the United Nations declares 1998 "International Year of the Oceans" and Portugal as host country for the last World Exposition of the century.

ECONOMY

Portugal's gross domestic product per resident is among the lowest in the European Economic Community (EEC), higher only than that of Greece. In terms of purchasing power, it is $12,850, while in neighbouring Spain this figure rises to $14,275. By comparison the GDP expressed as personal purchasing power is $20,000 in France, $21,000 in Canada, $26,600 in the United States and $18,300 in the United Kingdom.

By contrast, Portugal enjoys one of the lowest unemployment rates in the EEC: 7.2%. While far from the total employment that existed during the second half of the 1980s, this is a perfectly respectable rate compared to 22.6% unemployment in Spain, 11.7% in France or 8.5% in Great Britain.

After joining the EEC in 1986, Portugal experienced a formidable period of economic growth as a result of increased trade with EEC member nations. Portugal has also benefitted from EEC credit which has contributed to major infrastructure projects such as roadwork and restoration. An impressive railroad construction site, also funded by the EEC, is still underway and can be seen beneath the Ponte de 25 Abril. These EEC grants represent between two and four percent of the country's annual GNP.

At the beginning of the 1990s, Portugal's economic growth slowed. This phenomenon has been attributed to the extreme economic rigidity imposed by leftist governments since 1976, which created a system so inflexible that the constitution had to be amended to allow privatization of state-owned companies. Since 1995, however, economic growth has regained strength and now hovers at rates of about 2.5%. An excellent student, Portugal will succeed in bringing its public sector deficit below the fatal threshold of 3% of GDP, the cut-off set by the Maastricht Treaty as a condition of attaining the common European monetary unit, the famous Euro-dollar.

Inflation has also been reined in, falling from more than 13% in 1990 to a rate projected by government forecasts of less than 2.5% in 1997.

Portugal's principal clients and suppliers are the members of the European Community, which account for three quarters of the country's dealings in both cases. Its most important clients are France, Germany and Great Britain; its suppliers, Germany, Spain and France. Astonishingly, commerce with the Portuguese-speaking countries of Africa, all former colonies, which represented up to 25% of Portugal's international trade in the late 1960s, has dwindled to a mere 2%.

The primary industries (natural resources, agriculture and fisheries) employ a quarter of the population, but only generate 10% of the gross domestic product (GDP). This can be explained in part by the limited size of the country's farms, which has led to technological backwardness, in turn leading to low agricultural output.

The agricultural mainstays are wine, olives, wheat, corn, potatoes, tomatoes, cork and fruits of all sorts. Sheep is the most important livestock herd, with over three million head. As for energy needs, Portugal must import 20% of its electricity and all of its oil.

The manufacturing industry employs about a third of the population and generates about a third of the GDP. As this industry has never been strong in Portugal and is now undergoing profound changes world-wide, requiring more and more highly trained technical personnel, it is doubtful that the Portuguese will be able to catch up. Analysts claim that neighbouring countries create trademarks while Portugal is satisfied to manufacture products. This lack of innovation puts the country in competition with the Third World for manufacturing subcontracts. Finally, the service industries, which employ nearly half the population and generate over 50% of the GDP, are thriving due to a continued increase in tourism. Air travel has made distances much shorter, and it has become fashionable for northern Europeans to spend three or four days in Lisbon or Porto. The economic crisis of the 1980s had a negative impact on Portugal's tourist industry. The region hardest hit was the over-developed Algarve, where concrete buildings had been sprouting up unchecked for the previous two decades. Elsewhere, to visitors' advantage, the *pousada* network has fortunately continued to expand, with the restoration of abandoned heritage buildings. Tourists come mainly from Spain (4.5 million), Great Britain (1.3 million), Germany (0.8 million) and France (0.6 million).

POLITICS

In 1974, Portugal emerged from the obscurantism of Salazar with the Flower Revolution. After 48 years of dictatorship, democratic politics began to be practised here. From 1974 to 1982, the Portuguese voted Soares's socialists and Cunhal's communists in and out of office. A key figure on the political scene for 20 years, Mario Soares returned to power as prime minister in 1983, then became president in 1986. Anibal Cavaco Silva, a leader of the centre-right, has been prime minister since 1987. In 1991, both men were voted back into power—by an overwhelming majority (71%) in Mario Soares's case.

The local elections of December 1993 revealed that the population is polarized, with about 35% each for the socialists and the social-democrats. The latter party lost its majority in the general elections of 1995, and the presidential elections held in January 1996 brought to power the Socialist Jorge Sampaio.

Portugal continues to disengage itself from the Catholic Church, a transition that is still not fully completed, not even by the revolution of 1974. The new president, Sampaio, is an atheist who may continue to apply pressure in this direction in spite of the presence of Prime Minister Guterres, who is a practising Catholic. The rate of participation in Sunday mass remains 25%, but the church has acquired a television station, TVI, in an effort to restore its influence.

POPULATION

Portugal has 10,800,000 inhabitants (excluding Madeira and the Azores), with a population density of 106 inhabitants per square kilometre, therefore comparable to that of France, but half that of Great Britain. A total of only 3,000,000 people reside in the cities of Lisbon and Porto, which means that 70% of the country's population still live in rural areas or in small towns with fewer than 100,000 inhabitants. Almost 25% of Portuguese households do not have telephones, while over 10% do have personal computers.

A great many people emigrated up until the end of the Salazar regime, in the mid-1970s. As a result, over 3,000,000 Portuguese are now scattered all over the world, particularly in Brazil, France, the United States and Canada.

Although clearly on the decline, the illiteracy rate is still 15%. Accordingly, you might meet people who are unable to read something you show them or write down information for you.

In 1950, 48% of the population lived from the proceeds of agriculture; in 1990, this number had dropped to 10%. It is nonetheless important to remember that half of the Portuguese population has rural roots, although many of these people now live in cities. Agriculture, which represented 28% of the GDP in 1950, today accounts for only 8%. Life expectancy is 75 years. Infant mortality has greatly diminished in recent years, falling from 12.1 out of every 1000 births in 1989 to 7.9 per 1000 births in 1994.

The Portuguese have a few character traits that distinguish them from other Europeans. Travellers will surely appreciate knowing beforehand that most Portuguese are courteous, obliging, unaggressive and shy to the point of seeming unfriendly at first encounter. You are bound to notice the widespread *saudade*, a nostalgia that supposedly dates back to the end of the country's glorious era of exploration and colonization. Portugal's fall from power coincided with its military defeat in Morocco in 1578. King Sébastião I was killed in combat, but his body was never found. For many years, his people clung to the hope that he would return; it is said that as late as the 19th century, a significant portion of the population was still waiting for him to come back. This phenomenon is known as "Sebastianism."

Religious practice remains of central importance in Portugal, unlike other European nations. In fact, it is not uncommon to see young people in their twenties diligently attending service. This lack of curiosity about things foreign, including visitors, could be seen as a product of this conformity and of the absence of foreign influences, even at the level of cuisine – Lisbon is probably the European capital with the fewest foreign restaurants. Generally speaking, Portugal is probably the most conformist country in Western Europe. Accordingly, ancestral traditions, such as the Festa dos Tabuleiros in Tomar, have been preserved here better than anywhere else; this can prove to be an advantage for visitors. This conformity, which contemporary Portuguese author Torga calls "the creative penury of eight hundred years of litanies," is wonderfully described in his book *Portugal*.

Another earmark of Portuguese society is that even the tiniest bar in the tiniest town has a television, which seems to be left on 24 hours a day, broadcasting sports or, more often than not, Brazilian *novelas* (soap operas). These *novelas* serve as a rare example of reverse colonization: Portugal is being invaded by Brazilian culture — be it music, television, literature or even spelling. One of the Portuguese channels, SIC, even belongs to TV Globo, the Brazilian broadcasting giant. In any case, we have made a systematic effort to seek out the few television-free restaurants, cafés and bars in the country.

ARTS AND CULTURE

Architecture

Until the end of the 15th century, Portugal more or less followed the same architectural movements as the rest of Europe. At the dawn of the 16th century, however, an entirely original style emerged; it was named the **Manueline style**, after King Manuel I, who reigned from 1495 to 1521. An extension of the late Gothic style, revealing certain Muslim influences, it features complex lines and lavish ornamentation. It is worth noting that after the reconquest, many Muslims chose to stay in Portugal and adopt the Catholic religion. The artisans among them did not, however, abandon their decorative traditions.

The Manueline style was also inspired by contemporary issues. It coincided with the era of discovery, when the Portuguese ruled the sea. Accordingly, the stone used in buildings is often patterned with ropes, seaweed, nautical instruments, etc.

This style was born when the riches of America, Africa and India were being discovered. The nobility and the clergy were thus able to finance the construction of prestigious buildings, such as the Convento de Cristo in Tomar, the expansion of the Batalha monastery and the Mosteiro dos Jerónimos in Belém, which still command admiration today.

Portugal's prosperity attracted foreign artists, like French sculptor Nicolas Chantereine. Bringing news of the Renaissance, with its predilection for Roman antiquity, these individuals introduced Italian-style elements into the country's architecture. No pure, fixed style emerged, however, for Portugal had become the crossroads of the world, welcoming artists from Africa and the Orient, and letting its knights, merchants and members of religious orders draw inspiration from all they had seen elsewhere.

Portrait of Lisbon

Next, from the late 1600s to the early 1900s, came the Portuguese baroque, examples of which can be found all over, not only in churches, but also in palaces, like the one in Queluz (a part of which has been strikingly transformed into a *pousada*), and a number of charming hotels. This style continues to gain followers to this day, as evidenced by the decor of several nightclubs in Lisbon (the Alcantara Mar, the Fragil, the Kremlin, etc.). Portuguese baroque is characterized chiefly by the fanciful, extravagantly decorated gilded wood known as *talha dourada* (see box). It also features portals topped by pediments; arches and other geometric lines overlapping to form an intricate design. Toward the end of the 19th century, the baroque grew more elaborate and developed into the rococo style, one of whose characteristics is the frequent use of shells.

Talha Dourada

Talha Dourada

Talha dourada can be translated literally as "golden carving". It is an art form consisting mostly of wooden sculptures coated with golf leaf. Used individually (in statues, for instance) or in aggregate form (canopies, altars, retables, etc.) they are usually the work of several craftsmen, bringing together sculptors, painters and even architects. *Talha dourada* workshops flourished in the cities of Porto, Braga and Lisbon; they were governed in corporatist and very hierarchical fashion. Broadly promoted by the Catholic church in the Iberian peninsula, the art form served to impress and dazzle the faithful, emphasizing the special nature of religious ceremonies. Widely promoted in Portugal between 1670 and 1770, it experienced a particularly intense period during the reign of João V (1706-1750). To this day, art historians distinguish three different periods: the mannerist period, the baroque period, itself divided into two styles (the national and the Joãonian), and the rococo period. The mannerist period is characterized by decoration described as "minor". *Talhas douradas* are not there only for aesthetic reasons. Mostly geometric, they provide frames for paintings and enrich the elements without really modifying them. The only existing figurative motifs are limited to statues and to a few meagre natural motifs such as leaves. The "national" baroque period is characterized by an abundance of symbolic themes (vines, children, flowers, bunches of grapes, birds, etc.) and especially by the presence of numerous wreathed columns. Also, and this is unique to Portugal, the monstrance (a type of receptacle) is placed atop a stairway-shaped pyramidal group. The "Joãonian" baroque develops a decidedly Italian influence with a predominance of lively, exuberant scenes as a main characteristic. A multitude of faces, cherubs, birds, Atlas-like figures and harvest motifs are intertwined. King João V, enriched by the discovery of gold in his Brazilian colony, was one of the main promoters, hence the name, Joãonian baroque. Finally, the rococo period corresponds to what is known architecturally, with excessive curves and a sinuous and flamboyant decoration as its most visible elements.

Azulejos

These small ceramic tiles are found throughout Portugal, everywhere from historic buildings dating from the 15th century to restaurants in all different categories. Although definitely of Muslim origin, they were originally imported here from Spain; up until the 16th century, most of them came from Seville, and were only decorated with geometric or floral patterns. Then, around 1560, ceramists came from Anvers and began making *azulejos* in Lisbon. Their use of brushes to paint pictures on the tiles marked a shift away from the Moorish style, in which only non-representational decoration was permitted.

Surprisingly, it wasn't until the late 17th century that craftsmen began painting *azulejos* exclusively in cobalt blue, which then became extremely common, although multi-coloured tiles have come back into fashion from time to time. In the 19th century, *azulejos* began to appear on the outsides of buildings, giving certain urban areas in both Portugal and Brazil a distinctive look. The *azulejo* has naturally followed the major artistic trends, such as Romanticism, Art Deco, abstractionism, etc. Even the Lisbon metro is adorned with *azulejos*!

During the 19th century, there was a gradual shift away from the excesses of the baroque and rococo, and the neoclassical style became standard not only for official buildings, but for religious ones as well. Directly inspired by antiquity, this style is more austere and favours the use of "noble" materials, such as marble, over stucco and wood. The English introduced the Palladian style, a particular favourite of theirs, into certain northern cities, like Porto.

The Manueline style has nevertheless continued to influence Portuguese architecture to the present day. Some superb neo-Manueline palaces and villas, such as the Palace Hotel do Buçaco, have been erected in this century.

To date, over 2,500 buildings throughout the country have been classified historic monuments. A few places figure on UNESCO's list of World Heritage Sites: the monastery of Batalha, the Mosteiro dos Jerónimos in Belém, the Santa Maria monastery in Alcobaça and the historic centre of Évora.

Urban Planning

From an urban planning perspective, Lisbon can be divided into eleven areas. These zones correspond to periods of land use and help to make the fabric of the city understandable. All of these areas are discussed briefly here, even if not all of them appear on tourist's itineraries.

Zone 1: Original Lisbon

This zone that encompasses the Baixa and the Rossio and extends to the Castelo is the cradle of Lisbon, an area that was easy to access, as evidenced today by all of the wharfs, and that was easy to defend from the hill where the fort still stands. This zone, in large part destroyed by earthquake at the end of the 18th century, was rebuilt, in many cases in monumental style, and is still the object of fevered restoration work, most often successful.

Zone 2: Muslim and Working-class Lisbon

East of Baixa and behind the Castelo stretches this neighbourhood that includes the Alfama and Graça. Established a very long time ago and little affected by the earthquake, this zone has conserved its dense, often anarchic, settlement pattern.

Zone 3: Lisbon of Discovery

At the time when Portuguese navigators were pushing past the limits of the known world, Lisbon was coming out of its medieval walls and settling in Bairro Alto all the way to Armoreiras. This is the neighbourhood of the first wide avenues, of *miradouros* and of panoramic views. This is also the neighbourhood of the Sétima Colina (see p 128).

Zone 4: Elegant Lisbon

Past Barrio Alto stretches an upscale neighbourhood in which today are found many embassies and delegations. It is Lapa and Jardim da Estrela with its monumental basilica. Beyond, and with the same pattern of urban development, lies Campo Ourique.

Zone 5: Riverfront Lisbon

The old Lisbon of workers, docks and industry has been reborn of late, invaded by night by a hip crowd in search of new rhythms, new looks and new encounters.

Zone 6: Belém and Ajuda

An area of ancient settlement on the shore of the Tagus, across from the famous port of Belém which once guarded the river entrance to the city and to the country. The hills are much less densely populated and there are areas here that are still in the process of urbanization.

Arts and Culture

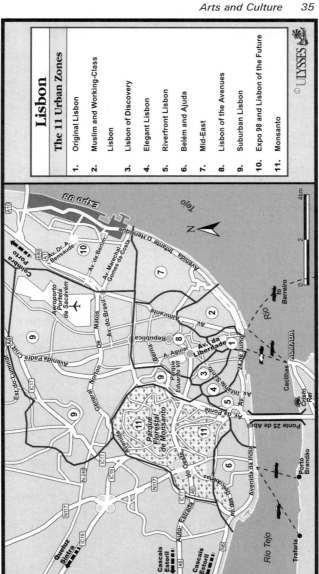

Lisbon
The 11 Urban Zones

1. Original Lisbon
2. Muslim and Working-Class Lisbon
3. Lisbon of Discovery
4. Elegant Lisbon
5. Riverfront Lisbon
6. Belém and Ajuda
7. Mid-East
8. Lisbon of the Avenues
9. Suburban Lisbon
10. Expo 98 and Lisbon of the Future
11. Monsanto

Zone 7: The Mid-East

This area is a sort of no man's land between the city and the refineries... For at least a few years it will remain so, interposed this time between the city and the site of EXPO 98, but if the plan for urbanization following the world fair succeeds, this neighbourhood could become quite interesting.

Zone 8: Lisbon of the Avenues

Liberdade, Marques Pombal, Picoas, Saldanha – all of these names evoke a grand Lisbon of avenues and squares aligned like those of Washington, according to the urban planning of the Marquês de Pombal. For a long time a rather reserved neighbourhood, it is beginning to come to life with bookstores, cafés and stylish restaurants.

Zone 9: Suburban Lisbon

New roads and the automobile have provoked in Lisbon, as in most cities around the world, the development of suburbs that are further and further from the city. The airport is in the east part of this zone, luckily not too far from the city.

Zone 10: EXPO 98 and Lisbon of the Future

An ambitious urban plan that seems likely to succeed includes the recuperation of an old industrial area in which EXPO 98 will be constructed on the principle that everything built for the fair must be usable afterward, thereby creating the Lisbon of the future. This is an exceptional achievement in urban planning: a railroad, a subway and a new bridge will access the new neighbourhood, which is near the airport and downtown. In one stroke a new city will have been created that will be much more attractive than the suburbs of Zone 9 and that will provide housing for 25,000 residents and employment for 18,000 people.

Zone 11: Monsanto

A sacred hill that has successfully evaded practically all construction, this is Lisbon's breath of fresh air. A wonderful place for walks, 20 minutes from downtown, this zone covers an area as large as Zones 1 to 5 combined.

Literature

In the late 15th century, a period of great upheaval all over the planet and great discoveries for Portugal, **Gil Vicente** pioneered the Portuguese theatre. Then, in the 16th century, **Luis de Camões** wrote an 8,000-verse epic poem describing the adventures of the explorers. Luis de Camões is to Portugal what Dante is to Italy or Shakespeare to England.

The 17th century sermons of **Padre António Viera**, an evangelist in Brazil, were masterpieces of religious oratory, and as such could not help but attract the attention of the extremely devout Portuguese.

In the 19th century, the Romantic movement emerged, led by writers like **Almeida Garrett**, **Alexandre Herculano** and **Camilo Castelo Branco**, who lampooned the clergy and the established order.

The beginning of the 20th century was marked by the publication of the first and only two issues of the literary journal *Orpheu* (1915). It was founded by **Fernando Pessõa**, the most celebrated Portuguese author of the 20th century, whose name means "person". In a way, he was more than one person, for he published a number of articles and longer works under various pseudonyms. Names alone were not enough for Pessõa, however; he actually developed a biography for each "author". Each one thus represents a different facet of his work, be it poetry, philosophy or aesthetics.

The Italian author Antonio Tabucchi describes the meeting of Pessõa with every one of his pseudonymous alter egos during the course of the last three days of his life. Tabucchi also wrote, in Portuguese, *Requiem*, in which the action is set entirely in Lisbon and which reveals captivating facets of the old city.

The relationship between Pessõa and his native city, which he had to leave at the age of seven when his widowed mother married the Portuguese consul to South Africa, is a veritable love story. Pessõa lived in this last country for ten years and was educated in English. At the age of 17 he returned alone to Lisbon and never again left. He endeavoured to make Lisbon and Portugal known the world over as he considered this culture to have been belittled by the superior attitude of its English "father-in-law". Pessõa even wrote a guide to Lisbon, in Portuguese and English, *What the Tourist Should See*, but astoundingly, this work was not discovered until the end of the 1980s. It is a rather banal work of too-detailed, soulless descriptions.

To learn more about the most famous Portuguese writer of the century, visit the museum dedicated to him in Lisbon: The **Casa-Museu Fernando Pessõa**, Rua Coelho da Rocho no. 16, 1250 Lisboa, ☎ 396 81 90, open Monday to Friday, 1pm to 6pm; from Rua Vitor Cordon, take tram 28, or form Rossio, bus 9.

Another important literary figure of the 20th century was **Miguel Torga**, who opposed the Salazar regime through his writing, which was repeatedly censored and seized. His book ***Portugal*** takes the reader on a whirlwind historical and poetic tour of the entire country.

One contemporary author who stands out is **Mario de Carvalho**, who skilfully blends the realistic and the absurd.

Although more than 200 million people across the world speak Portuguese, a book written in that language has never won the Nobel Prize for literature — a clear indication that the culture has yet to be duly recognized by the international community.

Painting and Cinema

Vieira da Silva is without question the most celebrated contemporary painter in Portugal. Born in 1908, he left his home town of Lisbon for Paris in 1936. There is a little bit of Lisbon in all of his work, though; a number of his paintings are made up of little squares reminiscent of *azulejos*.

At the age of 89, **Manoel de Oliveira** has just launched his latest film, *Viagem au Princípio do Mundo*. As in his last seven films, produced in seven years, Oliveira deals serenely with the subject of death as interpreted according to different philosophical visions. Bilingual, in French and Portuguese, this latest film is a posthumous homage to Mastroiani. Originally from Porto, Oliveira is already preparing *Inquiétude*, to be filmed in the north of the country. His films are characterized by slow rhythms, sumptuous images and literary scripts, aspects that do not generally contribute to the popularity of a film-maker. In fact, his films have been seen by an average of only 30,000 viewers in Portugal. Oliveira is the only director in the world still working whose career began in the silent age.

Music

Amália Rodrigues

Amália was born in 1920 and thus celebrated her 75th birthday in 1995. Television stations and cultural circles paid her the tribute she so richly deserves as a true national heroine. She began her career at the age of 19 in Lisbon's Retio da Severa, a *fado* club. Her unique way of singing, powerful stage presence and radiant beauty immediately set her on the road to success. She launched her international career four years later, in 1943, first in Spain and then in Brazil. Next, she appeared in the films *Capas Negros* and *Fado, história duma Contadeira*. She "created" rituals, her songs "became" *fado*, her black clothes, an "age-old tradition". She went to New York in 1952 and 1954, but, full of *saudade* (nostalgia) for Lisbon, refused to go to Hollywood to make movies afterward. In 1955, however, she appeared in the French film *Les Amants du Tage*, in which she sang *Barco Negro*. The song was an international hit, and as a result she was invited to perform at the Olympia in 1956. From that moment on, she was no longer simply the ambassador of a far-off, little-known country, but a prominent figure on the international music scene; she sang in English, Spanish, Italian and French, always in charming Portuguese tones. She can be credited with enriching the world of *fado*, giving it new poetry, from the Middle Ages to the present day; great musicians like Alain Oulman wrote for her, breathing new life into this form of music. In major English-speaking cities, you'll have no trouble finding the songs she recorded in English on compact disc. In Portugal, of course, you'll find her songs in Portuguese, but prices are higher than in North America. In either language, her outstanding voice and style of singing will go straight to your heart, making it easy to understand why she was the first Portuguese performer to earn worldwide recognition.

MadreDeus

MadreDeus was introduced to the world music scene by the Wim Wenders film *Lisbon Story*. The group's album *Ainda* is dedicated to Lisbon and serves, appropriately, as the soundtrack to Wenders' film. MadreDeus' sound is a mix of traditional and modern, layered on an aural background of medieval tones. The instrumentation includes voice, guitar, cello, accordion and keyboards. With its music full of sadness and *saudade*, MadreDeus proves archetypically Portuguese. A beautiful contribution to world music.

Tetvocal

Tetvocal got its start covering contemporary American songs. Still a cappella, the group now sings in Portuguese, drawing inspiration from everything that has anything to do with the Portuguese identity.

Rio Grande

The folk sound of Rio Grande is another example of the renewal of Portuguese music through exploration of its ancestral roots. The purity of the sound, the poetry of the lyrics and the allure of the melodies have made Rio Grande a success.

PRACTICAL INFORMATION

This chapter is intended as a reference of useful addresses for planning your stay in Lisbon.

Note that the area code for Lisbon is 01. Unless otherwise indicated, you do not need to dial the area code within Lisbon.

When calling from abroad, the area code for Lisbon is simply **1**.

ENTRANCE FORMALITIES

Citizens of the EEC or of Switzerland need only their national identity card to gain access to Portugal. North Americans must have a valid passport in their possession.

Canadians and Americans with a passport are admitted without a visa for stays of up to three months.

In addition, all travellers, except members of the European Union and of Switzerland, must have an ongoing or return ticket.

As these regulations are subject to change at any time, we recommend that you verify them with the Portuguese embassy or consulate nearest you before your departure.

Customs

North Americans over the age of 18 are allowed to bring one litre of spirits containing over 22% alcohol or two litres of wine, and 200 cigarettes (or 100 cigarillos, 50 cigars or 250 g of tobacco) into Portugal.

Tourists from the European Union or Switzerland are allowed to bring 1.5 litres of alcohol or 4 litres of wine, and 300 cigarettes (or 150 cigarillos, 75 cigars, or 400 g of tobacco) into Portugal.

PORTUGUESE EMBASSIES, CONSULATES AND TOURIST OFFICES ABROAD

On the internet: ICEP (Portuguese Tourist Office) www.portugal.org

In Australia
Portuguese Embassy: 60 Empire Circuit, Forrest, A.C.T. 2603, Canberra, ☎ 95 24 06, ⇌ 90 19 57 or 90 19 06.

In Belgium
Portuguese Embassy: 55 Avenue de la Toison d'Or, 1050 Bruxelles, ☎ 539 38 50.

ICEP (Tourist Office): Rue Joseph II, 5, B.P. 3, 1040 Bruxelles, ☎ 230 52 50, ⇌ 231 04 47.

In Canada
Portuguese Embassy: 645 Island Park Drive, Ottawa, Ont, K1Y 0B8, ☎ (613) 729-0883, ⇌ (613) 729-2270, Consular Services, ☎ (613) 729-2270.

Portuguese Consulate: 2020 Rue University, Suite 1725, Montréal, QC, H3A 3A5, ☎ (514) 499-0621, ⇌ (514) 499-0366.

Portuguese Consulate: 121 Richmond St., 7th floor, Toronto, Ont., M5H 2K1, ☎ (416) 360-8261, ⇌ (416) 360-0350.

Portuguese Consulate: 700 West Pender St., Suite 940, Vancouver, BC, V6C 1G8, ☎ (604) 688-6514, ⇌ (604) 685-7042.

ICEP (Tourist Office): 60 Bloor St. West, Suite 1005, Toronto, Ont., M4W 3B8, ☎ (416) 921-7376, ≠ (416) 921-1353.

In Germany
Portuguese Embassy: Dollendorfer Str. 15, 5300 Bonn 2, ☎ 35 29 37, ≠ 35 28 64.

ICEP (Tourist Office): Schäfergasse, 17, 60313 Frankfurt Main, ☎ 23 40 94 or 29 05 49, ≠ 23 14 33.

In Great Britain
Portuguese Embassy: 12, Belgrave Square, London, SWIX 8PT, ☎ 235 3688, ≠ 245 1287.

ICEP (Tourist Office): 2nd Floor 22-25A Sackville Street, London WIX 1DE, ☎ 494 1441, ≠ 494 1868

In Italy
Portuguese Embassy: Via della Camillucia, 730, 00135 Rome, ☎ 329 42 66, ≠ 841 74 04.

ICEP (Tourist Office): Largo Augusto, 3, 20122 Milano, ☎ 79 52 28 or 79 45 73, ≠ 79 46 22.

In the Netherlands
Portuguese Embassy: Tolweg, 1, 2517 Den Haag, ☎ 350 49 22.

ICEP (Tourist Office): Paul Gabriëlstraat 70, 2596 VG Den Haag, ☎ 326 43 71, ≠ 328 00 25.

In Spain
Portuguese Embassy: P.ª de la Castellana, 58, 28006 Madrid, ☎ 561 93 64, ≠ 411 01 72.

ICEP (Tourist Office): Gran Via, 27-1.ª, 28013 Madrid, ☎ 522 93 54 or 522 44 08, ≠ 522 23 82.

In the United States
Portuguese Embassy: 2125 Kalorama Rd., NW Washington DC 20008, ☎ (202) 483-7075, ≠ (202) 462-3726.

Portuguese Consulate: 899, Boylston St., 2nd Floor, Boston, Massachusetts 02115, ☎ (617) 536-8740, ≠ (617) 536-2503.

Portuguese Consulate: 1955 N. New England Avenue, Chicago, Illinois 60635, ☎ (312) 889-7405, ✻ (312) 493-2433.

Portuguese Consulate: 3300 South Broad St., Houston, Texas 77063, ☎ (713) 953-1255.

Portuguese Consulate: 1801 Avenue of the Stars, Suite 400, Los Angeles, California 90067, ☎ (310) 277-1491.

Portuguese Consulate: 100 N. Biscayne Boulevard, Suite 1602, Miami, Florida 33132, ☎ (305) 371-6333, ✻ (305) 444-7649.

Portuguese Consulate: 630 Fifth Avenue, Suite 310-378, New York, NY 10111, ☎ (212) 246-4580, 246-4581, 246-4581 or 765-2980, ✻ (212) 459-0190.

ICEP (Tourist Office): 590 Fifth Avenue, 4th Floor, New York, NY 10036-4704, ☎ (212) 354-4403 or 354-4404, ✻ (212) 764-6137.

FOREIGN EMBASSIES AND CONSULATES IN PORTUGAL

Australia
Embassy: Rua Marques sa da Bandera, 8/r/ce, 1000 Lisboa, ☎ 353 25 55, ✻ 353 63 47.

Belgium
Embassy: Praça Marques Pombal, 14, 6th floor, 1298 Lisboa Codex, ☎ 54 92 63, ✻ 353 57 23.

Canada
Embassy: Avenida Liberdade, 144, 3rd floor, 1200 Lisboa, ☎ 347 48 92, ✻ 347 64 66.

Germany
Embassy: Campo dos Martires da Patria, 38, 1100 Lisboa, ☎ 881 02 10, ✻ 885 38 46.

Great Britain
Embassy: Rua de S Domingos a Lapa, 37, 1200 Lisboa, ☎ 396 11 91, ✻ 397 67 68.

Italy
Embassy: Largo Conde Pombeiro, 6, 1200 Lisboa, ☎ 54 61 44.

Netherlands
Embassy: Avenida Infante Fanto, 435, 1300 Lisboa, ☎ 396 11 63, ⇌ 396 64 36.

Spain
Embassy: Rua do Salitre, 1, 1296 Lisboa Codex, ☎ 347 23 81, ⇌ 342 53 76.

Switzerland
Embassy: Travessa do Patrocinio, 1, 1399 Lisboa Codex, ☎ 397 31 21, ⇌ 397 71 87.

United States
Embassy: Avenida das Forcas Armadas, 1600 Lisboa, ☎ 726 66 00, ⇌ 726 91 09.

 TOURIST INFORMATION

In Lisbon

Portela de Sacavém Airport: The tourist office is located near the airport exit.

Downtown: Palácio Foz, Praça dos Restauradores; open Mon to Sat 9am to 8pm and Sun 10am to 6pm.

This building houses both the ICEP office (information on Lisbon as well as Portugal in general) and the tourist office of the Câmara Municipal (information on Lisbon only; relatively inefficient service). You'll find maps, brochures and a few guides here.

Around Lisbon

Estoril
Tourist office: Arcadas do Parque
Area code: ☎ 1

Cascais
Tourist office: Rua Visconde da Luz no. 14A
Area code: ☎ 1

Setúbal
Tourist office: Praça de Bocage et Largo do Corpo Santo
Area code: ☎ 65

Sintra Vila
Tourist office: Praça da República no. 3
Area code: ☎ 1

EXCURSIONS AND GUIDED TOURS

There are many options available to travellers wishing to explore the city with a guided tour. A few are mentioned below. Considering the frequent changes, we recommend contacting each of these organizations directly for information on the tours they offer and the prices.

Bus Tours

From May to September, the State-owned company **Carris** *(☎ 363 20 21 or 363 93 43)* offers visitors a double-decker guided bus tour, available in various languages. From the upper level, with the wind blowing through your hair, you'll be lead along a tour (the *Circuito Tejo*), which after making a loop towards the north from the Praça do Comércio, follows the Tagus from Belém to downtown. Departures are from the Praça do Comércio, and the tickets can be purchased on board. Rates are 2,000 ESC for adults and 1,000 ESC for children aged 4 to 10. Schedule: May to Jul and Sep, departures on the hour from 11am to 4pm; August, departures on the hour from 11am to 5pm.

Both **Cityrama** *(Avenida Praia da Vitória no. 12-B, 1096 Lisboa, Codex, ☎ 386 43 22 or 355 85 69, ≈ 356 06 68)* and **Portugal Tours** *(Avenida Praia da Vitória no. 14-A, 2nd floor, 1000 Lisboa, ☎ 352 29 02 or 316 02 99, ≈ 352 29 02)* offer guided tours of the capital and excursions to Cascais, Estoril, Sintra and Cabo da Roca.

Boat Tours

From April to October, **Transtejo** *(Estação Fluvial Terreiro do Paço, ☎ 887 50 58, ≠ 887 90 41)* organizes daily two-hour *cruseiros no Tejo* (cruises on the Tagus) which reveal another side of Lisbon. Departures *(11am and 3pm)* are from the Terreiro do Paço close to the Praça do Comércio. The cost is 3,000 ESC.

Eléctrico de Tourismo

From March 1st to October 15th, the State-owned **Carris** *(☎ 363 20 21)* company offers a guided tours in many languages aboard a pretty little tram called the Eléctrico de Tourismo. Departures are from the Praça do Comércio and tickets can be purchased on board the tram. The rates are fairly expensive, 2,800 ESC for adults and 1,500 ESC for children aged 4 to 10. As its Portuguese name suggests, the *circuito colinas* (hill tour) visits various picturesques areas of the city. Schedule: Mar to Jun and Oct, departures at 1:30pm and 3:30pm; Jul, departures at 11:30am, 1:30pm, 2:30pm and 3:30pm; Aug, departures at 11:30am, 1:30pm, 2:30pm, 3:30pm amd 4:30pm; Sep, departures at 11:30am, 1:30pm and 2:30pm. For those on a tighter budget, a ride (un-guided) aboard tram 28 provides an interesting look at Lisbon. Tickets bought in advance are only 150 ESC... quite a savings compared to 2,800 ESC for the tourist tram. Among the other routes worth trying are lines 25, 18 and 15.

 # GETTING TO LISBON

By Plane

Charter flights from Canada aboard TAP Air Portugal are offered out of major cities. Scheduled flights to Portugal are also available with Air France through Paris, KLM via Amsterdam, Swissair via Zurich, British Airways via London, etc. The majority of visitors land in Lisbon or Porto. Faro, in the

Algarve, is also served by planes from the continent and the United Kingdom.

Lisbon Airport (Portela de Sacavém)

Lisbon's international airport *(departures and arrivals information 24 hours a day ☎ 841 37 00; general airport information, www.anaep.pt/lisboa)* is located about eight kilometres north of downtown. Besides the tourist information counter and post office, you will find exchange offices, bank branches as well as automatic teller machines.

Several **car rental** companies have offices at the airport, these include: **Avis** *(☎ 849 48 36)*, **Hertz** *(☎ 849 08 31)*, **Budget** *(☎ 849 16 03)*, **Europcar** *(☎ 840 11 76)* and **Thrifty** *(☎ 847 88 03)*. Take note, however, that prices for car rentals at the airports are generally higher than downtown, except for those who have reserved in advance. An airport tax of 1,500 ESC is also added to each car rental.

To get downtown **by car**, take Avenida das Comunidades Portuguesas, which leads under Avenida Marechal Craveira Lopes to the Rotunda do Aeroporto. From there, take Avenida do Brasil to Campo Grande park. Turn left to go through the tunnel leading to Avenida da República, which comes to an end at the Praça Duque de Saldanha. Follow Avenida Fontés Pereira de Melo to the Praça Marquês de Pombal. From there, Avenida da Liberdade will take you into the centre of town.

To get downtown by **bus** if you are in a rush, take the 91, also known as the Aero-Bus *(one-day ticket: 430 ESC, 3-day ticket: 1,000 ESC or Passe Turístico)*, an express bus that goes by every 20 min. You must purchase a ticket ahead of time from the Carris counter at the airport. TAP passengers can take the Aero-Bus downtown for **free**; you must pick up your ticket at the TAP information counter, located near the customs exit. Slower but less expensive *(150 ESC)*, buses 44 or 45 will take you downtown by way of the Praça Marquês Pombal, Avenida da Liberdade, Praça Restauradores and the Rossio. Those wishing to go straight to the west part of the city (the Rato, Estrêla and Lapa) can take the bus 22.

As at most international airports, catching a **taxi** downtown is easy. The minimum fare is 250 ESC, and a second bag costs 300 ESC. Expect to pay about 1,500 ESC to get downtown.

By Car

If you are already in Europe, you can drive to Portugal, though it is a long trip through France and Spain and all costs (gasoline, highway tolls, wear on your vehicle) should be factored in when determining the best mode of travel.

This trip of at least 1,800 kilometres requires two to three days of driving and, unless you take the time to enjoy a bit of France and Spain along the way, will prove very taxing. If you want to have your car with you, you can always opt for the "car-train" offered by SNCF, the French railway company.

The most direct route from Paris is through Bordeaux then to Irún, Spain and into Portugal at Bragança, the more interesting option, or through Vilar Formoso. The latter border is open all night long, as are those at Elvas and Valença do Minho, though these are less practical.

Roads

Getting around by car is the best way to see all the little historic Portuguese villages. While Porto and Lisbon are both easy destinations for a short stay, the other way to visit Portugal, that is to explore its countryside, can only be done with a car.

The road network is still relatively undeveloped, even though much progress has been made. There is a lot of traffic and average speeds rarely exceed 80 kph. For this reason be sure to plan your excursions well, especially since in many regions the only lodging and restaurant possibilities are in the prestigious *pousadas*, which are run by the State and often only have a few rooms.

The only highway that is divided over its whole length is the one between Lisbon and Porto, as well as a few sections of road near Setúbal, Estoril, etc. The trip between Lisbon and

Porto costs 2,760 ESC on a toll road. Otherwise, narrow and winding sections of road are common. At press time the cost of a litre of gas was 170 ESC.

Drive with caution in Portugal: in populated regions, many of the roads have three lanes, the middle lane being a passing lane for both directions. A car with a powerful engine will be appreciated. The other reason to take special care is based on the fact that Portuguese drivers can be divided into two specific categories: those that seem incapable of driving faster than 50 kph (and there are a lot), and those, seemingly influenced by the *movida*, who drive at least 120 kph. Tourists generally find themselves precariously somewhere between these two extremes. Avoid driving at night or at twilight when farmers are returning from the fields with their animals and visibility is reduced. So... *precaução e bom viagem!*

Besides the highways, there is a considerable network of national, departmental and local roads that lead to the smallest most remote villages of the back country. Be careful, however, as national roads are not necessarily very wide roads, rather they tend to be quite narrow.

Theft in cars is common in Portugal so be sure to take note of the safety precautions on p 66.

A Few Tips

Drivers License: North American and European drivers licenses are valid in Portugal.

The Highway Code: North Americans are advised that at intersections, priority is given to cars arriving on the right, regardless of which driver arrived first. However, major roads are served by round-abouts and cars within them always have the right of way. Therefore, wait for the way to completely clear before entering the round-about.

The use of seat belts is mandatory in Portugal.

The major problem all over the city is parking. Students and people out of work often stand by the side of the road and point out empty spaces. The standard tip for this service is about 25 ESC. Parking lots are numerous throughout the city, but very costly (see p 53).

Car Rentals

All international car rental agencies have branches in the region. Most are represented in the airports and around the main train stations. It is generally more expensive to rent a car at the airport.

Foreign driver's licenses are generally valid for renting a car in Portugal.

If you rent a car upon arrival, expect to pay around 10,000 ESC per day (unlimited mileage) for a compact car, unless you can rent as part of a package deal. Better value deals are often offered for periods of a few days or a week; check with your travel agent or with the international reservations service before leaving. Get a written confirmation of the agreed-upon rate.

Table of Distances (km/mi)

Braga							
170/106	**Coimbra**						
625/388	460/286	**Faro**					
980/609	760/472	465/289	**Grenade**				
362/225	200/124	300/186	660/410	**Lisbon**			
580/360	510/317	730/454	425/264	630/391	**Madrid**		
50/31	120/75	570/354	920/572	310/193	620/385	**Porto**	

By Bus

The cities and towns of Portugal are served by an excellent network of buses. This mode of transportation is the most economical way to get around. There are several private companies and while some specialize in a certain region, others serve all locations in the country. In each city of some importance there is a *rodoviária* (bus station) where companies generally have their ticket offices. Below are the addresses of a few of these in Lisbon:

Rede Nacional de Expressos: Avenida Casal Ribeiro no. 18B, ☎ 357 79 15, www.rede-expressos.pt

Eva Expressos: Avenida Casal Ribeiro no. 18B, ☎ 314 77 10 or 314 77 13, www.eva-transportes.pt

Renex Expressos: Campo das Cebolas, ☎ 887 48 71 or 888 28 29, ≠ 887 49 42 or 886 45 48.

Hitchhiking

Hitchhiking is rare in Portugal, and is not recommended.

By Train

Large cities like Lisbon, Porto and Coimbra are served regularly by rapid and comfortable trains. It can be difficult, however, to reach the smaller cities and it is not feasible to imagine touring the entire country with this mode of transport. If you are arriving through France, remember that you must change trains at the Spanish border. This can be time-consuming and cumbersome, especially if you are travelling with a lot of luggage. Train fares are generally not that much cheaper than airfares. There are several single ticket packages (Eurailpass, Inter-Rail) but these carry certain restrictions and are really only useful for those who plan on visiting several cities.

The national railway company is called Caminhos de Ferre Portugueses (CP). It offers passes (*bilhetes turísticos*) which permit unlimited travel in 2nd class on the whole Portuguese rail network for seven to 21 days; the prices vary from 18,000 and 41,200 ESC. For more information, contact CP in Lisbon at ☎ (1) 888 40 25, 888 50 93 or 888 50 92.

GETTING AROUND LISBON

Generally speaking, it is not very complicated to get about in Lisbon by car, the only exception being the centre of the Alfama, which is inaccessible because it has so many dead-ends and streets with staircases. Similarly, the Bairro Alto, the triangular area bounded by the Praça Luís de Camões, the Miradouro de S. Pedro de Alcântara and the Miradouro de Santa Catarina, is accessible but better avoided by motorists. The streets are not only very narrow, but many are one-way, making driving here difficult. The major problem all over the city is parking. It is easier to find parking in the evening, however, since students and people out of work stand by the side of the road and point out empty spaces. The standard tip for this service is about 20 ESC. As a general rule, though, we recommend using public transportation or exploring the city by foot.

One last note: Private **parking** lots are outrageously expensive in Portugal. Oddly enough, furthermore, the hourly rate goes up the longer you leave your car. If you have no other choice, however, the lot on Praça dos Restauradores has the advantage of being located right downtown, making it easy to reach. Parking here will cost you about 225 ESC an hour. There is another lot next to the Praça Marquês de Pombal. Spread over five levels under Parque Eduardo VII, it has 1,454 spots and is open 24 hours a day. It costs about 140 ESC per hour to park here.

Public Transportation

The city of Lisbon has an extensive public transportation system operated by state-owned companies. Though the bus and the subway, called the metro, are the most common modes of transportation, the most pleasant means of exploring the city is definitely the tram, or *eléctrico*. Below, you will find a brief description of the various ways of getting around town.

54 *Practical Information*

Buses, Trams and *Elevadores*

Operated by the state-owned Carris company, about a hundred **buses** (*autocarros*) serve the city of Lisbon and its suburbs. Besides being comfortable, they are the fastest way of getting anywhere in town (along with the subway). If you plan on staying in Lisbon for a while, pick up a copy of the *Guia Informativo de Carris*. Laid out in a handy, pocket-sized format, it contains the schedules and routes of all buses and trams in the city, as well as the fares and various ticket options available, including those intended specifically for tourists. In addition to being very useful, it is a veritable souvenir in itself, since it is full of little pictures of local attractions. The *Guia Informativo* is available for the modest sum of 400 ESC at all Carris counters (see below).

Quaint little vehicles with wooden interiors and entertaining advertisements plastered outside, the **trams** (*eléctricos*) make their way up and down the streets in a slow, noisy and somewhat awkward manner. They are an essential part of life in Lisbon and add to the city's charm. It would thus be sacrilege to leave Lisbon without having taken the tram at least once. The Carris company recently acquired some new, ultra-modern trams, which are considerably more comfortable than

Eléctricos

the old ones, but are not, sad to say, always in the best of taste (line 15). Only six lines remain, and let's hope that the "melodious squeaking of wheels" will liven up the streets of Lisbon for many years to come.

Lisbon's four ***elevadores*** make it possible to go quickly from one area to another. They are not only practical, but also offer a very attractive view of the city, since they almost always lead to a *miradouro* (lookout). The fares are the same as for other means of public transportation: 150 ESC per trip. It should be noted that residents commonly use the term *elevador* for both funiculars and elevators. Of the city's four *elevadores*, listed below, three are actual funiculars.

The **Elevador de Santa Justa** *(every day 7am to 11:45pm)* links Rua de Santa Justa to Largo do Carmo.

The **Elevador da Glória** *(funicular; every day 7am to 12:55am)* links Praça dos Restauradores to the Miradouro de São Pedro de Alcântara.

The **Elevador da Lavra** *(funicular; Mon to Sat 7am to 10:45pm, Sun 9am to 10:45pm)* links Largo de Anunciação to Rua Câmara Pestana.

The **Elevador da Bica** *(funicular; Mon to Sat 7am to 10:45pm, Sun 9am to 10:45pm)* links Rua da São Paulo to Largo Calhariz.

Fares for buses, *elevadores* and trams:

Single ticket purchased aboard a bus, *elevador* or tram: 150 ESC per trip.

Ticket purchased in advance at a Carris counter: 150 ESC for two trips (this kind of ticket is called a Bilhete Único de Coroa, or BUC 2); 300 ESC for four trips (BUC 4).

Ticket good for one day of unlimited use: 430 ESC.

Ticket good for three days of unlimited use: 1,000 ESC.

Carris sales offices can be found all over town; here are a few locations:

Posto de Informação e Venda Carris
- Elevador de Santa Justa
- Praça de Figuera
- Largo do Rato
- Estrêla
- Alcântara
- Belém

Tickets can also be purchased from many local travel agents.

The Metro

Though fast and efficient, the metro system is not very extensive yet, and is most practical for travelling long distances in a short period of time. As a number of new lines are scheduled to open in 1999, some stations are being expanded and renovated, so make sure to pay attention to any notices you see. The metro map includes the new lines and future stations.

Fares: Single ticket purchased at a subway station: 70 ESC; 10 tickets: 550 ESC; Ticket good for one day of unlimited use (subway only): 200 ESC; Ticket good for one week of unlimited use (subway only): 620 ESC.

Each station is equipped with ticket machines. Theoretically, these machines give change, but they are sometimes empty (especially late in the evening) and will only accept the exact fare, so it is always wise to have some change on hand.

Passe Turístico

The *Passe Turístico*, can be used for buses, trams, *elevadores* and the subway; it costs 1,600 ESC for four days and 2,265 ESC for seven. These passes are sold at a number of subway stations (see subway map above).

Depending on how long you'll be staying in the capital and which types of transportation you prefer, some options are more cost-effective than others. For example, if you're staying in Lisbon for four days, you are better off purchasing a three-

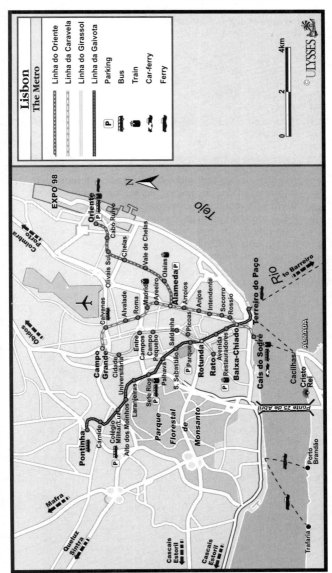

day ticket and a one-day ticket than a *Passe Turístico*, unless you plan on using the subway.

The *Lisboa Cartão*

This pass entitles its holder to unlimited use of the subway, buses and most trams and funiculars (except trams #15 and #18 and the Elevador de Santa Justa), as well as free admission to 25 museums and other attractions. Pass-holders also enjoy discounts of anywhere from 10 to 50% on cultural activities (shows, exhibitions, etc.) and 5 to 10% at certain stores. As it is quite expensive (1,500 ESC for a 24-hour-card; 2,500 ESC for a 48-hour-card; 3,250 ESC for a 72-hour-card), this card is most cost-effective for museum buffs who plan on spending at least six days in the capital. The *Lisboa Cartão* is sold at the following places:

- Posto Central, 50 Rua Jardim do Regedor (near Praça dos Restauradores)
- Mosteiro dos Jerónimos, Praça do Império
- Museo Nacional de Arte Antiga, 9 Rua das Janelas Verdes

By Taxi

Lisbon's taxis are among the least expensive in Europe, and are easy to find all over the city. Although they are all required to have meters and the fares are regulated, too often, the meter is hard to read, and sometimes it is already running when you get in. Be vigilant, and always make sure that the fare you are charged corresponds with the one on the meter. Asking for a receipt can help prevent drivers from overcharging you and, if necessary, make it easier to file a complaint.

Evening (from 10pm to 6am), weekend and holiday fares are slightly higher than those charged during daytime on weekdays. Expect to pay a flat charge of 250 ESC plus about 72 ESC/km at night and 57 ESC/km during the day. Extra luggage is 300 ESC per bag and there is a surcharge of 150 ESC for taxis ordered by phone.

On Foot

Lisbon is a delightful city with many different facets, and although there are all sorts of ways to visit it, its hidden beauties are best discovered on foot.

To make it easier for you to explore the city, we have divided up the local attractions by area. Furthermore, those who enjoy planned walking tours will find an itinerary for each of these areas. Visitors can thus explore each area separately or combine tours covering adjacent parts of the city.

If you plan on exploring the city on foot, it is important to remember that there are seven hills in Lisbon, and that climbing up and down them can be tiring. Visitors, like all good Lisboans, should therefore take the time to rest and sip a satisfying *bica* (espresso). To fully enjoy all Lisbon has to offer, wear comfortable shoes. Furthermore, the city is full of dead ends, passageways and streets with staircases, making it difficult to explore without a detailed map; make sure to bring one along.

Maps of the City

Unfortunately, although there are many maps of Lisbon (one of which is available free of charge at the tourist office), few of them are foolproof guides through this labyrinthine city. If your budget allows and you are spending an extended amount of time in the city, consider purchasing the *Lisboa Guia Urbano (2,800 ESC, available at ICEP, Praça dos Restauradores or in good bookstores)*, the most complete street atlas, with a detailed index.

Lookouts

There are many lookouts in the city, some quite isolated and hard to reach. The following are close to major attractions and fairly easy to get to:

- Miradouro de Santa Luiza (see p 98)
- Miradouro de São Pedro de Alcântara (see p 115)

Practical Information

- Miradouro de Santa Catarina (see p 128)
- Jardim do Torel (see p 126)
- Parque Edouardo VII (see p 118)
- Elevador de Santa Justa (see p 92)
- Castelo de São Jorge (see p 97)

By Boat

Transtejo *(Cais da Alfândega, Estação Fluvial Terreiro do Paço, 24-hour information line ☎ 310 31 31, ₼ 887 90 41)* provides ferry service between the capital and various cities south of the Tagus.

There are daily departures for the cities of **Montijo** *(one-way 270 ESC)*, **Seixa** *(210 ESC)*, **Cacilhas** *(90 ESC)* from the Terreiro de Paço, close to the Praça do Comércio. Ferries for the cities of **Porto Brandão** and **Trafaria** also leave from Belém.

The most interesting ferry from a tourist point of view is the one to Cacilhas. In a reasonable amount of time (30 minutes), you can cross the Tagus and enjoy a superb view of Lisbon. The trip is also possible from Cais do Sodré. Families or visitors out to make a day of it might be interested in a package deal with 10 crossings for 720 ESC. Transtejo also offers 24-hour service on the Cacilhas ferry *(motorcycle 180 ESC, car 200 ESC)* every 30 minutes during the day and evening and every hour at night.

 GETTING AROUND OUTSIDE LISBON

By Car from Lisbon

To reach the highway to **Cascais** and **Estoril** take Avenida da Liberdade to the Praça Marquês de Pombal, then turn left on Avenida Joaquim António Aguiar, which will take you directly to the A5 towards Estoril and Cascais.

For the scenic route, from the Praça do Comércio follow the docks heading west on Avenuda 24 de Julho then Avenida da

Índia. The latter joins the N6, which follows the coast all the way to Estoril and Cascais.

For **Sintra**, **Queluz** and **Cabo da Roca**, take Avenida da Liberdad to the Praça Marquês de Pombal, then turn left on Avenida Joaquim António Aguiar, which will lead directly to the A5. Once on the highway, after a few kilometres take the N117 towards Queluz or Sintra in order to get the IC19, which leads first to Queluz, then to Sintra. For Cabo da Roca, take the N247 from Sintra to Colares, then the N247-4 to Cabo da Roca.

For **Setúbal**, after crossing the Ponte 25 de Abril, continue heading south on the A2-E1-E90. After about 35 kilometres, a turn-off leads to the centre of Setúbal.

For **Palmela**, after crossing the Ponte 25 de Abril, continue heading south on the A2-E1-E90. After 37 kilometres, at the turn-off for Setúbal take the first exit on your right to get the H252 heading south. Less than one kilometre further, take the N379 heading west. Palmela is another kilometre further along.

By Train from Lisbon

For **Cascais** and **Estoril**, there are daily departures every half hour from the Cais do Sodré station, the platform west of the Praça do Comércio. Travel time: about 30 min for Estoril and 40 min for Cascais. Fare: 185 ESC.

For **Setúbal**, though this city is accessible by train, this is not the most practical way to get there because there is no direct route. You have to take the ferry (Estacão Fluvial Sul e Sueste) from the Praça do Comércio to reach the Barreiro station, in the suburbs on the other side of the Tagus, whence trains depart for the southern part of the country.

For **Queluz** and **Sintra**, there are several daily departures: from the Rossio station every 20 min. Travel time: about 30 min for Quelez and 45 min for Sintra. Fare: 155 ESC for Queluz and 185 ESC for Sintra.

By Bus from Lisbon

For **Cascais**, **Estoril**, **Queluz** and **Sintra**, since the train service is so good between the capital and these cities, there is no point taking the bus. For **Cabo da Roca**, there is no direct service from Lisbon, but there is a daily bus between Sintra, Cabo da Roca and Cascais.

Take note that there is no train service between Estoril and Cascais and between Queluz and Sintra. For those wishing to explore this magnificent region, the bus company Stagecoach offers a day ticket that allows you to make several stops. Thus by taking bus 403 you can get from Cascais to Sintra, passing through Cabo da Roca, in one day and with one ticket. There are many other connections between Sintra, Cascais and Estoril.

Stagecoach Portugal
Rua Capitão Rey Vilar no. 383
Alvide, 2750 Cascais
☎ 486 76 81
≠ 486 81 68

Setúbal and **Palmela** are served by various bus companies, and there are several daily departures from Campo das Cebolas, close to the Casa dos Bicos. Here are a few companies that make the trip:

Rede Nacional de Expressos
Avenida Casal Ribeiro no. 18B
☎ 357 79 15

Eva Expressos
Avenida Casal Ribeiro no. 18B
☎ 314 77 10 or 314 77 13

Renex Expressos
Campo das Cebolas
☎ 887 48 718 or 888 28 29

To get to **Costa da Caparica**, the closest beach to the city, take Carris bus 75 from the Praça Marquês de Pombal. It leads directly to the beach along the magnificent Ponte 25 de Abril for the modest sum of 480 ESC (ask for a *1-Dia-Praia* ticket). A family ticket *4 PAX* (four people) is also available for 1,440 ESC.

INSURANCE

Cancellation Insurance

Your travel agent will usually offer you cancellation insurance when you purchase your airplane ticket or vacation package. This insurance guarantees reimbursement for the cost of the ticket or package in case the trip has to be cancelled due to serious illness or death. Travellers with no health problems are unlikely to require such protection, and should weigh its advantages carefully.

Theft Insurance

Most home-owner's insurance policies in North America cover some personal possessions, even if they are stolen abroad. In order to file a claim, you must have a police report. Depending on what is covered in your policy, it is not always necessary to take out additional insurance. European travellers, on the other hand, should make sure their policies protect their property in foreign countries, as this is generally not the case.

Theft in cars is common in Portugal so be sure to take note of the safety precautions on p 66.

Life Insurance

Most airline companies include life insurance in the price of the airplane ticket, however, many travellers have a life insurance policy already. In these cases it is not necessary to obtain additional insurance.

Health Insurance

This is without question the most useful kind of insurance for travellers, and should be purchased before leaving. Look for the most complete coverage possible because health care costs in foreign countries can add up quickly. When you buy your policy, make sure it provides adequate coverage for all types of potentially costly medical expenses, such as hospitalization, nursing services and doctor's fees. It should also include a repatriation clause in case necessary care cannot be administered on site. As you may have to pay upon leaving the clinic, check your policy to see what provisions it includes for such cases. During your stay, always keep proof that you are insured on your person, as it will save you a lot of trouble if you are unlucky enough to require health care.

HEALTH

No vaccinations are necessary before entering Portugal, and health services are generally excellent. There are a significant number of AIDS cases, and as in other places, cases of venereal diseases are known, so be sure to take the necessary precautions.

The Sun

In spite of its benefits, the sun can cause numerous problems. Always wear sunscreen to protect yourself from the sun's harmful rays. Overexposure to the sun can cause sunstroke, symptoms of which include dizziness, vomiting and fever. Cover yourself well and avoid prolonged exposure, especially for the first few days of your trip, as it takes a while to get used to the sun. Even once you are used to the sun's intensity, moderate exposure is best. Wearing a hat and sunglasses can help shield you from the harmful effects of the sun. Lastly, don't forget that sunscreens are most effective when applied 20 to 30 minutes before exposure to the sun.

First-Aid Kit

A small first-aid kit can help you avoid many difficulties. It is best to prepare it carefully before setting off on your trip. Make sure you take along a sufficient supply of all prescription medications you take regularly, as well as a valid prescription in case you lose them. Other medicines, such as Imodium or its equivalent (for intestinal disorders and diarrhoea) may be purchased before leaving, but are also available in local pharmacies in the cities and even in the smaller towns.

SAFETY AND SECURITY

In case of emergency dial 115.

Though Portugal is not a dangerous country, it has its share of petty thieves, especially in resort areas and big cities. In Lisbon's busy areas (Bairro Alto, Alcântara and Santo Amaro) be particularly careful at night. As many establishments are located on dark side streets or near such places, muggings and thefts are common; one of the authors had just such an experience in the Bairro Alto. There is very little police presence in these areas and therefore we can only advise people to be extremely prudent at night. As the nightclubs open quite late, be sure to take a taxi to get there and to get back to your hotel, especially if you are travelling alone. If you choose to walk anyway, stick to well-lit and busy arteries and steer clear of dark side streets.

If you decide to visit one of the beaches near the coast, always keep an eye on your personal objects. These places are popular with tourists and by extension with professional thieves as well. Never leave anything in your car. Leave all your valuables in the safe at your hotel.

Conceal your traveller's checks, passport and some of your cash in a money belt. Remember, the less attention you attract, the less you risk being robbed. Pack a photocopy of your passport and the serial numbers of your traveller's cheques. If the originals are lost or stolen, knowing their reference numbers will make it much easier to replace them.

Victims' Rights in Portugal

Note that late at night or in the wee hours of the morning, the police will not come to the scene of the crime unless the circumstances are very serious. You must go yourself to the police station downtown *(Rua Capelo no. 13, ☎ 346 61 41)*, a station that, in theory, exists to come to the assistance of victims of theft or assault. In reality, however, no statements are taken at night, and you must wait to be taken to the central station in the Chiado. Once there, you'll have to wait while they wake up the officer on duty (!) in order to register your complaint. It goes without saying that this wake-up call is not appreciated and that the officer is therefore not very receptive to your account. Communications difficulties (officers' comprehension of English is sketchy) mean you will have to be very patient. Don't expect any sympathy or support, this type of assistance is not part of procedure and depends entirely on the officer. Finally, after enduring all of this, you have to find your own way back to your hotel. It goes without saying that some compassion and respect for victims' rights would go a long way in Portugal.

Theft in Cars

It may be hard for a North American to imagine the huge risk that exists in Southern Europe of having objects stolen from your car. Portugal is unfortunately no exception, and drivers would be wise to take the following precautions:

- Never leave your luggage in an unsupervised car. Thieves need only five minutes to get what they want without any trace, even in the most remote places. The authors were robbed in Portinho, south of Lisbon. Car door locks are no secret to these professional pilferers.

- Above all do not leave anything visible that might have any value: bags, jackets. The lock might be picked in hopes that the jacket contains a wallet.

- If you must keep your luggage in your car be careful when stopping for gas or for a quick bite. Place the car where you can see it constantly. In the city, pay for a parking lot, and choose a spot near the attendant.

- Always leave the glove compartment wide open, to avoid the supposition that your camera might be inside.

In general leave your bags at the hotel while you are sightseeing, even if you have checked out. The reception desk will usually keep them for you. Finally always remember that whatever precautions you've taken, you could still be robbed and avoid carrying valuables with you.

If despite all these precautions, you are unlucky enough to be robbed, be sure to file a police report. You will need it to be reimbursed by your insurance company. You will, however, have to deal with the inefficient bureaucracy.

CLIMATE

Generally speaking, there are advantages and disadvantages to Portugal's climate: it rains quite often, but temperatures are mild and relatively stable. It's latitude means that days are longer than in London or New York between September 21 and March 21. Any time of the year is a good time to visit Portugal, and when you go will ultimately depend on what kind of trip you are planning.

January, February and March

Above all, take note that Lisbon in January is twice a sunny as Paris or London, and 50% more than Montréal or New York. As far as temperature is concerned, newly arrived North Americans from the East often parade around in t-shirts, taking advantage of average highs around 15°C. Lisbon nights in January are cooler, around 8°C. Both Lisbon and Porto are rainy during this month, with 11 days of rain in the capital and 13 days in Porto, which is farther north and has an Atlantic climate. Half as much rain falls in Faro, in the Algarve, than in Porto in January, but there are still seven days of rain. This, combined with average highs of 15°C, means you won't be lounging around in your swimsuit all day, not to mention that the 16°C waters of the Atlantic are not very inviting. February and March are generally the same as January.

April and May

A look at the statistics may explain a few things about history and song. The weather starts to change in "April in Portugal", like during the Flower Revolution! The mercury climbs to an average of 20°C during the day in Lisbon and Faro, and only drops to 13°C at night. Perfect outdoor weather, especially when you consider that Faro only receives 30 mm of rain over five days in the month. Lisbon is less spoiled, and receives twice as much over eight days. In fact, it rains more in Lisbon in April than in Paris; it seems songs occasionally lead to false assumptions.

June

With only one day of rain in Lisbon and Faro (on average, of course!), and five in Porto and Miranda do Douro, this is a perfect time for a grand tour of the country. Especially since the tourist masses have yet to arrive, and temperatures remain very pleasant with maximum highs around 25°C throughout the country and minimums between 10 and 20°C.

July and August

This is the big tourist season, but not necessarily the most tolerable for those who don't value hot weather. Average highs hover around 28°C throughout the country, with almost no rainy days, except for four in Porto, where people wonder if the English didn't leave some of their weather behind.

September and October

Just like June..., except that we are in the northern hemisphere and therefore heading towards the shortest days of the year: in October, the whole country has an average of four hours less daylight than in June! Nevertheless, with close to eight hours of sunlight per day, on average, it's much more pleasant than London, New York or Montréal!

November and December

Temperatures drop everywhere, and the number of days of rain goes up. Nevertheless, the mercury does hover between 8 and 15°C in Lisbon and it only rains one out of every three days; urbanites could easily discover everything that Lisbon, Porto and their surroundings have to offer.

PACKING

Everything depends on the kind of trip you are planning and when you are going. Remember, however, that shorts and jeans are not always proper dress for visiting some churches and monasteries.

Southern Portugal lies at the same latitude as Sicily and the Carolinas, so sunglasses, sunscreen and a hat should always be included in your bags, no matter what time of the year it is.

MAIL

You can buy stamps at any post office, and also at the major hotels. Mail is collected on a daily basis.

There are two large post offices downtown:

Automated Post Office: Praça dos Restauradores no. 58; Mon to Fri 8am to 10pm, Sat, Sun and holidays 8am to 6pm.
Main Post Office: Praça do Comércio; Open Mon to Fri 9am to 5pm.

TELECOMMUNICATIONS

Telephones

Telephone numbers in the capital recently changed to seven digits, except numbers beginning with 60. For directory assistance dial 118.

To phone Lisbon from abroad dial the code for the international operator in your country then Portugal's country code and the area code (35-1), then the telephone number.

Remember that discount rates are available at certain times of the day.

Coin-operated public phones are easy to find in Lisbon. **Portugal Telecom** also has an office in the Rossio *(Praça Dom Pedro IV no. 68, northwest side of the square, next to the Valentim de Carvalho music store)*, which is open every day from 8am to 11pm. You can place calls from here and purchase *cartões telefónicos* (telephone cards) *(875 ESC for 50 units or 2,100 ESC for 120 units)*

To call abroad from Lisbon, you have two options. You can direct-dial and pay local phone rates or you can use your phone company's access code to reach an operator in your country. For direct-dialled numbers you must dial 00 for the international operator, the country code, the area code and the telephone number you wish to reach

Country Codes

- Australia: 61
- Canada and the United States: 1
- Belgium: 32
- Great Britain: 44
- Netherlands: 31
- New Zealand: 64
- Switzerland: 41

International access codes connect you with your phone company's operator and you pay your phone company's rates.

- Canada Direct 0517-1226
- AT&T Direct 05017-1288
- MCI Direct 05017-1234
- Sprint Direct 05017-1877
- British Telecom Direct 0505-00-44

When calling abroad from Portuguese hotels, keep in mind that hotels often charge much higher rates than the Portuguese phone company. It is much less expensive to call from a phone booth, using a Portuguese operator and even less expensive to use CanadaDirect or an equivalent. In the latter case you are charged approximately the same as you would pay to call Portugal from Canada or the United States.

In addition, most hotels offer fax and telex services, as do all post offices.

Internet

For internet access in Portugal, contact Telepac, a subsidiary of Portugal Telecom. They offer a service which gives access to the net for 30 hours over a two-month period for 6,900 ESC. Telepac offers the advantage of providing local access numbers in most cities of the country, which avoids long-distance charges. To reach Telepac, contact their business service at ☎ 0800 200 079 or by E-mail at internet.clientes@mail.telepac.pt. They offer good-quality technical support at ☎ 790 70 70. Normally you have to go to the head office of Portugal Telecom to get your user name and password. It is located at Avenida Fontes Pereira de Melo, edifício Forum, 1,000 Lisboa, ☎ 314 25 27 or 352 22 92, Picoas subway.

Of course you can always send E-mail, and sometimes receive it, from different internet cafés mentioned in this guide or at Portugal Telecom offices mentioned above.

A Few Internet Sites

For information on Portugal:
www.cidadevirtual.pt
www.cusco.viatecla.pt
www.ip.pt/top5
www.sapo.pt

Telecom white pages listings: www.telecom.pt; then click on the service icon 118.

MONEY AND BANKING

The local currency is the escudo (ESC; in Portugal the $ sign is occasionally used).

For easier on-the-spot reference, all prices in this guide are quoted in escudos.

Currency Exchange Rates

100 ESC = $0.81 CAN	$1 CAN = 124 ESC
100 ESC = $0.57 US	$1 US = 175 ESC
100 ESC = £0.33	£1 = 300 ESC
100 ESC = $0.82 Aust	$1 Aust = 122 ESC
100 ESC = $0.91 NZ	$1 NZ = 109 ESC
100 ESC = 0.80 SF	1 SF = 125 ESC
100 ESC = 20 BF	10 BF = 50 ESC
100 ESC = 0.98 DM	1 DM = 102 ESC
100 ESC = 83 pesetas	100 pesetas = 121 ESC
100 ESC = 959 lira	1000 lira = 104 ESC
100 ESC = 1.1 guilders	1 guilder = 91 ESC

Banks

Banks usually offer the best exchange rates if you're converting foreign currency into escudos. Most banks in Portugal are open from Monday to Friday 8:30am to 3pm.

Credit Cards and Travellers' Cheques

Visa and MasterCard are the most accepted. Be sure to ask in advance, however, if you plan on paying with a credit card.

Traveller's cheques are usually not a problem.

You can use your credit card in most automatic teller machines; small service charges apply ($2 in Canada) but you will generally get a better exchange rate than at the bank or exchange office. Plus you don't have to wait — these machines are open 24 hours a day.

ACCOMMODATIONS

The hotel infrastructure differs greatly from one region to the next in Portugal. In the big cities of Lisbon and Porto, you'll find all types of lodging for all budgets, except for bed and breakfasts, which are uncommon in the cities. In regions with many historic sites there is usually a *pousada* (see below).

Low budget accommodations are not always the best value when you consider the price. By spending just a bit more, about 8,000 to 12,000 ESC, you can find very comfortable accommodations with lots of charm and an excellent value for your money. **Breakfast is always included in the price of a room**, unless otherwise indicated, which is rare.

The season has a significant influence on the price. Below you'll find the low-, mid- and high-season prices for the *pousadas*. Keep this, as well as the climatic conditions, in mind when deciding on the best time to visit.

This guide lists what we found to be the best selections in each category. The prices given were valid at press time and are of course subject to change at any time. All prices, unless otherwise indicated, are for two people. We have also included the complete address of each establishment (postal address, telephone and fax number) in order to facilitate reservations before your departure.

Charges for calls made from a hotel room in Portugal are very high. It can cost as much as $7 per minute to call Canada! It is therefore a good idea to use the direct dialling services described on p 71; you will not have to pay anything in Portugal and it will cost only slightly more than you would pay from home.

The *Pousada* Network

Pousadas (or *posadas*) are State-owned establishments run by ENATUR, and there are three very distinct types. First, *pousadas* in national monuments, of which there are 10, are the most spectacular as they occupy heritage buildings like those in Óbidos, Évora or Estremoz. If there are no rooms available, be sure to at least stop for a meal or a drink. Next there are *pousadas* located in historic areas. There are eight of these, and though the building is more recent, it lies in the immediate vicinity of heritage buildings, like the *pousada* in Batalha. Finally, there are regional *pousadas*, of which there are 19. These are generally well located, often in the countryside and boasting exceptional views. Their locations allow you to visit even the most remote parts of the country while still enjoying quality accommodations.

In terms of rates, there are four price categories. The regional *pousadas* are generally the least expensive. The *pousada* network also has three different rates depending on the season:

Low season: from November 1 to March 31
Mid season: from April 1 to June 30 and October 1 to 31
High season: from July 1 to September 30

During the low season, rates for a double room with one bed vary between 10,600 and 24,400 ESC. During the mid-season, they vary between 14,300 and 29,600 ESC, and in the high season from 15,600 to 29,600 ESC. As with most Portuguese hotels, these rates include breakfast. An extra bed will cost between 3,300 and 8,500 ESC depending on the season. As for suites, like the one in the tower at Óbidos, they can run up to 48,500 ESC. **N.B. exceptionally during EXPO 98, the eight pousadas surrounding Lisbon will charge high season rates as of May 1.**

Exceptional quality is guaranteed when lodging in the *pousadas*, as is a unique cachet which comes from regionally-flavoured decor, a well-kept atmosphere and for the most part, very elegant architecture.

In terms of meals, *pousadas* are often an excellent solution: travellers will often find themselves far from the large centres, arriving late at their hotel in rural areas where locals rarely head out to restaurants after 8pm. Each *pousada* may have its own unique decor with dining rooms often located in architectural wonders, but the same cannot be said of the cuisine. Regional specialties are offered everywhere; but, after a few *pousada* meals you will begin to recognize a routine, ending with the same pastry trolley filled with the same egg and sugar desserts. Truly original dishes are sometimes offered, but 5,000 ESC a plate is a little steep. But like we said, in many cases the *pousada* restaurant is your only choice.

If you happen to find yourself in a city where we have recommended other fine restaurants, try them out for a break from the routine.

The *pousada* network is one of Portugal's riches, and we cannot recommend it enough. Several have limited space (sometimes as few as six rooms) and reservations are therefore strongly recommended.

For more information on the *pousadas*:

ENATUR
Avenida Santa Joana 10
1749 Lisboa Codex
Portugal
☎ 1-848 90 78, 848 12 21 or 848 46 02
≈ 1-848 92 57 or 848 43 49
www.pousadas.pt

Marketing Ahead, Inc.
433 Fifth Avenue
New York, NY 10016
U.S.A.
☎ (212) 686-9213
≈ (212) 686-0271

Keytel International
402 Edgware Road
London W2 1ED
England
☎ (171) 402-8182
≈ (171) 724-9503

Hotels and *Estalagem*

Portugal has several luxury hotels, generally concentrated in the large resort areas. Some of them are exceptionally charming, like the Lapa Hotel or the York House in Lisbon, or even the Palacio de Buçaco in the park of the same name, but many have nothing luxurious about them apart from the price. We have carefully avoided mentioning the huge charmless concrete towers, except where that was all there was. Take note that some luxury establishments are called *estalagem* and are sometimes comparable to *pousadas*; they are nevertheless private establishments.

Residencial and *Pensão*

These two appellations refer to a variety of different establishments, from the most inexpensive to the moderately priced. In Portugal, "budget" accommodations leave a bit to be desired in terms of comfort and above all in terms of charm. For this reason, fewer of these places are recommended in this guide; *residencial* and *pensão* generally do not offer good value for your money. For 1,000 or 2,000 ESC more you can get so much more.

 # RESTAURANTS AND FINE FOOD

Despite the almost infinite number of dining establishments in Lisbon, the variety of cuisines available is limited. Outside of Lisbon, the situation is even more marked, with the offerings summing up to the eternal *balcalhau*. We have thus made an effort to find something original, bearing in mind that after a few days of *bacalhau* (cod) you may be ready for a change. Another particularity, is that after so many discoveries, the

Portuguese tend not to be very interested in exotic cuisines, and in comparison to other European capitals, there are very few ethnic restaurants in Portugal.

Regional Portuguese cuisine actually boasts a fair number of dishes. Cafés sometimes charge different rates depending on whether you are standing at the bar, seated at a table or seated on the terrace. What seems commonplace to Portuguese seems unheard for Europeans from the north or for North Americans. Therefore, if you just want to grab a quick coffee, take it standing up at the bar, after all you'll be participating in a true Latin tradition.

Generally, restaurants serve food between noon and 2pm and from 7pm to 10pm. In smaller towns and villages, do not dawdle and arrive at the restaurant too late or you may have to content yourself with a sandwich and coffee. Dining later on is more feasible in the downtown area.

Restaurant Prices

$	less than 1,600 ESC
$$	1,600 ESC to 3,200 ESC
$$$	3,200 ESC to 5,000 ESC
$$$$	5,000 ESC to 7,000 ESC
$$$$$	more than 7,000 ESC

Tipping and Charges

The tip is included in the bill everywhere: restaurant, hotel, taxi. An extra 5 to 10% is nevertheless appreciated, especially when the service was particularly noteworthy.

ENTERTAINMENT

You'll find a bit of everything in Lisbon where weekend nights are endless. Elsewhere, however, except in the resort areas, people close in much earlier; perfect opportunity to catch up on all those books you've been meaning to read.

Gay Life in Portugal

Portugal's is a profoundly conservative society, where new ideas are not easily acepted, thus making like difficult for it's gay community. We can at least take comfort from the fact that the lack of gay places outside the city is more a result of ignorance than intolerance, as is the case in some places. On the other hand, there seems to be no problem of violence against gays.

In recent years, a core of militant gays has fought against discrimination and for better acceptance of openly-gay people. In fact, the International Gay and Lesbian Association includes a Portuguese contingent (www.ilga-portugal.org). This association organizes, among other things, a gay and lesbian film festival in Lisbon in September, whose first season took place in 1997. The first gay pride gathering in Portugal also took place in 1997, on June 28, at the Jardim do Principe Real, and brought together 3,000 people.

Of course, in Lisbon's bustling nightlife, and to a lesser degree in Porto, there are many gay or mixed nightclubs; the most prominent bars are proud to be frequented by gays. In the morning however, everyone conforms to their role at work or at home, in other words, to the heterosexual mold imposed by society. So nighttime is just an illusion and it will take many more years for this invisible minority to be able to expose their differences to the world and to fully participate in the construction of a society without discrimination.

A few gay publications:

Trivia: monthly information newspaper
Revista Lilás: magazine for lesbians

A few organizations:

ILGA-Portugal-Associação LesBiGay: Apartado 21281, 1131 Lisboa Codex

Associação Abraço: Travessa do Noronha no. 5, 4th floor, 1200 Lisboa, ☎ 60 38 35 or 395 79 21.

Internet:

International Gay and Lesbian Association:
www.ilga-portugal.org

Gay Portugal: www.ip.pt/~;p001704

SHOPPING

Shoppers will find arts and crafts treasures throughout the city: carpets, pottery, leather, ceramics. Of course, individual *azulejos* can be found everywhere. Besides these typically Portuguese items, the best buys are shoes and leather goods. Wine is an interesting souvenir, especially a good bottle of Port. Take note though, that prices are similar to those paid in Europe and just a bit less than in North America.

Antique-dealers and cabinet-makers are common throughout the country, but especially in Lisbon. Their shops are a delight for decorative art fans.

A few shops are affiliated with the "Tax Free for Tourists" system which allows anyone leaving the territory of the European Economic Community to be reimbursed for taxes paid on items being brought with them. Pamphlets for reimbursements are available at the Lisbon airport. Remember that in order to benefit from the reimbursement you must have spent a considerable amount of money.

There is also a tax-free system for non-residents of the European Community. Information is available from the Serviço de Administração do IVA, Avenida João XXI, 76, 1000 Lisboa, ☎ 1 793 66 73.

HOLIDAYS

January 1	New Year's Day
Variable	Shrove Tuesday
Variable	Good Friday
Variable	Easter
April 25	celebration of April 25, 1974 Revolution
May 1	Labour Day

Variable   Corpus Christi
June 10   Dia de Camões e das Comunidades
August 15   Feast of the Assumption
October 5   Republic Day
November 1   All Saints Day
December 1   celebration of Independence from Spain
December 25   Christmas

SPORTS CLUBS

There are many sports clubs throughout Portugal, and it is no secret that the Portuguese are big soccer fans. Visitors who want to stay in shape while staying in Lisbon might find this a bit difficult. Below are the addresses of a few clubs; the fees are unfortunately pretty high considering the facilities offered.

Clube de Ginásio: Pool, volleyball, aerobics and dance. Rua das Portas de Santo Antão no. 110-124. Access to the pool 800 ESC or monthly membership 7,500 ESC.

Clube de Ginásio Português: Aerobics, dance, yoga, judo, aïkido, fencing and weight-training. Praça do Ginásio Português no. 1, ☎ 385 60 45, ≈ 385 60 49.

Squash Soleil: Squash, pool, weight-training, gymnastics. Access to the pool 1,700 ESC or ten visits for 15,300 ESC. On the first floor on the Centre Commercial Amoreiras, ☎ 383 29 07 or 383 29 08.

Centro Viva em Forma: Pool, weight-training, gymnastics. Use of the weight-training machines 1,200 ESC or ten visits 10,800 ESC. Lisboa Sheraton Hotel, Rua Latino Coelho no. 1, ☎ 314 73 53

O Ginásio Holiday Inn: Gymnastics, pool, weight-training. Access to the pool and gym 1,500 ESC. Avenida António José de Almeida no. 28, 11th floor, ☎ 793 52 22, ext. 1184.

TIME ZONE

Portugal is in the same time zone as continental Europe and one hour ahead of Greenwich Mean Time. It is six hours ahead of eastern standard time. Therefore when it is noon in Montréal and New York it is 6pm in Lisbon. Portugal does observe daylight savings time (+ 1 hour in spring). From April to October, therefore, Portugal is one hour behind the rest of continental Europe, on the same time as Great Britain and five hours ahead of eastern North America.

ELECTRICITY

Electric plugs have two rounds pins and operate at 220 volts AC (50 cycles). Tourists from North America will need to bring along an adaptor and a converter.

Visitors from Great Britain will only need an adaptor with two round pins.

WOMEN TRAVELLERS

Women travelling alone should not encounter any problems. On the whole, women are treated with respect and harassment is relatively rare. Of course, a certain amount of caution is required; for example, women should avoid walking alone through poorly lit areas late at night.

LANGUAGE

Latin in nature, like Italian, Spanish or French, Portuguese might seem incomprehensible to an English-speaker's ear at first, even if they know a bit of Italian, Spanish or French. But to see it written is perhaps another story, and you only need a few hints about pronunciation and about the general differences from Spanish, and before you know it someone will be telling you *"O senhor(a) fala muito bem português"*. As in most countries, knowing a few Portuguese phrases will make your trip that much more enriching.

A language reveals so much about its speakers and their culture! Portuguese is often called an ancient language. Perhaps isolation and conservatism have preserved more of its Latin roots.

For example, throughout Europe, Monday is the day of the moon (Monday, *Montag, lundi, lunedi*) and all the other days refer to a different planet... except in Portugal. The church discouraged pagan references and many centuries ago imposed a way of saying the days that revolved around Sunday. Sunday is called *domingo*, while Monday is *segunda feira* (the second of the holy day), Tuesday is *terceira feira*, and so on. This custom has probably confused its share of travellers, who find themselves in front of a museum that is open from Monday to Friday, and the sign says *"seg-ses 9h - 17h"* or even *"2º - 6º 9h - 17h"*!

A short pronunciation guide and glossary can be found at the end of the guide. To develop your ear, pull out your João Gilberto records, even though the Brazilian pronunciation is a bit different, or look for a Portuguese radio or television station in your area.

WEIGHTS AND MEASURES

Portugal uses the metric system. Here are some equivalencies:

Weights
1 pound (lb) = 454 grams (g)
1 kilogram (kg) = 2.2 pounds (lbs)

Linear Measure
1 inch = 2.54 centimetres (cm)
1 foot (ft) = 30 centimetres (cm)
1 mile = 1.6 kilometres (km)
1 kilometres (km) = 0.63 miles
1 metre (m) = 39.37 inches

Land Measure
1 acre = 0.4 hectare
1 hectare = 2.471 acres

Volume Measure
1 U.S. gallon (gal) = 3.79 litres
1 U.S. gallon (gal) = 0.8 imperial gallon

Temperature
To convert °F into °C: subtract 32, divide by 9, multiply by 5
To convert °C into °F: multiply by 9, divide by 5, add 32

POLICE AND EMERGENCIES

In case of emergency dial **115**; an operator will direct your call.

EXPLORING

At the mouth of the Tagus, Lisbon, home to nearly two million inhabitants, lies along almost 16 kilometres of this majestic river flowing into the Atlantic Ocean. Stretched along the steeper bank of the river, its historic section, including the Castelo and the Alfama, is concentrated on the top and side of one of the seven hills that form the core of the city (São Viçente, Santo André, Castelo, Santana, São Roque, Chagas and Santa Catarina). Downtown Lisbon is divided into "upper" and "lower" sections, each made up of many different neighbourhoods. At the administrative level, the capital is divided into 53 *freguesias*, neighbourhoods: Lapa, Sé, Graça, São Mamede, etc. In the north, the suburbs sprawl all the way to the airport, eight kilometres from downtown; on the western shore, the city stretches to the municipality of Belém, the ancient outer harbour of the city and the royal suburb. The Ponte 25 de Abril, located halfway between Belém and Lisbon, has linked the two banks of the Tagus since 1966. To the northeast, the city opens onto a series of piers, in recent history the site of factories and refineries, that, after a project of complete restructuring, have now become the grounds of the Lisbon World Exposition, EXPO 98.

Below are a few suggested stops depending on how much time you have and what your interests are:

A Quick Stopover

The **Castelo** (p 97), the **Mosteiro dos Jerónimos** (p 138) and **Igreja Santa Maria** (p 139), and the **Torre de Belém** (p 141).

Two to Three Days

For churches: **Igreja Santa Maria** (p 139) and **Igreja da Madre de Deus** (p 106).

For museums: **Museu Calouste Gulbenkian** (p 120).

For the outdoors: **Parque da Pena** (p 179).

For palaces: **Palácio Nacional de Sintra** (p 153).

For *Azulejos*: **Museu Nacional do Azulejo** (p 105) and **Igreja e Mosteiro de São Vicente da Fora** (p 102).

For the Manueline Style: **Mosteiro dos Jerónimos** (p 138) and the **Torre de Belém** (p 141).

Three to Five Days

For churches: **Igreja Santa Maria** (p 139), **Igreja São Roque** (p 114), **Igreja da Madre de Deus** (p 106), and **Sé Patriarcal** (p 96).

For museums: **Museu Calouste Gulbenkian** (p 120), **Museu Nacional de Arte Antiga** (p 133) and **Museu Nacional dos Coches** (p 136).

For the outdoor: **Parque da Pena** (p 179), **Parque de Monserrate** (p 179), the **Castelo dos Mouros** (p 159) and **Serra da Arrábida** (p 182).

For palaces: **Palácio Nacional de Sintra** (p 153), **Palácio da Pena** (p 158) and **Palácio Nacional de Queluz** (p 149).

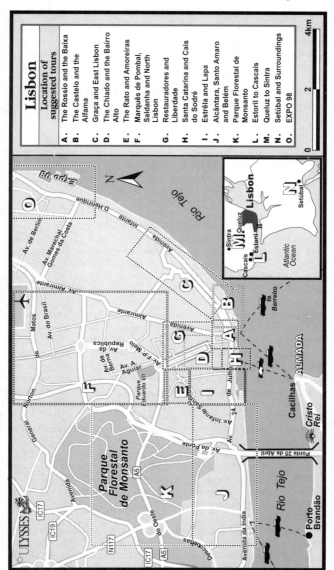

For *Azulejos*: **Museu Nacional do Azulejo** (p 105) and **Igreja e Mosteiro de São Vicente da Fora** (p 102), the **Pavilhão dos Desportos** (p 119) and the façade of the **Viúva Lamego** store (p 127).

For the Manueline Style: **Mosteiro dos Jerónimos** (p 138), **Igreja de la Conceição Velha** (p 95), the façade of the **Estação do Rossio** (p 91) and the **Torre de Belém** (p 141).

TOUR A: THE ROSSIO AND THE BAIXA

See map on p 89.

You can start off your tour of Lisbon in the heart of the city, at the **Rossio ★ (1)**, also known as Praça de Dom Pedro IV, after the first king of Brazil. This square, which dates back to the 13th century, owes its present design to the celebrated Marquês de Pombal. Today, it is lined with stores, banks, hotels and cafés. The nonstop flow of pedestrians and motorists makes for a perpetually noisy atmosphere, but take the time to walk around the square; there are several pretty shops here. At number 21, on the west side, the narrow **Tabacaria Mónaco** has a pretty interior, with lovely frescoes on the ceiling and an elegant counter made of dark wood. Right nearby, at number 23, the quaint little Art Nouveau façade of **Café Nicolas** is also worth a look. When this guide went to press, however, the famous café was closed for renovations, and the façade was being restored. Farther along, on the south side of the square, at numbers seven through nine, there is a **jewellery store** with a charming façade in the purest Art Nouveau style, advertising *Joias* and *Pratas* in elegant lettering. Next, walk through the arch (*Arco do Bandeira*) next to the jewellery shop to get to Rua dos Sapateiros. On the right side of the street, at number 229, you can admire the Art Nouveau ornamentation on the façade of the **Cinématografo** (now a pornographic theatre!).

There is a funny story behind the geometric patterns adorning the Rossio: rumour has it they were created on a whim by prisoners incarcerated in the Castelo, who had been sentenced to hard labour by the local authorities. It probably never

Tour A: The Rossio and the Baixa 89

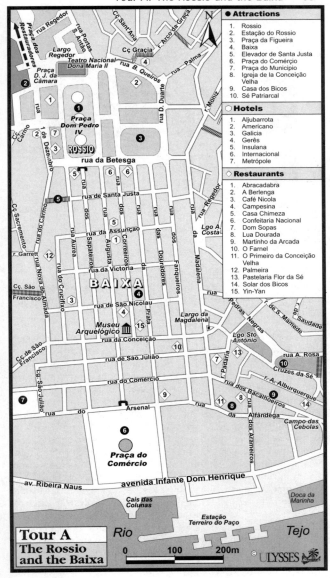

● Attractions
1. Rossio
2. Estação do Rossio
3. Praça da Figueira
4. Baixa
5. Elevador de Santa Justa
6. Praça do Comércio
7. Praça do Município
8. Igreja de la Conceição Velha
9. Casa dos Bicos
10. Sé Patriarcal

○ Hotels
1. Aljubarrota
2. Americano
3. Galicia
4. Gerês
5. Insulana
6. Internacional
7. Metrópole

◇ Restaurants
1. Abracadabra
2. A Berlenga
3. Café Nicola
4. Campesina
5. Casa Chimeza
6. Confeitaria Nacional
7. Dom Sopas
8. Lua Dourada
9. Martinho da Arcada
10. O Farnel
11. O Primeiro da Conceição Velha
12. Palmeira
13. Pastelaria Flor da Sé
14. Solar dos Bicos
15. Yin-Yan

90 Exploring

Cinématografo

occurred to the men who thought up the project that they were ushering in a new trend, and that these elegant patterns would one day cover many of the city's sidewalks.

On the north side of the square, you will see the neoclassical style **Teatro Nacional Dona Maria II** *(program ☎ 347 22 46 or 347 22 47)*, built during the first half of the 19th century. It was on this very site that auto-da-fés were declared in the Middle Ages. The statue of Gil Vicente at the top of the pediment serves as a reminder that he is the father of Portuguese theatre. In the centre of the square, set atop a pedestal, is a statue of the first king of Brazil, Dom Pedro IV, known in Brazilian history as Dom Pedro I. A strange rumour about this statue once spread throughout Lisbon. For many years, it was alleged that the statue was not actually Dom Pedro, but rather Emperor Maximilian of Mexico. According to the rumour, the statue had originally been destined for Mexico, but was altered to look like the king of Brazil after Emperor Maximilian was assassinated. The tale became such a subject of discussion and downright controversy that a Brazilian expert by the name of Stanislav Herstal decided to examine the statue to see if there was any truth to the rumour. He concluded that there wasn't, thus putting an end to the amusing story once and for all. On either side of the square, finally, two elegant baroque fountains, both sculpted in France, enhance the beauty of the setting.

It is worth stopping by little **Praça João da Câmara**, located alongside the Rossio, to see the façade of the **Estação do Rossio ★ (2)** *(to the left of the Teatro Nacional)*. Erected in 1887, this neo-Manueline building looks more like a palace than a train station. Particularly noteworthy is its curious central entrance, shaped like a pair of interlocking horseshoes.

Estação do Rossio

92   Exploring

On the other side of the train station, parallel to the Rossio, lies the **Praça da Figueira ★ (3)**. This square, too, is very lively, though the north side of it is off-limits to buses and taxis, making it a quieter place to enjoy a pleasant stroll. Praça da Figueira is known above all for its many outdoor cafés, which offer lovely views of the castle. A statue of King João I, founder of Portugal's second dynasty, the Aviz line, stands in its centre.

In addition to the presence of several impressive rococo buildings, the main attraction of the **Baixa ★ (4)** is its shops. Originally, a specific kind of merchandise could be found on each street, for example, Rua Aurea, also known as Rua do Ouro, was occupied primarily by jewellers, Rua dos Sapateiros by cobblers. Nowadays, however, you'll find an assortment of shops ranging from jeweller's and clothing stalls to pharmacies. There are several pedestrian streets here, the most pleasant of which is probably **Rua Augusta**. This street is not only flanked by shops with elegant window displays, but also offers an interesting view, due to its impressive triumphal arch.

The Baixa

Located between the Rossio and the Praça do Comércio, the Baixa (lower town) is unusual in that it consists of a group of buildings forming a rectangle, in which the streets are laid out in a perfectly symmetrical grid. This remarkable example of town-planning is to some extent a result of the terrible disaster of 1755. After the lower parts of Lisbon were completely destroyed by the earthquake, the Marquês de Pombal enlisted the help of three architects to rebuild the city using methods that were not only modern, but revolutionary at the time. Exemplifying what later came to be known as the "Pombaline-style", most of the buildings stand three or four stories high and feature uniform doors and windows, often with balconies. Lisbon thus became one of the first modern cities in Europe.

Rua de Santa Justa, which runs perpendicular to Rua Augusta, is also worth exploring to see the remarkable **Elevador de Santa Justa ★ (5)**. It was built by engineer Raul Mesnier du Ponsard, who received authorization from the city in 1899 to construct a vertical elevator that would make it easier to reach the Largo do Carmo. He was also awarded rights over the operation of the *elevador* for 99 years. It was inaugurated in 1902 and rented three years later to the state-owned Carris company, which took possession of it in 1939. The *elevador* is a metal tower that stands about 45 metres high and is topped by a proportionately large platform, where the steam engines that once drove the *elevador* were located. Connected to the Largo do Carmo by a 25-metre bridge, the *elevador* makes it possible to reach the Chiado (see p 55 and p 107) in just a few minutes. The tower, adorned with neo-Gothic details, seems to be modelled after a belfry. On your way up to the Chiado (150 ESC), take the spiral staircase to the top of the platform *(not recommended for visitors subject to dizzy spells)*, where you can enjoy a **magnificent view ★★** of the city, particularly the Castelo and the Igreja do Carmo (see p 107), not to mention, of course, the majestic Tagus River. Finally, if you enjoy lounging in the open air, walk along little Rua de São Nicolau which is lined with attractive patios.

If you are a history buff and your schedule is not too tight, make an appointment for a guided tour of the **Museu Núcleo Arqueológico** *(free admission, guided tours by reservation only; Thu 3pm to 5pm, Sat 10am to noon and 3pm to 5pm; Rua dos Correeiros no. 21, ☎ 321 17 00)*, located in the heart of the Baixa. This museum has a lovely collection of objects dating from the Roman era to the 18th century. A real treat for amateur archaeologists.

One of the loveliest squares in the city, the **Praça do Comércio ★★ (6)**, is of particular interest, not only because it is so charming, but also because numerous historic events have taken place here. Before the earthquake of 1755, the Paço da Ribeira (Riverbank Palace) stood here. A prestigious palace erected for Dom Manuel I, it was modified and embellished over and over, and housed one of the largest libraries in Europe. Today, this large rectangular square is surrounded by a series of classical buildings dating from the 18th century, which are arranged in a symmetrical manner and adorned with arcades. The pastel yellow hue of the buildings offsets the severity of their Pombaline-style architecture and creates an impression of great elegance. Today, as in the past, the edifices house a variety of administrative offices. The centre of the square is graced with a lovely **equestrian statue of Dom José I**, who was king at the time the buildings were reconstructed. It is the work of the celebrated sculptor Machado de Castro (see also p 96). At the foot of the statue, you will see a medallion depicting the Marquês de Pombal, a somewhat ironic reminder of that minister's key role in reconstructing the city. When this guide went to press, major construction was being carried out under the square. The city made the laudable decision to build a tunnel and an underground parking lot here to reduce traffic on the square, which used to serve as a parking lot itself. It should be covered with traditional paving stones by the time you visit.

On the north side of the square, an impressive baroque style **triumphal arch** ★ marks the beginning of Rua Augusta. This arch, which was not completed until 1873, features four illustrious figures (Vasco de Gama, Nuno Alvares, the mythical Viriath and the omnipresent Pombal) perched atop pedestals. They seem to be beckoning visitors to enter the heart of Lisbon in regal style. Dom Carlos I and his heir, Luis Philipe, were assassinated nearby in 1908. Just opposite, the **Cais das Colunas**, thus named for the marble columns on either side of the staircase, offers a **superb view** ★ of the Tagus, with the suspension bridge and statue of Cristo Rei in the distance. It is here that the bond between Lisbon and the Tagus is strongest; it is also from here that Portuguese navigators set out to discover the rest of the world. It is pleasant to linger here, where the slow moving tide seems to pause at the staircase before flowing from the city out to the open sea. In a continual cycle of glory and misfortune, kings fled from this quay, and caravels loaded with riches docked here. Perhaps it was here on the Cais das Colunas that the famous Portuguese nostalgia, or *saudade*, originated.

It is worth making a quick stop at nearby **Praça do Municipio** ★ (7) to see its lovely **cabled pillory** ★, topped by an **armillary sphere** (see inset). Opposite the pillory, the **neoclassical façade** of the city hall (Câmara Municipal) towers over the little square. Portugal was proclaimed a republic here on October 5, 1910. During our visit, major repairs were underway both to the square and to the Câmara Municipal, whose roof was damaged by fire. If you like Art Nouveau, be sure to pop over to tiny Largo de São Julião, right nearby, where you can admire the interesting **stained glass window** and elegant **façade** of the building next to Banco Borges & Irmão. Those whose tastes lean more toward rococo will find a fine

The Armillary Sphere

A symbol that appears frequently in Manueline art, the armillary sphere is a globe containing a set of rings showing the path of the stars. Dom Manuel adopted the sphere as the official emblem of the court.

example of that style at the corner of Rua Conceição and Rua do Crucifixo, where a residential building displays an elaborate façade, painted a pretty shade of green.

Head back toward the Praça do Comércio and take Rua do Alfândega, where you will see the **Igreja de la Conceição Velha ★ (8)** *(tram #18; bus #39 from Praça dos Restauradores; bus #46 from the Rossio, Alfânadega stop)* on your left. Its most noteworthy features are the **two front windows ★** and the **Manueline portal ★**: all that remains of an earlier church, which was destroyed in the earthquake.

If you walk a little farther along Rua da Alfândega, you will come to the Campo das Cebolas, and the **Casa dos Bicos ★ (9)** *(tram #13 from Praça Figueira, Alfândega stop; bus # 39A from the Praça do Comércio; bus #46 from the Rossio, Campo das Cebolas stop)*. This house has an unusual façade covered with diamond-shaped stones, hence the name (the House of Points). It once belonged to the viceroy of India, Afonso de Albuquerque. Partially destroyed during the earthquake, it was reconstructed while Pombal was in power. After being damaged again, this time by fire, it underwent a number of modifications, including the addition of the top two floors.

These do not match the style of the ground floor (especially as far as their proportion and window decorations are concerned), but the building is still attractive as a whole. Immediately to the right stands an interesting (but slightly run-down) residence adorned with numerous wrought-iron balconies, a fine example of the Pombaline style.

By taking Rua dos Bacalhoeritos, turning right on Rua da Madalena and then walking to the Largo da Madalena, you can either catch tram #28 or continue on foot up to the Sé (cathedral). On the way, at the Largo de Santo António da Sé, you will see the church of the same name, which houses a statue of St. Anthony of Padua. In keeping with local custom, a procession is held each year, where the statue is carried through the Alfama.

The **Sé Patriarcal** ★★★ **(10)** *(tram #28 from the Praça Luís de Camões, Sé stop; bus #37 from Praça da Figueira, Sé stop)*, erected around 1147 by order of Afonso Henriques, is one of the oldest monuments in the capital. Some historians claim that it was erected on the same site as an old mosque, but this remains a subject of debate. Having been damaged by several earthquakes (1337, 1344, 1531 and 1755), the cathedral has undergone numerous modifications. Although its exterior remains essentially Romanesque (with crenellations serving as a reminder of its defensive role and its gian, especially deep portal), a number of elements in other styles have been added, including a Gothic rose window, an ambulatory and a baroque sacristy.

Inside, to the left of the entrance, by the baptismal fonts, the walls are covered with beautiful *azulejos*. There is also an amusing panel showing St. Anthony preaching to the fish. In the neighbouring chapel, you will find an interesting **crèche**, or nativity tableau, by Machado de Castro. One of the chapels to the right of the choir (the fourth chapel in the ambulatory) shelters the 14th century tombs of Lopo Fernandes Pacheco and his wife. Finally, be sure to visit the **Romanesque cloister** ★★ *(100 ESC; Mon to Sat 9:30am to 5pm; enter through the ambulatory)*, built in the 13th century, to admire a group of lovely rose windows supported by elegant gemeled columns, each carved in a different way. In a remarkable turn of events, while excavating the foundations of Lisbon's first cathedral (built after the Moors were driven out of Portugal)

The Chiado is revealed from the Elevador de Santa Justa. (Câmara Municipal de Lisboa)

Lisbon's fortified cathedral, the Sé. (Tibor Bognar)

Lisboa, "daughter of the Tagus". (T.B.)

archaeologists recently discovered the foundations of a Roman temple dating from the Augustan age. A metal footbridge spans the site, enabling visitors to examine these impressive ruins. The cathedral also houses a small museum of religious art, the **Museu António** *(400 ESC; Mon to Sat 10am to 5pm; to the right of the main entrance)*, which exhibits an assortment of vestments, paintings and sacred objects. Aside from the ambulatory, nothing else that dates prior to the earthquake of 1755 has survived intact in the cathedral.

After visiting the Sé, make sure to stop in at **Espace Oikos** *(10am to noon and 2pm to 5pm; Rua Augusto Rosa no. 40)*, a beautiful, extremely modern multicultural centre set up inside the cloister stables. The centre is devoted to encouraging cooperation between developing countries.

TOUR B: THE CASTELO AND THE ALFAMA

See map on p 99.

The monument most known to Lisboans is the **Castelo de São Jorge** ★★ **(1)** *(bus #37 from Praça da Figueira, Castelo stop)* along with the Torre de Belém. When King Afonso Henriques drove out the Moors and took over the fortress in 1147, he seized the very cradle of the city. It was here, and on the hillside now occupied by the Alfama, that Lisbon first developed. The old fortifications had many occupants; first this was a Roman city, then a fortified Visigoth city and then a Moorish city (as of 716). Today, the ramparts shelter the old neighbourhood of **Santa Cruz**, whose souvenir shops and restaurants welcome tourists each year in a somewhat artificial atmosphere. To tour the area, go through the fortified São Jorge entrance, which faces onto Rua do Chão da Feira and offers access to the former parade ground, now a pleasant lookout. An imposing statue of King Afonso Henriques stands in the centre. Climb up the shady terraces opposite the statue to see what remains of the **royal palace of Alcáçova** (on the left), itself erected on top of an old Moorish palace. This was the home of the Aviz dynasty for many years, until a new residence was built on the banks of the Tagus. The building is now mainly used for receptions. The former palace chapel (São Miguel), which is rarely open, lies right nearby, as does the commanding officer's house. The latter has been converted into a wonderful restaurant (Casa do Leão, see p 219). To tour the Castelo, walk eastward across the terraces. On the other side of the drawbridge, inside the fortress, there are two squares with staircases leading up to the rampart-walk *(not recommended for those subject to dizzy spells)*, which boasts some **magnificent views** ★★ of the city and the Tagus. Each of the 11 towers connected to the castle serves as a scenic lookout. Given the historic significance of the Castelo, visitors might be surprised to learn that the place was neglected for many years, was a neighbourhood in itself and was even used as a prison. Although it was listed as a national monument in 1910, major repairs were not begun until 1938.

For a more in-depth tour of the neighbourhood, head down to pleasant **Praça Largo Contador-Mor (2)**, which is surrounded by houses with *azulejos*-covered façades. Continuing downhill, you'll reach **Largo das Portas do Sol**, adjacent to a small esplanade that offers a **splendid view** ★★ of East Lisbon, with the pristine dome of the Igreja de Santa Engrácia standing out sharply against the sky in the distance.

On Largo das Portas do Sol itself, visit the **Museu Escola de Artes Decorativas (3)** *(800 ESC; Wed to Mon 10am to 5pm; Largo das Portas do Sol no. 2, ☎ 886 21 83; tram #28 from Praça Luís de Camões; bus #37 from Praça da Figueira, Miradouro Santa Luzia stop)*, in the former residence of the viscounts of Azurara. Ricardo do Espírito Santo Silva purchased this little palace in 1947 in order to display his collection of decorative objects, and then established a foundation for the decorative arts. The museum boasts a particularly rich collection of 17th- and 18th-century furniture, enhanced by some magnificent bibelots. Make sure to take a look at the impressive *serviço de viagem*, a silver travel kit with its own special case. The splendid tapestry from Tournai, Belgium, showing a procession of giraffes and the elegant Chinese tapestry made of linen, silk and gold thread are remarkable as well. Finally, to prolong your stay in this pleasant setting, take a break at the museum cafeteria's pretty little patio.

Just next to the Largo das Portas do Sol is the **Miradouro de Santa Luzia (4)** *(tram #28 from Praça Luís de Camões; bus #37 from Praça da Figueira, Miradouro Santa Luzia stop)*, which offers a lovely **view** ★★ of the area, enabling visitors to see how very labyrinthine it is. The place itself is graced by a little

Tour B: The Castelo and the Alfama

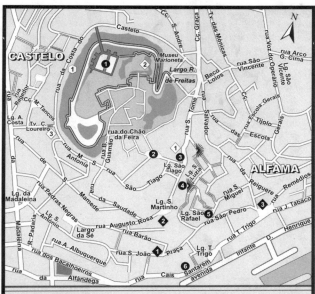

● Attractions

1. Castelo de São Jorge
2. Praça Largo Contador-Mor
3. Museu Escola de Arte Decorativas
4. Miradouro de Santa Luzia
5. Torre de São Pedro
6. Chafariz del Rei

○ Hotels

1. Ninho das Águias

◇ Restaurants

1. Cerca Moura
2. Casa do Leão
3. Costa do Castelo

◆ Bars and Nightclubs

1. Clube de Fado
2. Pé Sujo
3. Taverna d'El Rei

Tour B
The Castelo and the Alfama

0 100 200m

church and has a number of attractive terraces (refreshments available). This is a popular place for seniors to come and play cards. Finally, you'll find some beautiful *azulejos* ★ here; make sure to take a look at the ones showing a general view of the city (on the south wall of the lookout), as well as those depicting the capture of Lisbon in 1147 (on the right wall of the church).

To reach the Alfama from the Miradouro de Santa Luzia, go down the staircase immediately behind the Igreja Santa Luzia (tram #28 from Praça Luís de Camões; bus #37 from Praça da Figueira, Miradouro Santa Luzia stop).

The feeling of happenstance that prevails in the **Alfama** ★ (see map p 99) and the myriad reactions it elicits from visitors make it a delightful place to explore. There's surprise, when you head

---

The Alfama

Alfama: from the Arabic word *alhaman*, referring to the presence of hot springs. The name dates back to the era of the Moors, when a hot spring used to gush forth on the Largo do Charariz de Dentro. Along with Santa Cruz, the Alfama is the oldest part of the city. Essentially a working-class neighbourhood nowadays, it was originally inhabited by wealthy Moorish merchants and then, after the Moors surrendered control of the city, by Portuguese nobles. The character of the neighbourhood changed, however, when the earthquake of 1755 destroyed most of the opulent residences. The nobility gradually moved into the surrounding areas (particularly Belém), making way for sailors, artisans and workers, who slowly, and somewhat haphazardly, took over the area. Overpopulated, with no utilities, the Alfama slid into a long period of decline, eventually becoming a disgrace to well-heeled Lisboans. With the growth of the tourist industry, however, the city took a renewed interest in this neighbourhood. The Alfama now appears to be undergoing restorations, although many little "houses" (for lack of a better word) are still in an advanced state of disrepair, and a tour of the narrow and not always clean alleyways is best left to those with a genuine interest in the lifestyle of the Portuguese working class.

into one of countless little alleys and suddenly discover that it is only wide enough for one person to pass through at a time; pleasure, when you reach the end of an alley and find yourself in a little square surrounded by tiny houses decorated with *azulejos* and geraniums; despair, when you come to the end of a long climb uphill, only to discover another staircase that doesn't seem to lead anywhere; and finally a sense of adventure, as you stroll through unknown streets with only cooking odours and children's shouts to guide you. Although you don't need an itinerary to explore the Alfama, in fact you are better without one, make sure to visit the **Torre de São Pedro (5)** *(Largo de São Rafael)*, all that remains of the Moorish fortifications that once protected the city. At the top of the tower, in the back, is a pretty gemeled window, which can be admired from Rua da Judiaria. Back on the banks of the Tagus, on Largo do Terreiro do Trigo, you'll find an elegant public fountain **Chafariz del Rei ★ (6)** *(Rua Cais de Santarém)* built by order of Dom Dinis, it is one of the most ancient public fountains in Lisbon. Nearby, at the corner of Rua da Regueira and Rua dos Remédios, is a beautiful **Manueline door**.

TOUR C: GRAÇA AND EAST LISBON

See the map on p 103.

Heading east along the Tagus, you will come to the **Museu Militar ★ (1)** *(300 ESC, free on Wed; Tue to Sun 10am to 5pm; Largo do Museu da Artilharia, ☎ 888 21 31; bus #39A or 81 from Praça do Comércio, Estação Santa Apolónia stop; bus #46 from the Rossio, Estação Santa Apolónia stop)*, a sumptuous building containing a widely varied assortment of weapons, which is sure to fascinate anyone with an interest in the subject. It is worth coming here just to see the **beautifully decorated rooms** in which some of the collections are presented. These feature gilding, painted ceilings, carved woodwork and paintings by great Portuguese artists. Various artillery pieces are exhibited in a large, verdant, interior courtyard, the walls of which are decorated with lovely *azulejos*.

Of the many expressions used by Lisboans, *"obras de Santa Engrácia"* is probably one of the most colourful. It is used to designate a work in progress that seems as if it will never be completed. The origin of this expression can be traced back to the construction of the **Igreja-Panteão de Santa Engrácia (2)** *(200 ESC; Campo de Santa Clara; bus #39A from Praça do Comércio, Estação Santa Apolónia stop; bus #46 from the Rossio, Estação Santa Apolónia stop)*, which was begun in the 17th century and finished in the 1960s! It now presents its virtually immaculate white dome proudly for all the city to see. Declared the National Pantheon in 1966, it contains cenotaphs to major Portuguese figures like Afonso de Albuquerque, Camões and Vasco de Gama.

Just uphill from the Pantheon, you'll find the **Campo de Santa Clara (3)** *(tram #28 from Praça Luís de Camões, Rua da Voz do Operário stop)*, a charming little square with a covered market at its centre. In addition to the usual vegetable stalls, you'll find all sorts of second-hand goods displayed all around the building (see "Shopping", p 272). Several handsome government buildings, including the stately military courthouse, face onto the square, and an attractive little park completes the layout. Be sure to take a look at the beautiful façade covered with *azulejos* in trompe-l'œil motifs at numbers 124-126.

Located, as its name indicates, outside the city walls, the **Igreja e Mosteiro de São Vicente da Fora (4)** *(Largo de São Vicente; tram #28 from Praça Luís de Camões, Rua da Voz do Operário stop)* is worth the detour along narrow Rua Arco Grande da Cima, with its pretty archway. Not only does the church boast a lovely **marble interior**, a high altar topped by an impressive baldachin, and a beautiful choir floor, but the huge monastery is adorned with numerous *azulejos*. The church was built during the reign of Afonso Henriques, as a gesture of thanks to St. Vincent, the patron saint of Lisbon, after the Moors were driven out of the city. Upon entering the **cloister ★** through the ground floor *(300 ESC; Mon to Sat 10am to 1pm and 3pm to 5pm; to the right of the church)*, take a look at the immense cistern illuminated by the skylights of the cloister. It is also interesting to see how well the vestiges of a 12th century monastery were incorporated into the present structure. The two large cloisters on the first floor are decorated with ***azulejos* ★** depicting pastoral scenes. Don't miss the remarkable *azulejos* illustrating La Fontaine's *Fables* in the south cloister. On the second floor is the the longest panel of *azulejos* in Portugal. The tiles in the caretaker's quarters depict various historic events, including the capture of Lisbon. At the

Tour C: Graça and East Lisbon

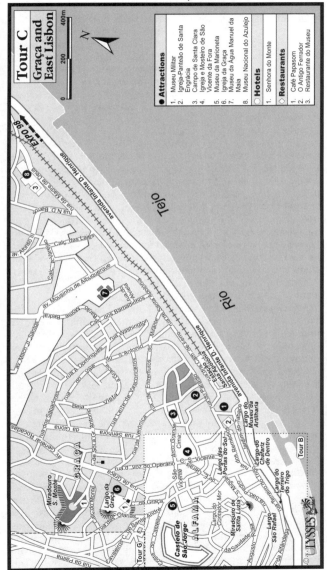

Tour C
Graça and East Lisbon

Attractions
1. Museu Militar
2. Igreja-Panteão de Santa Engrácia
3. Campo de Santa Clara
4. Igreja e Mosteiro de São Vicente da Fora
5. Museu da Marioneta
6. Igreja da Graça
7. Museu da Água Manuel da Maia
8. Museu Nacional do Azulejo

Hotels
1. Senhora do Monte

Restaurants
1. Café Papasom
2. O Antigo Ferrador
3. Restaurante do Museu

far end of the cloister, the former refectory has been converted into a mausoleum for the Bragança dynasty. Here lie the remains of Portugal's last monarchs, including Queen Amélia (died in 1951) and her son, the country's last king, Manuel II, who died in exile in 1932. Before leaving, make sure to take in the lovely view of the city from the terrace accessible from the ground floor *(on your way back downstairs from the cloister, take the left-hand exit and then the staircase immediately to the right)*.

By taking Rua de São Vicente then Rua de Santa Marinha, you'll come to Largo Rodrigues de Freitas, home of the **Museu da Marioneta (5)** *(300 ESC; Tue to Fri 10am to noon and 2pm to 6pm, Sat and Sun11am to 6pm; Largo Rodrigues de Freitas no. 19, ☎ 888 28 41)*. On a guided tour of this museum, you can learn all there is to know about these mischief-makers.

Just steps away, on Largo da Graça, the Miradouro da Graça commands a remarkable **panoramic view ★★** of the city and the castle. This pleasant esplanade lies in front of the **Igreja da Graça (6)**, whose **Manueline baptistery ★** and numerous chapels decorated with *talhas douradas* are worth a peek.

Like *azulejos*, water is an integral part of Lisbon's history, as the Águas Livres (see p 143) aqueduct, the Mãe d'Água reservoir and the city's numerous fountains remind us. Therefore, no history buff would want to miss a visit to the remarkable **Museu da Água Manuel da Maia ★ (7)** *(300 ESC, guided tour of both sites mentioned above by request only; Mon and Wed to Sat 10am to 12:30pm and 2pm to 5pm; Rua do Alviela no. 12, ☎ 813 55 22; bus #39A or 81 from Praça do Comércio, Estação Santa Apolónia stop; bus #46 from the Rossio, Estação Santa Apolónia stop; bus #12 from Marquês de Pombal, Estacão Santa Apolónia stop)*, located in the heart of the Xábregas neighbourhood in East Lisbon. Through documents, photographs and various kinds of machinery, visitors explore the complex history of the city's water supply system. The city's first residents drew water freely from small springs in the Alfama. The lovely Chafariz del Rei fountain (see p 101), which dates back at least to the era of Muslim rule, is a beautiful example from this period. However, as demand for water increased and supply diminished, water distribution became regulated. Originally, slaves had carried water to their masters' homes in wooden casks; now, this activity became a full-time occupation, mainly of Galician labourers. The rules were very strict, and certain people were given water before others, depending on their rank on a list: workers were first, and women were fifth! Later still, after a number of springs dried up and the demand for water continued to increase, King João V ordered the construction of the Aguas Livres aqueduct so that water could be brought in from springs outside the city. Starting in the mid-18th century, the owners of springs located on the outskirts of the capital were obliged by royal decree to contribute to the city's water supply via a network of aqueducts. In return, a certain amount of water was distributed to their Lisbon homes at no charge. In some cases, this arrangement is still in effect today! As the demand for water continued to rise, a new aqueduct, the Aqueduto de Alviela, was built in 1871. When it became apparent that the pressure was too low in certain places, French engineers from Rouen were hired to install a **pumping station** ★★, which can be admired today at the museum. If you have a chance, go and see the machines in operation (ask the employee on duty), and make sure to climb up to the second floor to admire the huge hydraulic pistons in action; it's truly a sight to see! Today, in addition to the Alviela aqueduct, another conduit starting at the Tagus and a supply pipe connected to Castelo do Bode provide the city with water.

Portugal's inescapable *azulejos*, with their countless depictions of historic events and social realities, are like an open book on the country's past. If you find these tiles truly fascinating, make sure to visit the Convento da Madre de Deus to see the **Museu Nacional do Azulejo** ★★★ **(8)** *(300 ESC; Tue 2pm to 6pm, Wed to Sun 10am to 6pm; Rua da Madre de Deus no. 4, ☎ 814 77 47 or 814 77 99; bus #39A from Praça do Comércio, Igreja Madre de Deus stop; tram #17 from Praça do Comércio)*. Founded in the early 16th century by Queen Leonor (the widow of João II) as a place where she could retire from public life, the **Convento da Madre de Deus** was once so luxurious that it looked more like a palace than a convent. The convent and the adjacent church have undergone numerous modifications over the centuries. During the reign of João III (1557-1578), the buildings were raised in order to protect them from the frequent floods of the Tagus. Then, under João V, the convent was given a major facelift, and a new sacristy was erected. The building escaped only partially damaged from the terrible earthquake of 1755. A century later, in 1867, after the convent had become government property, large sections of both the cloister and the church were destroyed by a fire while extensive renovations were being carried out. Thanks to public donations, however, the structure was quickly reconstructed and restored. In 1959, the Gulbenkian Foundation came up with the idea of opening an *azulejo* museum here, an idea that was fully realized in 1980, with the official inauguration of the Museu Nacional do Azulejo.

Inside, on the ground floor, there are two **cloisters**, the larger of which contains a great number of *azulejos* accompanied by written explanations of the various ways of making the tiles. Before going upstairs, make sure to visit the **Igreja da Madre de Deus** ★★★, adjacent to the large cloister. The remarkable interior of the church is decorated with a harmonious combination of *azulejos* and sculptures. *Talhas douradas*, statues, Flemish and Portuguese paintings, and other baroque decorations seem to be vying for the dazzled eyes of visitors. At the entrance of the church, on the left, there is a remarkable group of *azulejos* depicting Moses receiving the Ten Commandments on Mount Sinai. As the church is dedicated to the Virgin Mary, a lovely representation of the *Madre de Deus* graces the high altar. After gaining access to the second floor through the **small cloister** ★, which is completely covered with beautiful *azulejos* in a rich shade of blue, you'll find yourself in a small room, where your attention will be drawn to a group of **Dutch tiles** ★★ dating from 1740, all in pretty brown hues. Each tile shows a scene from Jesus's life, with the various figures depicted in a manner reminiscent of a child's drawings. A real little wonder to behold!

Next, you'll visit the *coro-alto* ★★, at the back of the church, where the decoration of the ceiling and the walls, completely covered with big paintings with fantastically ornate gilt frames is outstanding. On your way out of the *coro-alto*, immediately to the right, is a large panel of 576 *azulejos* re-creating a panoramic view of **pre-1755 Lisbon** ★. Finally, don't leave the premises without taking a look at the group of *azulejos* illustrating scenes from the life of **Chapeleiro António Joaquim Carneiro** ★★, known as Odito, an amazing social portrait written in old Portuguese.

TOUR D: THE CHIADO AND THE BAIRRO ALTO

See maps on p 109 and p 110.

Though its boundaries are somewhat vague, the Chiado, with its pretty little central square called Largo do Chiado, essentially lies between Rua do Carmo and Praça Luís de Camões. From the Rossio, start off your tour by walking up **Rua do Carmo**. Along with Rua Garrett, which intersects with it, this street was long home to the most elegant shops in the capital. In August of 1988, however, a terrible fire that lasted several days destroyed all of the buildings on Rua do Carmo and a number of those on Rua Garrett, reducing many luxurious, near-centenarian stores to ashes. With the help of celebrated architect Álvaro Siza Vieira, the city reconstructed as many buildings as possible, always striving to retain the spirit of the area. Strolling along Rua do Carmo, you will see many façades that escaped complete destruction and are now being preserved so that they can be incorporated into new buildings. When you reach number 87A *(on the right side of the street as you head uphill)*, stop for a moment to admire the tiny Luvaria Ulisses, a lovely little glove shop dating from the turn of the century.

Before continuing your tour on Rua Garrett, turn right onto the Calçada do Sacremento to reach peaceful little **Largo do Carmo**. The atmosphere was livelier back when tram #25 used to stop here. In addition to an elegant fountain, you'll find the **Igreja do Carmo ★ (1)**. Miraculously, only the church's vault collapsed during the great earthquake of 1755. Today, with its arches that seem to defy the heavens, the church stands its ground proudly, as if to show that it is still keeping a close watch over the lower parts of the city. Built in the late 14th century at the instigation of Nuno Álvares Pereira (Grand Officer of the Crown), in honour of Portugal's victory in the Battle of Aljubarrota (see p 20), it was the largest church in Lisbon for many years. The open-air **Museu Arqueológico do Carmo** *(Largo do Camo, ☎ 346 04 73; take the Elevador de Santa Justa from the Rossio)* used to display Visigoth and Roman artifacts, Arab sculptures and even a Manueline window from the Mosteiro dos Jerónimos (see p 138). However, when this guide went to press, the museum was closed for repairs. Though it is scheduled to reopen in 1998, its future role remains uncertain.

Tour D - The Chiado and the Bairro Alto

● Attractions

1. Igreja do Carmo
2. Largo do Chiado
3. Praça Luís de Camões
4. Teatro Nacional de São Carlos
5. Galeria Nacional do Chiado
6. Igreja São Roque
7. Miradouro de São Pedro de Alcântara
8. Praça do Príncipe Real
9. Jardim Botânico
10. Museu da Ciência

○ Hotels

1. Borges
2. Casa de São Mamede
3. Globo
4. Londres
5. Príncipe Real

◇ Restaurants

1. A Brasileira
2. Adega do Teixeira
3. Ali-a-Papa
4. Bachus
5. Bizzaro
6. Brasserie de l'Entrecôte
7. Café no Chiado-Ciber Chiado
8. Casa Nostra
9. Cervejaria da Trindade
10. Chacuteria Francesa
11. Chez Degroote
12. Consenso
13. El Último Tango
14. Estadio Silva Seixas
15. Flor do Duque
16. Guillaume Tell
17. Hell's Kitchen
18. Huá Li Tou
19. Janela do Bairro
20. Majong
21. Massima Culpa
22. Novo Bonsai
23. O Capuchinho
24. O Paço do Principe
25. O Sol
26. O Tacão Pequeno
27. Pap'Açôrda
28. Pastelaria São Roque
29. Pato Baton
30. Pedro das Arábias
31. Pizzeria Mama Rosa
32. Poeta na Bicha
33. Porta Branca
34. Rua em Rua
35. Securas
36. Tagide
37. Tapas-Bar El Gordo
38. Tavares Rico

◆ Bars and Nightclubs

1. A Capela
2. A Tasca-Tequila Bar
3. Adega do Ribatejo
4. Agua no Bico
5. Bachus Bar-Restaurante
6. Bar-106
7. Bricabar
8. Cafediário
9. Café Webs
10. Céu de Lisboa
11. Finalmente
12. Frágil
13. Fremitus
14. Gráfico's
15. Keops
16. KGB
17. Memorial
18. Mezcal
19. O Forcado
20. Páginas Tantas
21. Pavilhão Chinês
22. Pedro Quinto
23. Pintaí
24. Portas Largas
25. Satyros
26. Solar do Vinho do Porto
27. Suave
28. Targus
29. Tatoo
30. Trumps

Tour D: The Chiado and the Bairro Alto 109

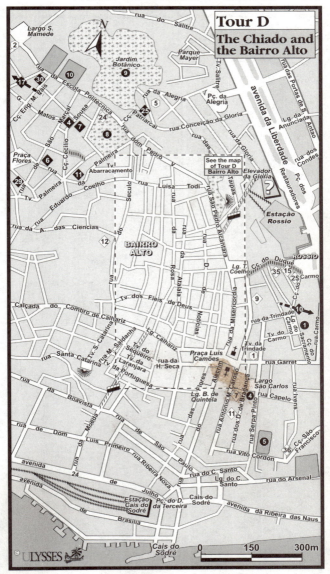

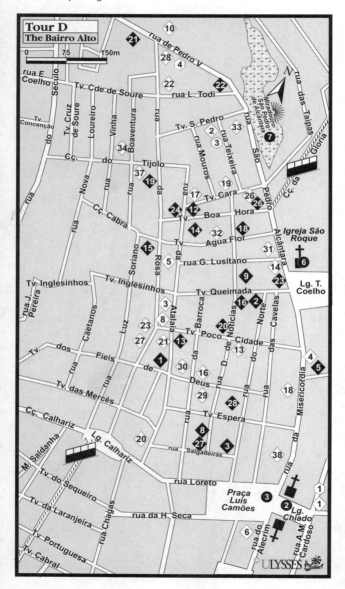

Tour D: The Chiado and the Bairro Alto 111

Before heading back to Rua Garrett, *azulejo* aficionados will want to stop by numbers 28-34 on Rua da Trindade *(on the north side of the Largo)*, where allegorical figures representing water, earth, commerce and industry adorn a superb ***azulejo-covered façade*** ★.

Now, take **Rua Garrett** to Largo do Chiado, the best-known square in the area. On the way, stop at numbers 50-52 for a peek inside the Ourivesaria Aliança. This goldsmith's shop is a survivor from the days when luxury shops abounded in the area. Farther along, at number 77, the window of the Paris em Lisboa shop is adorned with pretty signs and a copper-plated, Art Nouveau guardrail. Finally, make sure to go inside the Ramiro Leã notions shop (number 83) for a look at the magnificent Art Nouveau-style elevator and the stairwell adorned with stained glass and frescoes.

It is on **Largo do Chiado (2)** *(tram #28 from Rua da Conceição in the Baixa; tram #24 or bus #15 from the Rato, Praça Luís de Camões stop)*, once a favourite haunt of the literary crowd, that you'll find the famous café A Brasileira (see p 227). Such celebrated Portuguese poets as António Ribeiro and Fernando Pessõa used to be regular customers here. On the patio, you can have your picture taken with Pessõa (the bronze version, of course!), unless you'd prefer to be seen with that famous Renaissance poet Antonio Ribeiro, whose statue stands in the middle of the square. As a crowning touch to this beautiful spot, two churches, **Nossa Senhora de l'Encarnação** and the Italian community's **Nossa Senhora do Loreto**, stand, with freshly restored façades, across from each other on the square.

In keeping with the literary theme, **Praça Luís de Camões (3)** *(tram #28 from Rua da Conceição in the Baixa)* has a statue of Portugal's most celebrated poet, Luís de Camões (see p 37) in its centre. This square, which is surrounded by dilapidated buildings, most certainly deserves better. There is a certain harmonious quality about the buildings, and the trees lining the square, along with the view of the two churches flanking Largo do Chiado, make this quite a pleasant spot. Take a few moments to observe the bustling activity going on about you.

It is worthwhile to walk farther down Rua Serpa Pinto to take a look at the **Teatro Nacional de São Carlos (4)** *(Rua Serpa Pinto, near Rua Capelo, program ☎ 346 84 08, tickets*

☎ 346 59 14; tram #28 from Rua da Conceição in the Baixa, Largo do Chiado stop), a handsome Italian-style building built in the late 18th century. The interior was modeled after the Scala in Milan.

If you like painting or modern architecture, you simply must visit the Chiado's brand-new museum. Set up inside the former Museum of Contemporary Art, the **Galeria Nacional do Chiado** ★★ **(5)** *(400 ESC; Tue 2pm to 6pm, Wed to Sun 10am to 6pm; Rua Serpa Pinto nos. 4-6,* ☎ *343 21 48 or 343 21 49; tram #28 from Rua da Conceição in the Baixa, Rua Vitor Cordon stop)* displays paintings and sculptures by major Portuguese artists like Columbano, Silvo Porto, João Voz, Soares dos Reis, Malhoa, etc. Despite its name, the museum is devoted mainly to works from the 19th and early 20th centuries. The interior design, by the Wilmotte firm (a French architecture firm already well-known for having designed the furnishings for the Champs-Élysées in Paris), successfully combines metal and glass structures with stones and bricks, some of which date back to the 17th century. Particularly noteworthy pieces include José de Almada Negreiro's *Gato Felix*, which you'll see as you come in, and, on the second floor, the panels entitled *Bar de Marinheiro* and *Jazz*, which were part of a set of 12 Art-Deco panels that used to adorn a Spanish movie theatre. These are the only two to have survived, and they narrowly escaped destruction. Part of the museum is laid out in the former São Francisco da Cidade monastery. After being abandoned by the church then put to several other uses, the buildings served as a *bolacha* (cookie) factory from 1855 to 1898. The only noteworthy vestiges from that period are the four ovens in the José-Augusto França room, which have been perfectly integrated into the decor. Among the other works on display, Eduardo Viano's remarkable paintings are not to be missed. The museum has an attractive cafeteria with an outdoor seating area graced with a number of modern sculptures. Make sure to go to the top floor, where a huge terrace offers a partial view of the Tagus. Overall, the ultra-modern decor is a bit cold, and there is a woeful amount of wasted space.

The **Bairro Alto** ★★, was originally (in the 16th and 17th centuries) made up of palatial residences, which lay stretched in front of small public squares and parks. These were later replaced by working-class houses occupied by artisans and

Azulejo-*covered façade*

shopkeepers. In the evening, local prostitution increased, giving the area a bad reputation. Presently undergoing yet another transformation, the Bairro Alto has come to be known for its nightlife (family restaurants, *fado* taverns), and more and more shops, discos and fashionable restaurants are popping up here, attracting young Lisboans in search of *movida*.

Take your time as you stroll down Rua da Rosa, located opposite the Largo, or Rua da Atalaia, a bit farther along, so that you can soak up the peaceful atmosphere that prevails in the Bairro. A sudden change comes over these streets after dark (especially on weekends, see also "Safety", p 65), with bars, nightclubs, *fado* taverns and nighttime restaurants appearing as if by magic.

Farther along, at the edge of the Chiado, the **Igreja São Roque** ★★ **(6)** *(Largo Trindade Coelho; from Praça dos Restauradores, take the Funicular da Glória, beside the Palacio Foz, or bus #100)*, does not look very inviting at first glance, due to its nondescript façade. Its interior, however, is not to be missed. Built by the Jesuits in the 16th century, partially destroyed in the earthquake of 1755 and reconstructed shortly thereafter, this is one of the most richly decorated churches in the capital. Its nave and wooden ceiling painted in trompe-l'œil are both very elegant, while the walls are lavishly decorated with carved woodwork and marble. There is a series of chapels, each decorated in a different manner. The **Capela de São João Baptista** ★★★ *(from the chancel, first chapel on the left)* is a veritable marvel of Italian art. Commissioned by King João V and constructed in Rome by numerous artisans and artists, it was transported here piece by piece by boat. Amethysts, bronzes, lapis-lazuli, ivory, silver, alabaster and all sorts of other splendid materials make this chapel look like a museum of sacred art. It is almost as if everything that Italian baroque art has to offer were concentrated here. Before leaving this magical place, stop in at the second chapel on the right (from the chancel) to see some beautiful Renaissance-era *azulejos* ★★ made in Seville.

It is also worth visiting the **Museu de Arte Sacra de São Roque** ★ *(150 ESC, free Sun; Tue to Sun 10am to 5pm; entrance from the church or from outside, immediately to the right of the church, ☎ 346 03 61 or 342 08 50)* adjoining the church, which contains a rich collection of sacred objects made

Tour D: The Chiado and the Bairro Alto 115

of silver and gold, as well as all sorts of vestments. One of the most interesting items is a 14th-century silver Virgin from Germany.

Nearby, on Rua de São Pedro de Alcântara, you can enjoy a magnificent view from the **Miradouro de São Pedro de Alcântara ★ (7)** *(to the right when you get off the Funicular da Glória; from Praça dos Restauradores, take the Funicular da Glória, beside the Palacio Foz)*. This pleasant little garden and lookout lies opposite the Castelo and offers a view of downtown Lisbon below, with the Tagus in the distance.

Heading back up Rua de São Pedro de Alcântara to Rua da Escola Politécnica, you will find a pretty square on your left. This is **Praça do Príncipa Real (8)** *(from Praça dos Restauradores take the Funicular da Glória, then bus #100 or #58, Príncipe Real stop)*, whose little park is a pleasant place to relax. If you come here in the afternoon, you'll find many locals playing cards on the park's little tables. In the centre, there is a remarkable cypress tree, which has been shaped into a bower and offers welcome shelter from the sun. Located right nearby is the pleasant restaurant Café O Paço do Principe (see p 228), where you can have a bite to eat while admiring the surroundings.

Just opposite, at the corner of Rua da Escola Politécnica and little Calçada da Patriarcal, stands the **Palacete Ribeiro da Cunha**, a beautiful mansion that was built in 1877 and now belongs to the University of Lisbon. After admiring the lovely façade with its Arab accents, go inside for a peek at the pretty covered patio, also influenced by Arab architecture *(take the door on the right, just past the main entrance)*.

If you have a penchant for a calm setting lush with greenery, continue up the street a little farther to the **Jardim Botânico (9)** *(200 ESC; winter, Mon to Fri 9am to 6pm, Sat and Sun 10am to 6pm; summer until 8pm; Rua da Escola Politécnica no. 58; from Praça dos Restauradores take the Funicular da Glória, then bus #58, Rua da Escola Politécnica stop)*, laid out alongside the former Faculty of Science. A path lined with palm trees seems to beckon visitors to enter this pleasant garden. Established on a hilly site, the garden offers numerous interesting views of the city. For those wishing to go

Exploring

to Avenida da Liberdade, a second exit is located on Rua da Alegria.

Right near by, the **Museu de Ciência (10)** *(free admission; Mon to Fri 10am to 1pm and 2pm to 5pm, Sat 3pm to 6pm; Rua da Escola Politécnica no. 58, ☎ 396 15 21 or 396 15 22; from Praça dos Restauradores, take the Funicular da Glória, then bus #58, Rua da Escola Politécnica stop)* will appeal mainly to those interested in exact sciences. Throughout the museum, all sorts of devices are on hand so that visitors can test the basic principles of physics and chemistry themselves. Though the explanatory text is written only in Portuguese, this little foray into the scientific world is quite entertaining.

TOUR E: THE RATO AND AMOREIRAS

See the map on p 117.

This neighbourhood, most of which was built after the earthquake of 1755, was once known for its royal earthenware factory and large silk factory. Founded in 1767 due to the efforts of the Marquês de Pombal, the Real Fábrica de Louça was one of the first large-scale factories in the country, producing large numbers of *azulejos*. Today, the Rato is essentially a shopping area, located between the Bairro Alto and the Amoreiras.

Because it offers direct access to the Bairro Alto, the **Largo do Rato (1)** *(from Praça dos Restauradores, take the Elevador da Glória, then bus #15, Rato stop)*, the true heart of the Rato, is constantly bustling with activity. All around the square, you'll find a wide variety of shops selling reasonably-priced merchandise, as well as a number of snack-bars.

Heading back up Rua das Amoreiras, you'll see **Praça das Amoreiras (2)** on your right. This pretty square has a park, which is a pleasant place to idle away some time. To get there, you have to walk under the Aqueduto das Águas Livres (see p 143). You will notice its pillars are adorned with lovely *azulejos*.

Facing onto the Praça das Amoreiras, the **Museu Arpad Szenes-Vieira da Silva (3)** *(300 ESC, free Mon; Mon and Wed to Sat*

Tour E: The Rato and Amoreiras 117

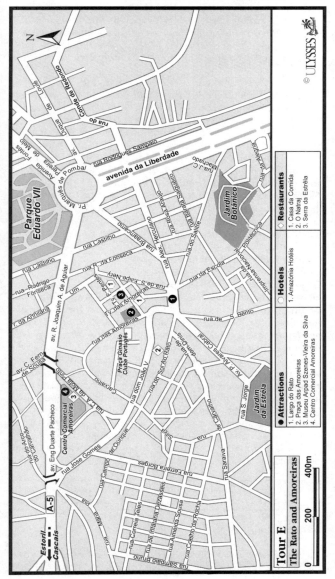

noon to 8pm, Sun 10am to 6pm; Praça das Amoreiras nos. 56-58, ☎ 388 00 44; from Praça dos Restauradores, take the Elevador da Glória, then bus #15, Jardim Amoreiras stop) features works by the two famous painters after which it is named.

The **Mãe d'Água reservoir** *(guided tour upon request; inquire at the Museu da Água Manuel da Maia, Rua do Alviela no. 12, ☎ 813 55 22)*, located right next to Praça da Amoreiras, is the last link in the capital's water supply system. It was constructed in 1834 to collect water from the impressive Águas Livres aqueduct (see p 143), to which it is directly connected. With a capacity of 5,500 cubic metres, it supplied water to as many as 64 fountains by means of three conduits running under the city. Three fountains, including the one in the middle of Largo do Carmo and the one on Largo Dr. José Figueiredo, opposite the Museu Nacional de Arte Antiga, are still connected to this system. Aside from its own pretty fountain, the site's main attraction is its vast pool of water, sheltered by elegant vaults.

Continuing north in the Amoreiras neighbourhood, you cannot help but be surprised by the futuristic **Centro Comercial Amoreiras ★ (4)** *(from the Rossio or from the Praça dos Restauradores, bus #11, Amoreiras stop; or, from the Praça dos Restauradores, take the Elevador da Glória, then bus #15, Amoreiras stop)*. This group of ultra-modern buildings, whose blend of shapes and colours is oddly reminiscent of the Art Deco style, is the work of architect Tomás Taveira. A veritable shopping mecca, it has over 350 shops (don't expect bargain prices), 50 restaurants and cafés (see p 228) and several movie theatres. Although this place is not to everyone's taste, we strongly recommend a visit to see how dramatically its architecture contrasts with the rest of the city. You can decide for yourself whether it is striking, hideous, fantastic or simply pleasant.

TOUR F: MARQUÊS DE POMBAL, SALDANHA AND NORTH LISBON

See map on p 121.

Vast **Parque Eduardo VII ★** is perhaps the most distinctive part of this quarter, which might strike visitors as little more than

Tour F: Marquês de Pombal, Saldanha and North Lisbon 119

one big crossroads (Praça Marquês de Pombal). A tour of the park starts off beautifully at the top, in the middle of Avenida Cardeal Cerejeira *(bus #2 from the Rossio, Marquês da Fronteira stop)*, where a large terrace overlooking a stretch of greenery offers a lovely **view ★★ (1)** of the park, with Praça Marquês de Pombal, the Baixa and the Tagus in the distance. A formal garden graces the centre. Although it was created on the occasion of King Edward VII of England's visit to Portugal, this carpet of greenery now seems more like a tribute to the Marquês de Pombal, whose statue occupies a place of honour at the far end. Opposite the lookout, on the other side of Avenida Cardeal Cerejeira, stands a castle-like building, which looks rather pleasant but is actually a prison, so you are better off not visiting it!

On the right side of the park as you walk down the esplanade, you'll see the **Estufa Fria e Quente ★ (2)** *(80 ESC; open every day 9am to 5:30pm during summer, 9am to 5pm during winter)*, dating from 1910. Originally located in an old quarry, this greenhouse contains two gardens, one with exotic plants. Its cleverly designed bamboo roof creates a microclimate in which lush vegetation from countries as varied as Australia, Peru and China can flourish. It is extremely pleasant to stroll along the numerous pathways that wind their way through the heart of this domesticated jungle.

Closer to downtown Lisbon, but on the left this time, you'll see the dazzling baroque-style **Pavilhão dos Desportos ★ (3)** (Sports Stadium). It is worth making a detour to admire its exterior, which is covered with *azulejos* ★★, most depicting historical scenes like the famous Battle of Ourique (see p 19). Particularly noteworthy is the magnificent grouping entitled *Cruzeiro do Sul*, in which five female figures, half-angel, half-fairy, seem to be showing the path of discovery to a caravel heading out to sea. Right beside the stadium, in the park, there is a picnic area where visitors can have a bite to eat and relax a while before returning to the feverish activity of the city.

Praça Marquês de Pombal (4) *(you can take any number of buses here from Praça dos Restauradores and the Rato)*, also known as the Rotunda, is a large traffic circle with a lovely central monument honouring the Marquês de Pombal and his talents as a statesman. The Praça has an elegant design and is

● Attractions

1. Lookout
2. Estufa Fria et Quente
3. Pavilhão dos Desportos
4. Praça Marquês de Pombal
5. Museu Calouste Gulbenkian
6. Praça de Touros
7. Museu da Cidade
8. Museu Nacional do Traje
9. Instituto Nacional de Estatística

⬡ Hotels

1. Avenida Alameda
2. Avenida Parque
3. Dom Carlos
4. Dom Manuel I
5. Excelsior
6. Fénix
7. Flamingo
8. Holiday Inn Lisboa
9. Méridien
10. Miraparque
11. Rex
12. Ritz
13. Sheraton and Towers Lisboa
14. Suite Hotel Dom Rodrigo
15. Vila Nova

◇ Restaurants

1. Galeto
2. Marcado Original
3. Pastelaria Versailles
4. Pub Eduardo VII

adorned with many interesting statues. Unfortunately, however, it is difficult to get to the middle of it.

The **Museu Calouste Gulbenkian ★★★ (5)** *(500 ESC; Tue to Sun 10am to 5pm; Avenida de Berna no. 45, ☎ 795 02 36 or 793 51 31; bus #31, 41 or 46 from the Rossio, Gulbenkian or São Sebastião or Palhavã metro stop)* is located in the Praça de Espanha area, in a lovely park adorned with numerous modern sculptures (Parque de Palhavã). It has a large collection of decorative objects (paintings, sculptures, earthenware, bibelots), mostly from Europe and the Orient. All of the objects in this modern building are beautifully displayed in a series of rooms, each devoted to a different era. Almost all of these rooms are fascinating and merit a visit. In one, you can admire some lovely Egyptian pieces; in another, an interesting collection of ancient coins (mainly Greek and Roman). Then there is a collection of articles (earthenware, carpets, books, etc.) from the Near and Middle East, as well as a room containing objects and paintings from the Far East. At the end of your tour, you will pass through a series of rooms devoted

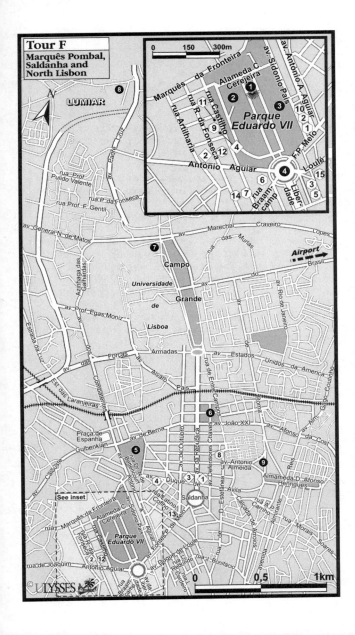

> ## Calouste Sarkis Gulbenkian
>
> The **Calouste Gulbenkian Fundação** was created by a wealthy Armenian businessman named Calouste Sarkis Gulbenkian, who made his fortune in the oil industry. After living in London and Paris for a while, he settled in Lisbon in 1942. A true art lover, he accumulated an impressive number of genuine works of art (6,000) over the course of his lifetime. Upon his death in 1955, a large portion of his assets went to the government and to his foundation, which now organizes many exhibits and concerts, and even has its own ballet company.

to European art, covering the Renaissance all the way through Art Nouveau, and including decorative objects from the 18th and 19th centuries. This museum, where modern technology has been put to wonderful use in the interest of art, also contains a large library and space for temporary exhibitions.

Right nearby, in the same park, the **Centro de Arte Moderna** *(same ticket used for admission to museum, same schedule; Rua Dr. Nicolau Bettencourt)* exhibits paintings and sculptures by contemporary Portuguese artists and foreign artists working in Portugal.

If you are interested in bullfighting, go to **Praça de Touros (6)** *(Praça de Touros; bus #21 from the Rossio, Campo Pequeno stop; Campo Pequeno subway station)*, where an unusual building houses the city's arena. Built in 1892, it has onion domes and horseshoe arches, which lend it a distinctly Moorish look. Between May and October, there are "shows" twice a week.

History buffs will enjoy the **Museu da Cidade (7)** *(330 ESC; Tue to Sun 10am to 1pm and 2pm to 6pm; Campo Grande no. 245, ☎ 759 16 17; bus #7 from Praça Figueira; bus #1 or #36 from the Rossio, Campo Grande-Norte stop, or metro Campo Grande-Norte)*, which traces the history of Lisbon from prehistoric times to the birth of the Republic. The exhibit includes an interesting model of the city the way it looked before the earthquake of 1755.

Tour F: Marquês de Pombal, Saldanha and North Lisbon   123

The **Museu Nacional do Traje** ★ **(8)** *(400 ESC; Tue to Sun 10am to 6pm; Largo Júlio Castilho-Parque do Monteiro-Mor, in Lumiar, ☎ 759 03 18; bus #7 from Praça Figueira; bus #36, from the Rossio, Lumiar stop)* displays a vast array of fabrics and clothing dating from the 4th century through the 15th. Artisans using various weaving techniques can be observed in the workshops surrounding the museum.

The **Instituto Nacional de Estatística (9)** is housed in a beautiful Art-Deco building of gleaming green metalwork and golden-hued glass that blocks off the vista down Avenida António José de Almeida.

TOUR G: RESTAURADORES AND LIBERDADE

See map on p 125.

Upon the death of Cardinal Henrique, in 1580, Portugal came under the yoke of the Spanish. About 60 years later, however, on December 15, 1640, a revolt instigated by the nobility brought the Duke of Bragança (João IV) into power, thus restoring the country's independence. In commemoration of these events, an obelisk flanked by two bronze statues was erected on **Praça dos Restauradores (1)** in 1886. This square is an important crossroads and a stop on many bus routes, but will probably be of little interest to visitors. Numerous hotels, banks and travel agencies are located here, as is a large underground parking lot.

The most noteworthy building on the square is the **Palácio Foz** *(on the left side of the square, towards Praça Marquês de Pombal)*. A former palace dating back to the 19th century, it now houses the tourist office (ICEP) (for opening hours, see p 45). Its lovely façade, the work of Francisco Fabri, is yet another testimony to the savoir-faire of Italian architects. Right next door, in the Calçada da Glória, the **Elevador da Glória** takes passengers straight into the Bairro Alto. This was Lisbon's second funicular (1885), and the first powered by an electric motor. It is the only one of the city's *elevadores* to have once been equipped with a long bench on the roof to provide extra seating. Trivia buffs might also be interested to know that the cable car used to be lit by candles at night. It now transports up to three million passengers a year.

Art Deco fans are sure to notice the huge façade of the former **Teatro Eden** ★, located alongside the Palácio Foz. The top is decorated with lovely frescoes. The façade is fine example of preservation, unlike the rest of the building, which now houses the Orion hotel (see p 197) and a Virgin store.

The continuation of Praça dos Restauradores, the immense **Avenida da Liberdade** ★ **(2)**, is probably the longest and widest avenue in Portugal. Ninety metres across, it was clearly intended to serve as a showy, romantic route into the city. Those who designed it, however, probably never imagined that it would one day become a noisy major artery. In any case, it is still an impressive tree-lined avenue with several stately buildings facing onto it. Among these stand the elegant façade of the building at numbers 206-216, whose ground floor, now occupied by a Fiat dealership, has been atrociously disfigured, and the charming Moorish façade of the building at numbers 226-228, adorned with splendid stained-glass windows. Lisboans come here for the movie theatres and travel agencies; tourists, for the hotels. Beneath the trees along the side roads, you can still find some outdoor cafés bordered with grass. Despite the noise of the traffic, these are pleasant places to relax and quench your thirst (see p 231). The Liberdade's mosaic sidewalks with maritime motifs are an indication of just how sophisticated the city was at the time the avenue was laid.

If you walk across the middle of the Praça dos Restauradores, you will come to the Travessa Santo Antão, which leads to the **Rua das Portas de Santo Antão**, a pleasant pedestrian street lined with restaurants. Here, you will find a social club called the **Casa do Alentejo** ★ **(3)** *(Rua das Portas de Santo Antãono. 58)*, an opulent 19th century building, part of which is open to the public. The interior is decorated in the Mudejar style, which was very much in fashion at the time of the building's construction. As you enter through the front door, you will find yourself in a lavish inner courtyard that will set your mind wandering to exotic Arabian locales. A majestic staircase embellished with *azulejos* leads up to the second floor. When you reach the top, go into the large room to your left, whose rococo decor, featuring stucco, gilding, crystal chandeliers and a lovely floor, is fit for a palace. Alongside this room, you'll find a restaurant (see p 231), whose beautiful *azulejos* merit a visit

Tour G: Restauradores and Liberdade

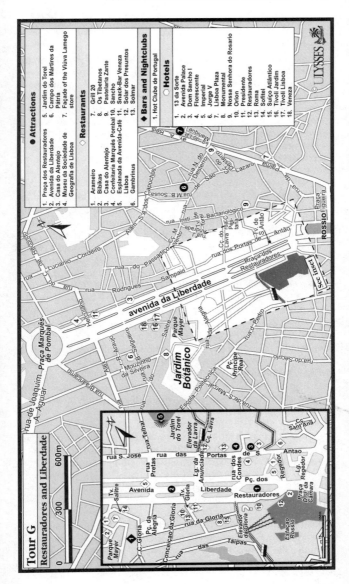

all on their own, while at the far end, to the right, is a smaller, less interesting room, which serves as a cafeteria.

Farther north on the same street is the **Coliseu dos Recreios** *(located between Travessa Santo Antão and Rua dos Condes, on the right side as you head north up the street)*, an immense auditorium often used for concerts, among other events. It also houses the **Museu da Sociedade de Geografia de Lisboa (4)** *(free admission; Mon, Wed and Fri 11am to 1pm and 3pm to 6pm; Rua das Portas de Santo Antão no. 100, ☎ 342 50 68)*, a rather outdated-looking ethnographical museum displaying all sorts of objects accumulated by the Portuguese during their great era of exploration.

Still farther north, you will end up at the Largo da Anunciado, where you will find the Elevador da Lavra *(Calçada da Lavra)*. This funicular, the first to be built in Lisbon, was a huge success right from the start. On its first day, April 19, 1884, it was in operation for 16 hours straight and transported 3,000 passengers. To avoid accidents, the operator used to have to alert people that the *elevador* was coming by blowing repeatedly into a horn. Thanks to this funicular, Lisboans (and tourists, of course) can reach the **Jardim do Torel (5)** *(when you get off the elevador, turn left onto Rua Câmara Pestana, then left again onto Travssa do Torel, to reach Rua de Júlio de Andrade, on the right)*. This pleasant garden, laid out in the centre of a charming old neighbourhood (best avoided at night), offers some **lovely views** of the northern part of the city. However, before going there, shutterbugs should be sure to stop off on **Calçada do Lavra** *(take the funicular halfway up)*, where they can capture some especially romantic views.

Afterward, you can walk a short distance farther down Rua de Julio de Andrade to the **Campo dos Mártires da Patria (6)**, an immense square, with a park and a statue honouring a celebrated Portuguese doctor, Dot Sousa Martins. Many women come here to lay pictures of ill or deceased relatives all around the statue and kneel to pray, hoping to benefit from the good graces of the doctor.

If you have a passion for *azulejos* and don't mind a good walk, continue your tour by taking Rua Manuel Bento Sousa, then Rua de São Lazaro, where quaint little Calçado do Desterro will lead you straight to bustling Avenida Almirante Reis. There, at

Tour G: Restauradores and Liberdade 127

the corner of Largo do Intendente Pina Manique, a handsome building proudly displays its Art-Nouveau-inspired **azulejos** and its whimsical **ironwork accents**, shaped like dragonflies, scarabs and swans. On Largo do Intendente Pina Manique itself you can admire the **façade** ★★ **(7)** of the Viúva Lamego store (see p 273), a real little gem that is a wonderful reward for the effort of your long excursion. You can catch a train straight downtown at the Intendente subway station, right nearby, thus winding up this lengthy tour.

TOUR H: SANTA CATARINA AND CAIS DO SODRÉ

See map on p 129.

As with most parts of Lisbon, there are a number of itineraries to choose from when touring the Bairro Alto. The one below is a continuation of the tour of the Chiado and includes an enjoyable ride on the Elevador da Bica.

From Largo do Chiado, head south on bustling Rua do Alecrim. On the way downhill, make a brief literary stop at **Largo Barão de Quintela (1)**, where novelist José Maria Eça de Queirós is immortalized by a **sculpture entitled *Truth***. Farther downhill, you'll cross a small bridge with typical Lisbon trams running both across and under it, the perfect spot for some lovely snapshots. You'll notice many wrought-iron fences, just before the bridge, protecting nearby houses.

By continuing downhill toward Praça Duque da Terceira, you'll end up at **Cais do Sodré (2)** *(tram #15 from Praça da Figueira, tram #18 from Praça do Comércio, Cais do Sodré stop)*, one of the nerve centres of the capital. In addition to a railway station *(Estaçao Cais do Sodré)* that offers frequent service to the seaside resorts of Setúbal and Cascais, there is a ferry terminal where passengers can board boats heading across the Tagus to Cacilhas (also see p 60). There are several bars and restaurants along the wharves, and you can have a drink or a good meal on one of their pleasant terraces.

Retrace your steps back to Rua da Ribeira Nova, then continue on to Rua da Moeda. The latter leads straight to the **Elevador da Bica (3)**, which provides a fun ride up to Largo Calhariz. Once there, go to the **Biblioteca Camões (4)** *(Tue to Sat 10am*

La Sétima Colina

While visiting the Bairro Alto or the Chiado, you might hear about the Sétima Colina, or Seventh Hill, which was one of the many projects organized by the city to celebrate its role as the "European Cultural Capital" in 1994. It was the brainchild of art historian José-Augusto França, who wanted to draw Europe's attention to his city's rich architectural heritage by creating a tour leading from the Cais do Sodré (pier) to the Largo do Rato. The route is a string of five streets, all heading in the same direction, but running through very different types of neighbourhoods. These streets are lined with buildings of all different styles and eras, ranging from the Mudejar style to the baroque interior of the 17th century Igreja de São Roque and the neoclassical style of the 19th century. Thanks to this project, a large number of buildings were restored or touched up and continue to be maintained, giving Lisbon's rather dated charm a brand new vitality.

to 6pm; Largo do Calhariz no.17, entrance opposite the tram stop; tram #28 from Rua da Conceição or bus #100 from Praça da Figueira, Calhariz stop), where a lovely **stairwell** ★ with a ceiling made entirely of carved wood and walls adorned with *azulejos* is sure to send fans of this type of ornamentation into raptures.

Continue your tour on Rua Marechal Saldanha. The little lanes that intersect this street are among the most picturesque in town. Make sure to pause for a moment in front of the **Travessa da Laranjeira** and **Travessa da Portuguesa**, both genuine postcard material. Farther along, at the **Miradouro de Santa Catarina** ★ **(5)**, which is closely watched by Adamastor, the sea monster so vividly described in Camões' *Lusiads*, you can wind up your tour with a pleasant view of the Tagus and Ponte 25 de Abril.

Tour H: Santa Catarina and Cais do Sodré

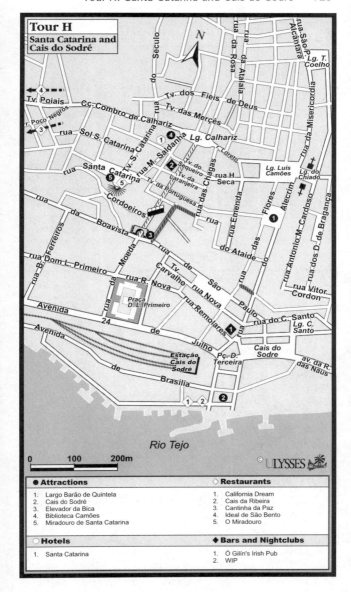

TOUR I: ESTRÊLA AND LAPA

See map on p 131.

If you walk down **Rua São Bento** from Largo do Rato, heading towards the Palácio da Assembleia Nacional, you will pass by many **antique dealers** and **second-hand shops**. This street is known by residents as an excellent place to find all sorts of treasures from the past, and is thus sure to please anyone with an interest in antiques. The **Palácio da Assembleia Nacional (1)** *(bus #6 or 49 from the Rato, São Bento stop; tram #28 from Rua da Conceição in the Baixa, Rua São Bento stop)*, the former Mosteiro de São Bento, lies all the way at the bottom of the street, on the right side. Its monumental neoclassical façade, set back from the square onto which it faces, seems to dwarf its surroundings. The prime minister's residence is located behind the Palácio, on the adjoining piece of property.

● Attractions

1. Palácio da Assembleia Nacional
2. Praça das Flores
3. Jardim da Estrêla
4. Basílica da Estrêla
5. Palácio dos Valenças
6. Casa Visconde de Sacavém
7. Museu Nacional de Arte Antiga

○ Hotels

1. As Janelas Verdes
2. Da Lapa
3. York House

◇ Restaurants

1. Assóporco
2. Casa México
3. Conventual
4. Embaixada
5. Flor da Estrêla
6. Foxtrot
7. Frei Contente
8. Gringo's Café
9. Joe Spaghetti
10. O Leão da Estrêla
11. Pastelaria Apolo XI
12. Picanha
13. Siesta Brava
14. Umpuntocinco
15. Xêlê Bananas
16. Xico's Bar Restaurante
17. York House
18. Zutzu

◆ Bars and Nightclubs

1. A Lontra
2. A Última Ceia
3. Akade Nykos
4. Até Qu'Enfim
5. Café Central
6. Café Santos
7. Foxtrot
8. Kapital
9. Kremlin
10. Pérola
11. Plateau
12. Senhor Vinho

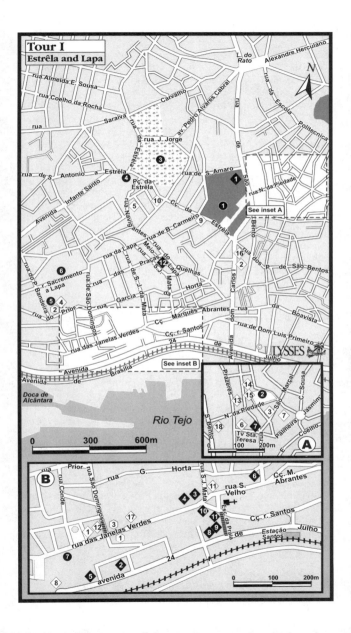

It is worth making a short detour along Rua Nova da Piedade to **Praça das Flores (2)**, a pretty little tree-lined square. This is a charming area, where you can enjoy a pleasant stroll at any time of the day. What's more, the square is surrounded by excellent restaurants, so you can please your palate here as well.

Retrace your steps and turn onto Calçada da Estrêla, located to the left of the Palácio da Assembleia Nacional.

Despite being a centre of political activity, Estrêla is known for its quiet atmosphere and green spaces. If you like beautiful gardens, make sure to visit the **Jardim da Estrêla ★ (3)** *(tram #28 from Rua da Conceição in the Baixa, Estrêla stop; various buses from the Rato)*. Not only is it one of the oldest parks in the city, but its pretty sculptures, pools, poplar-lined paths, plane-trees and cedars make it one of the most romantic as well. The crowning touch is a small bandstand decorated with lacy ironwork.

Opposite the garden, the baroque style **Basílica da Estrêla ★ (4)** *(tram #28 from the Baixa, Estrêla stop; various buses from the Rato)* was erected between 1779 and 1790 by Dona Maria I to give thanks for the birth of an heir to the throne. Unlike the rather elegant exterior, the interior has little charm and is decorated with pink and blue marble, which make it seem somewhat cold. Dona Maria I's tomb is located here.

Although the **Lapa ★** area has few attractions as such, it is fascinating to stroll about here and look at the numerous *hôtels particuliers*, known as *Palacetes* (little palaces), many of which are surrounded by lovely gardens. Most of these buildings are now embassies, consulates and offices.

For an interesting walking tour, start at number 37 on Rua de São Domingos, a lovely old palace by the name of **Porto Covo**. Built in the 17th century, it is now the British Embassy. Farther along, at Rua do Pau da Bandeira 4, you'll find the former **Palácio dos Valenças (5)** dating from 1870. Although it has been converted into a luxurious hotel (the Hotel da Lapa, see p 200) its owners wisely preserved its façade. On the second floor, furthermore, there is a banquet hall sumptuously decorated with gilding, stucco and imitation marble, which is bathed in light filtered through period stained-glass windows.

Tour I: Estrêla and Lapa 133

Now take Rua do Pau da Bandeira to Rua do Sacremento a Lapa and turn right. At number 27, the elegant Fundação Luso-Americana boasts a pretty garden. Just opposite stands the **Casa Visconde de Sacavém ★ (6)**, worth a trip in itself. Its doors and windows are adorned with a unique mixture of *azulejos* and other ceramic decorations. To complete your whirlwind tour of the neighbourhood, walk along Rua Garcia da Orta and Rua S. João da Mata, then Rua das Janelas Verdas. You will end up near the wharves and the Museu Nacional de Arte Antiga.

If you don't feel like walking, take tram #25 across the neighbourhood; from the Baixa, go to the terminus of tram #25, on Largo do Corpo Santo.

Partially housed in a palace once occupied by the Marquês de Pombal, the **Museu Nacional de Arte Antiga ★★ (7)** *(500 ESC; Tue 2pm to 6pm, Wed to sun 10am to 6pm; Rua das Janelas Verdas no. 9, ☎ 367 60 01 or 396 41 51; bus #40 from Praça Figueira, Rua Presidente Arriaga stop; from Praça do Comércio, tram #15, Cais da Rocha stop)* boasts a rich collection (the largest of its kind in Portugal) of art and other articles dating from the 14th century all the way through the 19th. These include sculptures, tapestries, furniture, silver and gold objects, ceramics and most importantly, a large number of paintings from the great European schools. Highlights include a triptych entitled **The Temptation of Saint Anthony ★** by Hieronymus Bosch and, in the collection of gold and silver, a magnificent **monstrance from Nossa Dama de Belém ★**, a true Manueline masterpiece. Most of the pieces displayed in the museum were confiscated when the country's monasteries were closed in 1834, and a number of others came from royal collections.

TOUR J: ALCÂNTARA, SANTO AMARO AND BELÉM

See maps on p 135 and p 137.

On its way to Belém, tram #15 runs along the banks of the Tagus and passes through Alcântara. Once an industrial area crowded with old warehouses and factories, it is now, like the Bairro Alto, undergoing a metamorphosis. More and more local buildings are being converted into discotheques, bars and fashionable restaurants. If you go club- or bar-hopping in

Alcântara at night (see p 262), you'll find yourself in an unusual atmosphere amidst trendy Lisboans, who stroll through this industrial area looking for fun and excitement. A daytime ride aboard the tram, between the gigantic concrete pillars supporting the Ponte 25 de Abril, is an equally strange experience, albeit of a different variety. The striking view of the bridge overhead, with the houses below it, is worth a brief stop.

Before moving on to the next part of the city, history buffs can head to the Alcântara to see the impressive façade of the **Palácio das Necessidades (1)** *(Largo das Necessidades; bus #27 or 49 from the Rato, Praça da Armada stop; bus #40 from Praça Figueira, Praça da Armada stop)*, the former residence of almost every member of the Bragança dynasty up until Manuel II went into exile. A whole series of dramatic events took place here, including Pedro V's death from typhus, Queen Maria II's death at the age of 27, the assassination of Carlos I and his son. When Manuel II fled the country in 1910, the Portuguese monarchy came to an end. Now occupied by the Ministry of Foreign Affairs, the palace is closed to the public.

If a king were visiting Lisbon, he would surely choose to enter the city by way of **Ponte 25 de Abril ★★ (2)** *(250 ESC per car; from Praça Marquês de Pombal, take Avenida Joaquim António de Aguiar and follow the signs for Alcântara or Sétubal, or take bus #53 and get off at the tollbooth)*. This bridge is to the capital what the Eiffel Tower is to Paris or the Golden Gate Bridge to San Francisco. Indeed, no one could imagine the city today without the Ponte 25 de Abril. Built from 1962 to 1966 and inaugurated under Salazar (it used to be called Ponte Salazar), it was an immediate success. Previously, it had been necessary either to drive a fair distance up the Tagus in order get across or to take one of the numerous ferries that constantly shuttle back and forth from one shore to the other. In celebration of the Flower Revolution, the bridge was rebaptized Ponte 25 de Abril. Technically speaking, it is a masterpiece of its time. Up until January 1995, with the opening of the Normandy Bridge, it was the longest suspension bridge in Europe. It is 70 metres above the water, its central span measures 1,013 metres, and every day 140,000 cars use it to cross the Tagus, sometimes causing traffic jams that last several hours. For those visiting Portugal, the Ponte 25 de Abril not only offers rapid access to the lovely beaches on the Bay

Tour J: Alcântara, Santo Amaro and Belém

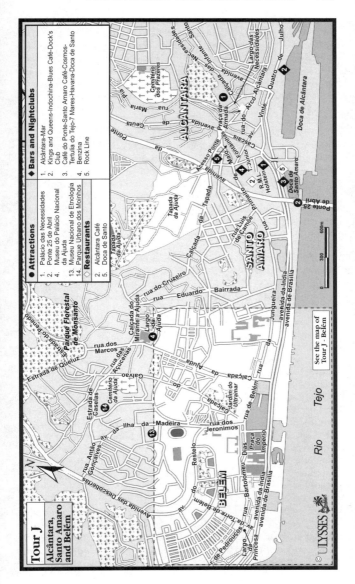

of Setúbal, but also affords some **magnificent views** ★★ of Lisbon and the Tagus. We especially recommend crossing the bridge at night, when the city looks more romantic than ever, glittering with thousands of lights. With the financial support of the European Economic Community, major construction is presently being carried out on the bridge; a lower level is being built for the train. When this project is completed, Lisbon will finally be directly linked to the southern part of the country by rail.

Belém ★★★, whose name is a contraction of the word Bethlehem, was once a suburb of Lisbon. As far as monuments and museums are concerned, it is one of the richest parts of the city. It was from here that the caravels set out, and the area's development was financed mainly by the riches brought back from the Indies. Flush with money, the nobility built opulent palaces here, most of which miraculously survived the earthquake of 1755.

The **Museu Nacional dos Coches** ★★ **(3)** *(450 ESC; Tue to Sun 10am to 5:30pm; Praça Afonso de Albuquerque, ☎ 361 08 50; tram #15 from Praça da Figueira, Rua de Belém stop, or bus #14 and 43, Altinho stop)* is devoted chiefly to royal coaches. As the Portuguese royalty had accumulated quite a few state-coaches, Queen Amelia decided to put them all in the former riding school of the Palácio de Belém and open a museum. Founded in 1905, this museum boasts one of the richest and most complete collections of its kind in the world. Visitors will find coaches dating from the 17th century to the 19th. Some are so lavishly decorated that it is hard to believe that they were used for transportation. Among the most elaborate are the three baroque coaches (1716) used by the Portuguese ambassador to the Vatican under Pope Clement XI. As if the coaches were not extravagant enough on their own, the ceiling of the large room is covered with countless medallions and paintings. On the second floor, there are a number of galleries, which offer an excellent overall view of the place.

Those with a taste for opulent decors should make a detour through the Ajuda area to visit the **Museu do Palácio Nacional da Ajuda** ★ **(4)** *(500 ESC; Thu to Tue 10am to 4:30pm, closed during official receptions; Calçada da Ajuda ☎ 363 70 95 or 362 02 64 #18 from Praça do Comércio, Calçada da Ajuda*

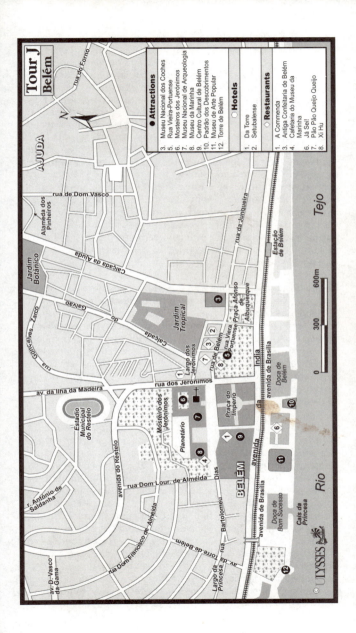

stop; bus #60 from Praça da Figueira, Largo da Ajuda stop), the royal residence from 1862 to 1910. The present palace was begun in 1802; it was originally supposed to be twice as big, but remained unfinished for financial reasons. When Dom Luís moved in here in 1862, he probably never suspected that his spendthrift Italian wife, Dona Maria Pia, would turn the place into a veritable museum of decorative arts. She had little interest in antiques, but adored modern design, and furnished the palace with pieces by Europe's finest artisans. The rooms thus feature a diverse sampling of the continent's 19th century decorative output. Make sure to visit the winter garden, a gift from the viceroy of Egypt, which is perhaps the most remarkable and most modern room of all. The massive-looking neoclassical exterior of the palace is of little interest. Since the palace is often closed for official receptions for foreign heads of state, be sure to check whether it is open to the public before visiting it.

Before visiting the Mosteiro dos Jerónimos, make a short detour down **Rua Viera-Portuense (5)** to see the pretty row of old working-class houses that once lined the docks, and which have been fixed up and transformed into cafés, restaurants and shops. Along the way, take a look at those between numbers 52 and 40, whose projecting second floors are supported by small columns, forming a covered passageway. Next, cross Rua de Belém and go to the back of the restaurant Pão Pão Queijo Queijo, where you'll see the *pelourinho de Belém* ("the pillory of Belém"), curiously tucked away on a tiny street.

If there is one place that you simply have to see while you're in Lisbon, it's the **Mosteiro dos Jerónimos ★★★ (6)** *(Praça do Império, ☎ 363 00 34; tram #15 or bus #43 from Praça da Fiegueira, Mosteiro Jerónimos stop)*. It was begun by Boytac in 1502, by order of Dom Manuel I, and was not completed for nearly a century. Thanks to the riches accumulated by the Portuguese after the discovery of a route to India, Manuel I and his successors were able to invest huge sums of money in the project, hiring the best artisans and architects of their time. These included João de Castilho (the Spanish architect of the Monastery of Christ in Tomar) and French sculptor Nicolas Chantereine, who, according to some historians, first introduced the Renaissance style into Portugal. The Mosteiro dos Jerónimos, made up of the monastery itself, its adjoining cloister and the Igreja Santa Maria, is a true architectural

Tour J: Alcântara, Santo Amaro and Belém 139

masterpiece featuring a nearly perfect fusion of Manueline art and Renaissance style. It has been listed as a World Cultural Heritage Site by UNESCO.

Before entering the **Igreja Santa Maria** ★★★ *(free admission; Tue to Sun 10am to 5pm)*, take a good look at its two portals. The enchanting **south portal** ★★, adorned with statuettes and carved with maritime motifs is a work of great intricacy, complemented by the richly decorated windows on either side. The equally intricate **west portal** ★★ features two lovely statues of King Mantel and Queen Maria (by Nicolas Chantereine), as well as numerous religious scenes. Inside, the lofty vault is adorned with a complex network of ribs and supported by finely worked columns (by João de Castilho). Its construction was a true feat of engineering; considering how wide it is, it is amazing that it survived the earthquake. In the choir and the transepts, you'll find a number of tombs supported by elephants and containing the remains of several kings. On either side of the entrance, under the *coro-alto*, are the beautifully carved tombs of the celebrated poet Camões and explorer Vasco de Gama. From the *coro-alto*, which can only be reached through the cloister, you can admire the lovely series of ribs covering the vaults of the central nave. The church was once topped by a pyramidal bell tower, which collapsed during the earthquake of 1755; the dome you see now dates from the 19th century.

To continue your tour of the premises, head to the **cloister** ★★★ *(400 ESC; Tue to Sun 10am to 5pm; entry adjacent to the west entrance of the church, ☎ 363 00 34)*, which, along with Batalha's, is one of the most beautiful in the country. Upon entering the building, you'll feel as if you've just stepped into a magical place. There are two levels of deep, richly carved bays adorned with just as finely worked columns. The Gothic-style first floor was designed by Boytac, the less elaborate upper floor by João de Castilho. It is particularly interesting to visit the cloister in the late afternoon, when the soft natural light gives the stone an ochre hue. Make sure to take a look at the *azulejos* and beautifully decorated vault of the **refectory** ★.

The **Museu Nacional de Arqueologia (7)** *(350 ESC, free Sun 10am to 2pm; Tue 2pm to 6pm, Mer to Sun 10am to 6pm; Praça do Império, ☎ 362 00 00)*, housed in the long 19th

Manueline Art

century building adjacent to the Igreja Santa Maria, will appeal to visitors interested in the period extending from the Paleolithic age to the Roman era. A large collection of objects (statuettes, pottery, etc.) discovered on Portuguese territory is displayed here.

In the same building, in the west wing of the monastery, the **Museu de Marinha ★★★ (8)** *(300 ESC; winter, Tue to Sun 10am to 5pm, summer open until 8pm; Praça do Império, ☎ 362 00 10)* is one of the most comprehensive maritime museums in the world. Model boats, navigational instruments and sea-charts are exhibited in an interesting and original manner. Don't miss the room devoted to royal barges, which contains an impressive barge used by Maria I. The same room also contains the *Santa Cruz*, the first airplane to cross the South Atlantic (1922). A copy of the *Santa Cruz* was placed in the park opposite the Torre de Belém to commemorate this event.

Opposite the Museu de Marinha, the new **Centro Cultural de Belém (9)** *(Praça do Império, information in Portuguese only, ☎ 361 24 00; tram #15 or bus #43 from Praça da Figueira, Mosteiro dos Jerónimos stop)* is remarkable both for its size and its futuristic lines. This cubic colossus, built in 1993 by architects Vittorio Gregotti and Manuel Salgedo, clashes a bit with its immediate surroundings. It contains a number of theatres and exhibition spaces, as well as several shops and restaurants. It is a challenge not to get lost in this place, which is a veritable labyrinth.

On the pier opposite the monastery's museum stands a huge, stately monument, the **Padrão dos Descobrimentos** ★★ **(10)** *(Avenida de Brasília)*, erected in 1960 on the occasion of the 500th anniversary of the death of Henry the Navigator. It shows Henry with a little caravel in his hand, standing in front of a number of famous Portuguese figures (explorers, kings, cartographers, writers, etc.) who participated either directly or indirectly in the country's great discoveries. You can take a short elevator ride to the top of the monument to enjoy a **lovely view** of the Mosteiro dos Jerónimos and better appreciate the interesting **mosaic** *(at the foot of the monument)* depicting a map of the world in two hemispheres, which shows the major steps in Portugal's age of discovery and the names of the men who led the voyages.

Farther along the pier, right before the Torre de Belém, lies the **Museu de Arte Popular (11)** *(400 ESC; Tue to Sun 10am to 12:30pm and 2pm to 5pm; Avenida de Brasilia, ☎ 301 16 75)*, which displays clothing, furniture, pottery and other articles from different parts of the country, all related to Portuguese folklore.

Of all of Lisbon's attractions, its most emblematic is definitely the **Torre de Belém** ★★★ **(12)** *(400 ESC; Tue to Sun 10am to 5pm; Praça do Império, ☎ 362 00 34; tram #15 or bus #43 from Praça da Figueira, Largo da Princessa stop)*. This handsome Manueline tower was built between 1515 and 1521 by order of Manuel I to defend the mouth of the Tagus. It was originally located in the middle of the river, but the tidal wave that followed the earthquake of 1755 shifted large amounts of sand, thus altering the course of the water. Architecturally speaking, it is a marvellous blend of styles, combining the Moorish (architect Francisco Arruda's little domes on the turrets) with the Romanesque (the gemeled windows) and the Italian Renaissance style (the second-story windows with little balconies, which are adorned with Christian crosses). To top off all this ornamentation, which is quite elaborate for an old prison (convicts were kept here until 1828), the entire tower is

142 Exploring

Torre de Belém

adorned with the rope motifs so characteristic of the Manueline style, as well as coats of arms of the Order of Christ. Particularly noteworthy inside is a lovely carved niche sheltering the Virgin with Christ in her arms, which is topped by an armillary sphere (see p 95). It is patterned with bunches of grapes, an unusual touch that gives it an exotic look.

Continuing your tour farther north, in the Restelo neighbourhood, where new apartment buildings seem to pop up every day, you'll reach the **Museu Nacional de Etnologia (13)** *(price of admission varies depending on the exhibition; Tue 2pm to 6pm, Wed to Sun 10am to 6pm; Avenida da Ilha da Madeira, ☎ 301 52 64; bus #32 from the Rossio, Avenida da Ilha da Madeira stop)*, which presents temporary exhibitions. To find out what's on while you're in Lisbon, check the *Agenda Cultural* (see p 267).

Finally, if you like the great outdoors, head to the new **Parque Urbano dos Moinhos (14)** *(winter 9am to 5:30pm, summer to 8pm; Estrada de Caselas, tram #18 from Praça do Comércio, Cemitério da Ajuda stop)*, a lovely hilltop garden with some **beautiful views** ★ of the Tagus and even, in clear weather, of the sea off in the distance. There are two pretty **windmills**, a small artificial lake, a playground and a snack bar in the park. Tram #18, which runs to the park, has a very interesting route that crosses several neighbourhoods, each with its own distinct social make-up.

TOUR K: PARQUE FLORESTAL DE MONSANTO

See map on p 144.

At the edge of the Parque Florestal de Monsanto, the majestic **Aqueduto das Águas Livres** ★★ **(1)** *(guided tour upon request; inquire at the Água Manuel da Maia museum, Rua do Alviela no. 12, ☎ 813 55 22; Bairro Alto da Serafina; bus #2 from the Rossio, bus #13 from Praça do Comércio, Serafina stop)* is probably Lisbon's most impressive monument. Though the idea of building an aqueduct was entertained as early as 1571, it wasn't until 1729 that precise plans were actually drawn up. In a royal decree dating from 1731, King João V authorized construction of the aqueduct, which began in 1732. Over the next 16 years, no less than 5.8 kilometres of conduits were installed in order to transport water to the capital. The most impressive part of the aqueduct is definitely the section running over the Alcântara valley, a true feat of engineering for its time. Its 35 arches stretch over nearly a kilometre and rise 65 metres at their highest point. The aqueduct was finally put to use for the first time in 1748, conveying water from a spring located at an altitude of 178 metres to the Mãe Água reservoir, 94 metres above sea level. Remarkably enough, the aqueduct was a functioning part of the city's water-supply system until 1967.

Located in the northwest part of the capital, **Parque Florestal Monsanto** *(Bairro Alto da Serafina entrance, bus #2 from the Rossio or bus #13 from Praça do Comericio, Serafina stop; Cruz das Oliveiras entrance, bus #11 from the Rossio, Cruz Oliveiras*

144 Exploring

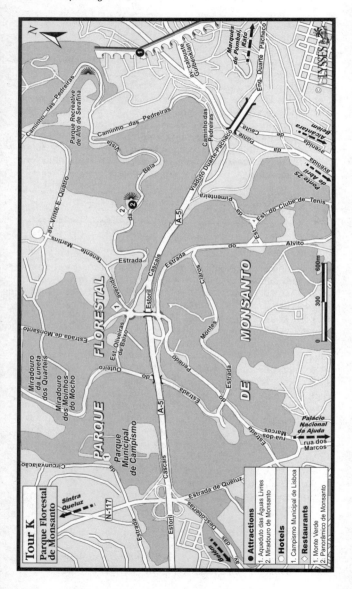

stop) stretches across several hills, covering nearly one fifth of the area of Lisbon. Reforested and laid out as a park between 1938 and 1942, this gigantic recreation area is now home to several government and military buildings, various private athletic clubs, a towering radio antenna and several lookouts which afford interesting views of Lisbon and the Tagus. Among the last-mentioned, the **Miradouro de Monsanto (2)** *(Estrada da Bela Vista, accessible only by foot or by car)* not only offers a pretty panorama, but also has a restaurant where visitors can have a meal while taking in the pleasant view. Parque Florestal de Monsanto appeals mainly to outdoor enthusiasts and people who enjoy picnicking. It is inadvisable to explore the park after sundown, as parts of it are reputed to be unsafe.

TOUR L: ESTORIL TO CASCAIS

See maps p 146 and p 148.

Estoril

Once visited for the benefits of its curative waters, Estoril really took off in the 1950s when several famous figures took up residence here, among them deposed kings such as King Humberto of Italy and King Juan of Spain (father of the current Spanish king). Though the construction of an impressive casino, preceded by an elegant park lined with luxury hotels, has drawn a wealthy clientele, its renowned sporting competitions (the Tennis Open, Formula One grand prix auto racing, and sailing regattas) have conferred upon it an international reputation. All these attractions, combined with an intense cultural life (theatres, concerts, festivals and so on) and a mild winter climate, have long attracted a sophisticated public, composed in large measure of artists, politicians, business people and sports stars. Estoril's star, however, seems to be fading these days, and its old prestigious hotels and mansions bear witness to a bygone decadent era. There are no special attractions for tourists, apart from the **casino** and its **park** as well as the many luxurious **mansions** lining its avenues. Estoril will suit people who appreciate a comfortable and traditional holiday in a sophisticated but somewhat artificial setting. Prices at this resort, as a general rule, are

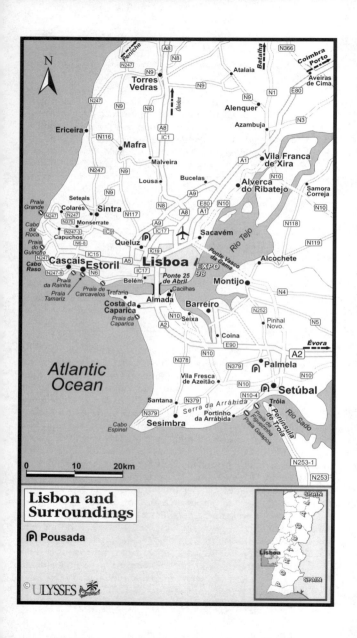

Tour L: Estoril to Cascais 147

exaggeratedly high for what you get. See also "Parks and Beaches", p 178.

Cascais

Few traces remain of the prosperous little fishing village that Cascais once was. A victim of its strategic location and twice ransacked by foreign troops (in 1580 by the French occupiers and in 1589 by the English), the city also had to endure the terrible earthquake of 1755, obliterating it once again. Despite this succession of setbacks, Cascais has always boasted a consistently mild climate, and thus benefited more than any other from the vogue for seaside vacations that flourished in the late 19th century. Each autumn the royal court, seeking eternal spring, moved to this spot, bringing in its wake the Portuguese nobility and a crowd of courtiers. Between 1930 and 1950, many secondary residences were built here, bringing the town a certain degree of wealth and a renown that spread far and wide. Toward the 1970s, when mass tourism began its crusade, Cascais once again fell victim to its geographic location and was among the first resorts to suffer from this devastating assault. Less than 30 kilometres from the capital and easy to reach, Cascais is besieged by day-trippers year-round, turning it into one of the country's busiest resorts. For those who enjoy a lively scene and constant crowds, Cascais is a dream come true. Even if prices here are more reasonable than in Estoril, Cascais remains a rather expensive beach resort. See also "Parks and Beaches", p 178.

In terms of tourist attractions, besides its prettily cobbled **pedestrian streets**, which are good for strolling, Cascais has rather few interesting monuments. Listed below are some that justify a brief visit, nonetheless.

Igreja Nossa Senhora da Assunção (1) *(Largo do Assunção, just near the citadel of Cascais)* is worth a look for its fine ***azulejos*** and its beautiful *talha dourada* altar.

The **Câmara Municipal (2)** boasts an elegant *azulejo*-adorned **façade**.

The **Palácio-Museu Condes Castro Guimarães (3)** *(250 ESC for a guided tour, free Sun 10am to 12:30pm; Tue to Sun 10am*

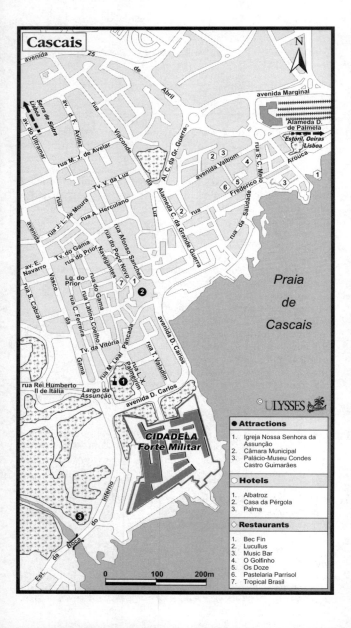

to 5pm; west of town, off the N247-8, along the coast, Estrada da Boca do Inferno). Hidden within a small bay topped by a picturesque stone bridge, this curious dwelling unfailingly conjures up images of a fairy-tale castle. Dating from the beginning of the 20th century, this noble residence was transformed by the municipality into a museum and library, now housing Portuguese furniture and knickknacks mostly dating from the 18th and 19th centuries and, of course, an important collection of very old books.

TOUR M: QUELUZ TO SINTRA

See maps p 146 and p 155.

Queluz ★★★

Located halfway between the capital and Sintra, the **Palácio Nacional de Queluz ★★★** *(400 ESC, free Sun 10am to 1pm, 50 ESC admission to garden only; Wed to Mon 10am to 1pm and 2pm to 5pm; access by the IC9, Largo do Palácio Nacional)* is considered by many to be Portugal's Versailles, and with reason. Its gracious rocaille-accented baroque façade, softened by soothing Portuguese colours, makes it one of the most elegant baroque palaces in the country. Also, as at Versailles, the palace is fronted by perfectly ordered gardens, worthy of the purest French tradition. It was at the initiative of Dom Pedro, the second son of João V, that the work began in 1747. Portuguese architect Mateus Vicente de Oliveira is responsible for the façade as well as the wing in which the throne room is located. After a brief interruption because of the 1755 earthquake, the work was turned over to the French architect Jean-Baptiste Robillon who, with the help of his Portuguese colleague, completed the main buildings. From 1786 to 1807, Dona Maria I brought several additions to the interior decoration and had another section built, thereby completing the building as we see it today. The Queluz palace became a royal residence with the accession to the throne of Dom Pedro III and was inhabited until 1807, when Napoleonic troops invaded and the royal family fled to Brazil. The Queluz palace is the last great prestigious undertaking of the royal family. Despite the opulence of its decoration and the freshness of its gardens,

Palacio Nacional de Queluz

Queluz bears memory to the sad end of Queen Dona Maria I, struck with madness toward the end of her reign. Nowadays, the building belongs to the government and serves as a residence for foreign dignitaries on official visits. An excellent restaurant (see p 245) is now housed in the same wing as the palace's former kitchens.

A tour of the **palace apartments ★★** will appeal mainly to those with a taste for period furniture and objects. Among the many rooms that may be admired, make sure to visit the **throne room ★★★**. Oval-shaped and adorned with numerous mirrors, it is reminiscent of the Galerie des Glaces in Versailles. Imposing Venetian crystal chandeliers hang from the attractively decorated ceiling, which seems to be held up by four Atlases. From May to October, concerts are held here on weekends *(usually around 6pm)*, making the place that much more enchanting *(concert information ☎ 435 00 39 or 436 38 61, ≈ 435 25 75)*. Among the other rooms open to the public, the **Queen's dressing room ★** and the **Don Quixote room ★**, both graced with superb parquet floors, are lovely as well. Finally, in the little oratory next to the Don Quixote room, the magnificent Indo-Portuguese ivory **calvary ★★** is a real little masterpiece.

A tour of the premises wouldn't be complete without a stroll through the magnificent **gardens ★★**. In addition to the **Neptune pool ★**, designed by the architect Robillon, visitors can admire numerous alabaster statues, ceramic vases and a whimsical fountain adorned with hydras and statuettes of clothed monkeys. In the background, the elegant **ceremonial façade ★★** completes this majestic, fairy-tale setting. Below the gardens is a canal with a small stream flowing through it. The low walls running along its banks and the little bridge over the Jamor river are covered with beautiful *azulejos* ★.

Sintra ★★★

Along with Buçaco and the Serra de Monchique, the Serra de Sintra constitutes one of those magical places of wonderfully dense and varied vegetation. Besides tropical flora, you can find one of the most charming palaces in Portugal, the **Palácio Nacional de Sintra**, as well as another building, the **Palácio da Pena**, notable for their whimsical architecture. Though these

Palacio da Pena

two national monuments are often mentioned as must-see tourist attractions, Sintra Vila has much more to recommend it, including courtly dwellings, *quintas*, convents, gardens, and so on, that also deserve a visit and that make this area among the most interesting in the general region of the capital. Sintra is also a veritable Eden; its beauty has been praised by numerous noblemen, writers and artists, including Lord Byron and William Beckford, English writers famous for *Childe Harold's Pilgrimage* and the *Sketches of Spain and Portugal*, respectively. Sintra today is made up of three distinct areas. Visitors arriving from Lisbon by train will disembark in Estefânia, the modern part of town. Those arriving from the capital by road will pass through the São Pedro area, famous for its antique shops (prices are out of sight, however) and for its bi-weekly market. Finally, the historic district, called Sintra Vila or Vila Velha, is where you will discover the pearl of the oyster that is the Sintra area. If damp weather is enough to ruin your day, avoid visiting when it is cloudy, for the Serra da Sintra is often shrouded in a heavy fog and is the first area to "welcome" the rain. On a brighter note, however, Sintra's delicious little locally made pastries, called *queijadas*, are the perfect consolation to a rainy day. These sweet, cheese-based cakes, made since the 13th century, are the pride of local inhabitants.

If you are pressed for time, start off at the **Palácio Nacional ★★★ (1)** *(400 ESC, 30-minute guided tour without narration, free Sun 10am to 1pm; 10am to 1pm and 2pm to 5pm, closed Wed; in the centre of Sintra, Terreiro da Rainha Dona Amélia)*, a wonderful summer residence formerly inhabited by the kings of Portugal. Although some visitors may rightly detect a certain lack of architectural unity, this is a unique palace. Its mixture of styles, ranging from the Gothic to the Mudéjar to the Manueline, gives it a certain character, enhanced by two enormous chimneys that are as surprising as they are elegant. Currently, some rooms in the palace are reserved for the president of Portugal for protocol purposes.

Before going in, take the time to examine the exterior, where the evolution of styles in Portuguese history is revealed. The central buildings, set on the site of a Moorish palace of which scarcely any traces remain, are the oldest parts. Dating from the end of the 14th century, they were built by order of João I. By expanding the existing buildings, he wanted to make them a summer residence for the Avis dynasty. You can still make out a few Gothic-style elements, even if the whole group underwent substantial modifications later on. An interesting aside: the building had not yet been completed when important royal decisions were already being taken here, for example the order to launch an expedition to capture Ceuta, on the Moroccan coast. Next, observe the right wing, added in the 16th century during the reign of King Dom Manuel I. These Mudéjar-influenced gemeled windows show the attraction that the Hispano-Moorish style, very fashionable at the time, held for the bourgeoisie. The two gigantic conical chimneys, located in back, are fine examples of this. Finally, in a purely Portuguese touch, the Manueline windows have ship's rigging as motifs, recalling the influence of the great expeditions on architecture. Thus, unlike the Palácio da Pena, whose exterior architecture seems inappropriate in the Portuguese context, Sintra's national palace is a page of history, and one can easily imagine the dramas and joyful events that went on here: joy when Dom Sébastião was proclaimed king here and when Camões read the Luisiades here for the first time, and drama as the feeble-minded King Dom Afonso VI was held prisoner here until his death.

Inside, amongst the ample crowd (this palace is one of the most visited in the country, although groups are limited to 30 persons), you can wander through an impressive number of rooms, each with its own character. Several Moorish-looking patios are also visible. Here are a few rooms not to miss:

The impressive **kitchen**, especially to admire the interior of its hearths whose breadth is astonishing.

The **Quarto de Hôspedes** (guest room), where you can see what may be the world's first sofa-bed.

The wonderful *azulejos* ★ in the **Capela-Mor**, some dating from the 15th century.

The **Sala dos Brasões** ★★★ (heraldry room), the most beautiful room in the palace, to admire its 74 coats of arms representing the Portuguese nobility. Magnificent *azulejo* **panels** ★★ representing hunting scenes may also be viewed.

The **Sala das Pegas** ★★ (magpie room), including an interesting ceiling painting that portrays 136 magpies holding in their

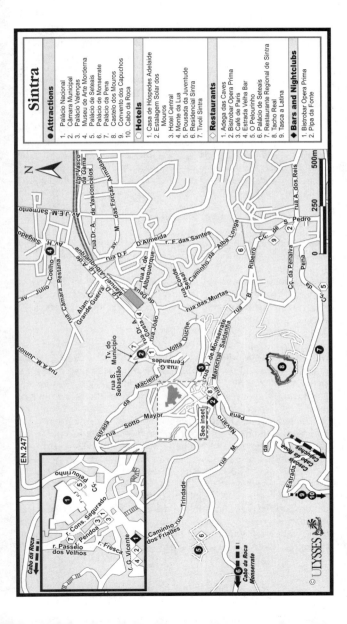

beaks a rose with the inscription "*por bem*" (for the good). These strange birds, painted by order of João I, in fact represent the 136 ladies-in-waiting of the court. These ladies, victims of rumours relating to a spicy adventure between one of them and the king, are thus besought to speak only the truth: the king's acts were "*por bem*" of the kingdom!

The **Sala dos Cisnes** ★ (swan room), the biggest in the palace, with portraits of 27 crown-bearing swans, each in a different position. These paintings honour the coat of arms of the de Lencastre family, whose members included the wife of João I. Also on view are a superb sideboard table as well as fine Chinese vases.

Head now to the Camâra Municipal.

The **Câmara Municipal (2)** *(Largo Dr. Virgilio Horta)* is worth a short stop to admire its very pretty **Manueline façade**.

The **Palácio Valenças (3)** *(Rua Visconde da Monserrate)*, now housing the town library, also has a pretty façade decorated with an imposing coat of arms. The town archives are kept here.

Just a few steps away from the station lies the brand-new **Museu de Arte Moderna** ★★ **(4)** *(600 ESC; Tue 2pm to 6pm, Wed to Sun 10am to 6pm; Avenida Heliodoro Salgado, Estefânia, ☎ 924 81 70)*, formerly the Sintra casino. Completely remodeled, this stately neo-baroque building dating from 1920 proudly displays its pretty façade, which is painted white and pastel yellow and strangely topped by a bull's-eye window that serves as a niche for a statue. Displayed inside are no fewer than 400 works of modern art (paintings, sculptures, photographs and video installations) dating from the post-war period to the 1980s. Visitors can admire pieces by such renowned artists as Vieira da Silva, Bissière, Riopelle, Michaux and many others. A significant portion of the museum is devoted to pop art, highlighting the work of several masters of that movement, including Roy Lichtenstein and Tom Wesselman. Anyone who appreciates modern art should definitely make a pilgrimage here!

Seteais ★ *(2 km from Sintra)*

Located in the Serra de Sintra, less than two kilometres from the village of Sintra, the **Palácio de Seteais ★ (5)** *(along the N375; Rua Barbosa Bocage no. 10)* is a very elegant palace formed by two buildings connected by an imposing arch. The buildings now house a luxurious hotel (see p 206) which is well worth a visit. In the 18th century, each wing formed a distinct property. While the right wing housed the elegant Quinta da Alegria, the more recent left wing was built by the Dutch consul as a residence. It was he who laid out the grand esplanade facing the two buildings. The two properties became one at the beginning of the 19th century when the marquis of Marialva acquired all the lands and had the imposing central arch built to link the two wings. Besides a remarkable **interior decoration ★** where frescoes, ancient tapestries and period furniture incite admiration, we suggest a little stroll on the **terrace**, with its beautiful French-style gardens and its **panoramic view**, romantic to perfection. Some say the origin of the palace's name may be explained as follows: the word Seteais is the contraction of "sete aïes", in other words seven repetitions of the exclamation "aïe" created by echoes from the valleys facing the terrace. Sceptics can decide for themselves while here!

Returning from the Seteais palace toward Sintra, on the right side of the N375 (Rua Barbosa Bocage), notice the fine residence located at number 9, adorned with an imposing lichen-covered grill at the entrance. A little further down, at the curve, is a sumptuous **residence ★** *(visits not allowed)* at number 5. This astonishing palace, with its mixture of neo-Manueline and Moorish styles, is a true wonder. Although it seems to come from another era, it dates from the beginning of the 20th century.

Monserrate ★★ *(4 km from Sintra)*

Set on vast grounds, the **Palácio de Monserrate (6)** *(along the N375; during our visit, work was in progress for an indeterminate period and only the garden was accessible to the public)* was built for Francis Cook, a wealthy English businessman who held the noble title of First Viscount of Monserrate. The name seems to originate from the existence of a little church of the same name, now gone, that may have been built to commemorate a pilgrimage to Monserrate, in Catalonia, made by a monk in the 16th century. Throughout the 17th and 18th centuries, many buildings occupied this site, among them a neo-Gothic building inhabited by the famous writer William Beckford. The last important modification took place in 1856 when Francis Cooke decided to have a Mongolian-influenced oriental palace built and to turn the garden into a park, the **Parque de Monserrate** ★★ (see "Parks and Beaches", p 179).

Palácio da Pena ★ *(4 km from Sintra)*

Perched 500 metres high, on one of the hilltops in the Serra da Sintra, the **Palácio da Pena** ★ **(7)** *(400 ESC, free Sun 10am to 1pm; Tue to Sun 10am to 1pm and 2pm to 5pm; from the centre of Sintra, take the Estrada da Pena)* cannot fail to draw attention with its lively, provocative colours.

Before continuing with a brief description of this spot, keep in mind two pieces of advice for a pleasant visit. First, go early in the morning, for the site is quickly overrun by hordes of tourists and Portuguese families all year long. Second, if you are driving, park your vehicle in the Castelo dos Mouros parking area, the first one you come to on your way up the Estrada da Pena (on the left). If you are the sort who hates walking, you can always try to find space in the second parking area, located further up near the entrance to the grounds. The entrance to the actual castle is then less than 500 metres away. If you truly hate walking, there is another spot (fee for parking) just next to the castle, but you will really need the blessing of the gods to find a space here! Whatever solution you choose, be prepared for a memorable crowd scene. For a pleasant stroll, walk to the palace across its magnificent **garden** ★★★ located below (see "Parks and Beaches" p 179), where extraordinary flora awaits.

We cannot say for sure whether it is the whimsical shapes or the appearance of a Bavarian castle that attracts so many people, but this is among the most extravagant examples of what "Prusso-Portuguese" architecture could produce. It was in 1839 that Ferdinand II of Bavaria's house of Saxe-Cobourg-Gotha, the husband of Dona Maria II, bought the ruins of a monastery with the aim of turning it into a summer residence. A Prussian engineer, Baron Ludwig Von Eschwege, was put in charge of the project. Starting with the former Manueline monastery dating from 1503, the engineer erected a genuine castle with a happy mixture of a great number of styles: Moorish, Gothic, Manueline and Renaissance, all combined with a Germanic flair. Although they may look like something out of Hollywood, the bright colours that now grace the palace do tone down its rather severe countenance.

After a careful look at its extravagant exterior architecture, it is no surprise to discover just as extravagant an interior, where furnishings and rococo knickknacks mix with stucco carvings and other Moorish-inspired sculptures. A visit here will be of particular interest to those who enjoy a rich interior, with the exception of Dom Manuel II's bedroom, practically empty in comparison with the other rooms in the palace. All that remains of the primitive convent is its Manueline cloister, in which beautiful *azulejos* may be seen; also, its chapel contains an elegant **retable**, a work by Nicolas Chantereine.

Located right near the Palácio da Pena, the **Castelo dos Mouros** ★ **(8)** *(free admission; every day 10am to 4:30pm in the winter, until 5:30pm in the summer)* is an ancient Moorish castle built during the 8th and 9th centuries, whose walls have been saved almost intact. Conquered by Afonso I in 1147, the castle later fell into oblivion and was left in an increasingly abandoned state. It was only toward 1860 that Ferdinand of Saxe-Cobourg-Gotha decided to restore its walls and to reforest the surroundings of the castle. Walking across the site today, you can see the ruins of a pretty Roman chapel and reach the castle's spectacular **circular road**. The road is literally attached to the sides of steep hills, making this a photographer's delight with its many **panoramic views** ★ of Sintra and of the Palácio da Pena.

Capuchos *(9 km from Sintra)*

The **Convento dos Capuchos (9)** *(every day 10am to 5pm in the winter, until 6pm in the summer; from the Palácio da Pena, go 8 km along the N273-1, then go right and follow the sings for* *about 1 km)* is a curious monastery founded in 1560 where you can admire the monks' minuscule cells carved out of the rock and covered with cork to protect them from the cold. During your visit, leave nothing in your vehicle, for the parking area is unguarded and the spot is rather isolated. This excursion will allow you to explore the thick, lush forest covering the Serra da Sintra. Also, for those wanting to see the site of Cabo da Roca, the route along here makes for a pleasant little jaunt.

Cabo da Roca *(19 km from Sintra)*

Although someone may actually offer you a certificate (costing 400 to 600 ESC, no doubt!) testifying to your presence at this, the most westerly point in continental Europe, the site of **Cabo da Roca (10)** (Rock Cape) is nothing special. Overlooking the sea from 140 metres above, this promontory offers fine **viewpoints** of the coast, with an often violent sea smashing against jagged cliffs. This vista will invigorate lovers of dramatic scenery. A lighthouse has been built here, along with a tourism office. This is an ideal excursion for those who appreciate the sea air.

TOUR N: SETÚBAL AND SURROUNDINGS

See map on p 146.

Setúbal

Little is known to this day about the pre-Roman period, but it has now been proven that this area was inhabited by humans back in prehistoric times. In the coastal region, however, the oldest traces still visible today go back to the Roman period, falling between the 1st and 4th centuries AD. At that time, Romans settled both shores of the Rio Sado and founded Cetóbriga, a major port and fish processing centre. Toward the 5th century, however, a powerful landslide destroyed the town and actually transformed the configuration of the Sado's mouth. This, combined with frequent barbarian invasions, left the area long bereft of human activity, as people preferred to seek refuge inland. It was not until the consolidation of the

The romantic charm of Lisbon seen from the Calçada da Lavra. (Marc Rigole)

The constant bustle of the popular Alfama neighbourhood. (T.B.)

Tour N: Setúbal and Surroundings 161

reconquest and the full confirmation of Portuguese sovereignty that a fortified village was developed in the 14th century, this time, only on the right bank of the Sado. Later, the era of great discoveries led to the enrichment and progressive growth of the village, with its port serving as the embarkation point for several expeditions. Among the great achievements to follow, the Igreja de Jésus, built in the 15th century, and the Castelo de São Felipe, dating from the 16th century are worthy of mention.

Today Setúbal is the country's third most important seaport and has become home to many factories, ranging from cement mills to chemical plants and including fish processing plants and automobile assembly operations. Moreover, the construction of an expressway running straight to the capital has spurred a considerable population increase, and Setúbal, located less than 50 kilometres from Lisbon, is slowly becoming a bedroom community. Across from the port, on the other side of the Sado, the Tróia peninsula and the mouth of the river together create a vast interior sea; great expanses of saltwater marsh as well as a wildlife reserve form its estuary. Besides salt production, many oyster shoals are cultivated here, with nearly all production exported to other European countries. West of Setúbal is the beautiful Serra da Arrábida, part of which has been turned into a nature park, offering magnificent hilly scenery as well as lovely beaches in hidden coves. During your visit to the town and its surroundings, you can taste an absolutely delicious local cheese, Queijo de Azeitão. And do not miss sampling the area's excellent wines, not the least of which is a delicious, very sweet muscat wine called *Moscatel de Setúbal.*

Despite its respectable size, the country's third biggest city, ranked by population, really has rather little to offer tourists. The number of tourist attractions in the centre of town is rather limited, although it could be interesting to stay at the beautiful *pousada*. Two hours are more than sufficient to explore the heart of the city. The many shopping streets, some of them for pedestrians only, will delight avid shoppers. You will probably enter the city along Avenida Luísa Todi, named after a famous Portuguese singer who came from Setúbal.

Go first along Avenida 22 de Dezembro to the jewel of the city, **Igreja Jésus** ★ *(at press time the church and museum were* *closed for renovations; Rua Acácio Barradas)*. Dating from 1491, this church is worth visiting especially for its remarkable **interior**, where Boytac, one of the master architects who worked on the Belém monastery, first achieved a type of decor that would later be called the Manueline style. You can see impressive **wreathed columns** ★ as well as fine ribbing surrounding vaults and windows. Outside, take a glance at the fine Gothic portal made of marble from the Serra da Arrábida. Just adjacent, in the cloister attached to the church, the **Museu de Setúbal** exhibits a series of **primitive works** by an unknown artist, commonly referred to today as the Master of Setúbal.

Continuing along Avenida 5 de Outubro, facing the Praça Miguel Bombarda and taking the second street on your right, you will come to the **Praça de Bocage**, named after the well-known Portuguese poet Manuel Barbosa de Bocage, who was born in Setúbal. Built in the centre of this charming square, the **Igreja de São Julião** is worth a brief stop to contemplate its two **Manueline portals**. Walking by the church toward the east, you can explore a series of little alleyways which are pleasant for a stroll. They make up the town's historical district. People interested in the town's Roman past should not miss going to the **Posto de Turismo da Região de Setúbal** *(Largo Corpo Santo)*, near the Igreja de Santa Maria da Graça, to look through a cleverly designed glass floor at the foundations of a Roman building which was used to preserve fish.

Located away from the centre of town, the **Castelo de São Filipe** ★★ *(Estrada de São Filipe)* is one of the few must-see attractions here. To reach it, go to the western end of Avenida Luísa Todi and, once there, take the last street on your right, then Rua de São Filipe immediately on the left. Continue climbing and follow the signs to the *pousada*. Built in 1590 on orders from King Filipe I, better known as King Felipe II of Spain, this castle and fortress were built not to protect the town but rather to keep watch over the coast. The king of Spain greatly feared the English navy, a power with which Portugal had built long-standing alliances. The inhabitants of Setúbal, for their part, had little appreciation for the Spanish seizure of the country. Today, the fortress houses a *pousada* (see p 209) with an impressive entrance. After passing through its imposing fortified gate, you reach the central part of the building by a long vaulted passageway. One of the arches is decorated with beautiful *azulejos* showing baroque motifs. On the top floor, a big terrace offers a spectacular **panoramic view** ★ of the city and the Tróia peninsula. The buildings which now house the *pousada* used to provide lodgings for the guards and also for the region's governor. On the side, is a little **chapel** *(unfortunately, opening hours are very irregular)* dating from the 18th century and displaying a remarkable **interior** ★ entirely covered with *azulejos* simulating a three-dimensional baroque decor. In the centre of the vault, you can see the emblem of João V, seemingly placed there to exorcise the memory of an affront that remains unforgotten.

Península de Tróia *(98 km from Setúbal)*

Facing the city of Setúbal, the 17-kilometre-long **Península de Tróia** is made up of a narrow band of sand at the end of which is the village or, rather, the tourist complex of Tróia. Although this extraordinary tourist development came about because of its fine beaches, the spot is not really very interesting. In fact, there are many other beaches in the area that are just as beautiful and easier to reach, and which are not marred by such unpleasantries as smoke-belching factories far off on the coast, or the sight of countless towers being erected on the peninsula. The only attractions worthy of attention are the various **ruins** that have been uncovered, and these are limited in number. There are a few modest vestiges of Cetóbriga, the ancient Roman seaport built between the 1st and 4th centuries and destroyed by a landslide in the 5th century. You can observe what remains of the baths and of several buildings used for fish preservation, as well as the ruins of a temple.

Palmela ★ *(8 km from Setúbal)*

Although the discovery of prehistoric grottos in the area (near Quinta do Anjo) has shown that the human presence here goes back to about 5000 BC., the village of Palmela owes its place in Portuguese history mostly to its fortress and its sinister dungeon, in which the bishop of Évora lay dying.

Built by the Moors on the foundations of Roman buildings, the castle was conquered by Dom Afonso I in 1148, recaptured by the Moors in 1165, and then captured for good by Dom Sancho I in 1166. Expanded, modified, destroyed and then rebuilt, the castle and fortress would undergo many modifications over the centuries, with the result that the vestiges now go back to a period stretching between the 14th and 18th centuries. Before beginning your climb toward the fortress, take a moment, while at the top of the village, to admire the very elegant façade of the **Câmara Municipal**, adorned with a fine colonnaded gallery, as well as the **pillory** in front dating from 1645.

Once at the top of the hill, you enter the fortress by an imposingly large fortified gate. After a hairpin turn, visitors face the ruins of the former **Igreja Santa Maria do Castelo**, destroyed by the 1755 catastrophe. By looking carefully, it is still possible to see a few yellow and blue *azulejos*. Just beside the church, a stairway leads to the ancient dungeon of the fortress, which still has the "tank" in which the bishop of Évora was imprisoned for having conspired against the king. Some say it was on the orders of João II himself that the bishop's mysterious elimination was carried out, by poisoning, it seems. Whatever one makes of this, going to the top of the dungeon, you can enjoy a breathtaking **view** ★. For those who suffer from vertigo or who shun long climbs, an esplanade located in front on the dungeon also allows for the enjoyment of absolutely magnificent viewpoints. Also on the esplanade, beyond the ruins of various buildings, a corridor leads to a souvenir shop and an art gallery.

Retracing your steps, go now in front of the former Santiago monastery, transformed in 1979 into a wonderful ***pousada*** ★. It is well worth a look; having a drink or a meal there (see p 249) is certainly an excellent pretext for exploring this spot (or vice versa!). Lovers of the baroque will not want to neglect visiting the church attached to the monastery *(unfortunately, it is often closed)*, where beautiful ***azulejos*** may be seen.

Praia do Portinho da Arrábida ★
(18 km from Lisbon)

After travelling along a lovely **panoramic highway** ★ and down a steep hill, you will come to the **Museu Oceanográfico** *(200 ESC; Tue to Fri 10am to 4pm, Sat and Sun 3pm to 6pm)*, which lies on the right, in a particularly impressive bend of the road. Housed in a 17th-century fortress, this modest museum displays several specimens of marine life. Continuing down to the bay, the road comes to a dead end in front of a **lovely beach** with a few services and facilities. Unfortunately, thieves are known to prowl the area, so don't leave ANYTHING in your car.

TOUR O: EXPO 98

See map on p 167.

At Portugal's suggestion, the General Assembly of the United Nations officially declared 1998 the "International Year of the Oceans". On the same occasion, the Bureau of International Expositions chose Lisbon as the site of EXPO 98. This fair will follow an updated version of the old system, under which each country had to build its own pavilion. From now on, the host country will provide pavilions for participating countries, who will only have to pay for their indoor facilities. This new procedure will make it possible for even the poorest countries to take part at a relatively affordable cost, thus ensuring greater participation in the event and prompting suggestions that EXPO 98 may be the first true "world's fair". In order to implement the project, the state-owned company Parque EXPO 98 was established by the Câmara Municipal de Lisboa,

The Oceans, a Legacy for the Future

The official themes of EXPO 98 will be:

• Portugal's role in the great discoveries that led to European expansion in the 15th and 16th centuries;

• The present state of knowledge of the oceans and their resources;

• The preservation of ecological equilibrium and the rational exploitation of marine resources;

• The ocean as a place of leisure and artistic inspiration.

in conjunction with the Portuguese government. The event is scheduled to start officially on May 22, 1998 and end on September 30, 1998. At the same time, Portugal will also celebrate the 500th anniversary of Vasco da Gama's discovery of a route to India.

The General Assembly of the United Nations also approved two scientific projects involving the ocean, to be carried out concurrently with the Expo.

The Maris Project

The goal of the Maris Project, financed by the G7 and coordinated by the European Economic Community and Canada, is to create a world-wide communication system for the purpose of protecting the ocean and its resources. To that same end, there are plans to develop a data bank on marine animal life. These tools will also serve to facilitate and improve the regulation of maritime traffic, and to tighten controls on the transportation of substances that are hazardous to the environment.

The Independent World Commission on the Oceans (IWCO)

In 1995, a committee of 42 key figures was assigned the task of preparing a major study with the participation of scientists and many different countries. The goal: to draw up an overview of the state of the world's oceans and the various ways in which the exploitation of their resources is affecting the planet. This report, entitled *Oceans and Society on the Threshold of the Third Millenium* will be published for the inauguration of EXPO 98 and presented to the United Nations. The document should thus lead to the creation of a new branch of the United Nations, the Independent World Commission on the Oceans. Among the notables responsible for the report are Mario Soares, former president of the Republic of Portugal, and 1987 Nobel Peace Prize laureate and former president of Costa Rica, Óscar Arias Sánchez.

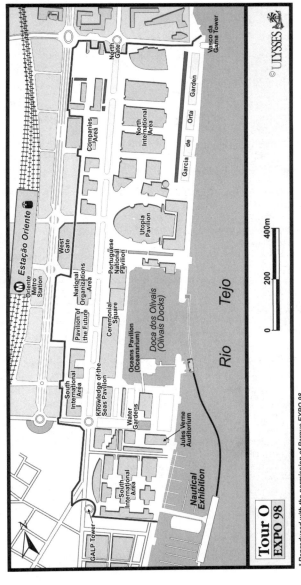

Some EXPO 98 Statistics

• With over 130 countries and six international organizations present, Portugal will boast the largest number of participants of any Expo to date.

• Over eight million visitors are expected to attend EXPO 98, half of them from abroad.

• No fewer than 330 hectares have been set aside for the occasion, 60 of which are exclusively for the Expo. This area stretches nearly 5 km along the Tagus.

• No fewer than 30,000 trees and 70,000 bushes have been planted.

• About 800 kilometres of cable have been installed.

• By the year 2010, 10,000 apartments will be built on the site.

 Finding Your Way Around

By Car

For motorists, the most direct route from downtown to the EXPO 98 site is to head northeast on Avenida Infante Dom Henrique, which, after changing names several times, will take you straight there. If you are at the airport, take Avenida Marechal Gomes da Costa from the Rotunda do Aeroporto. This road will lead you straight to the south gate of EXPO 98, three kilometres away. Motorists arriving from the southern part of the country should cross the brand-new, 13-kilometre-long Ponte de Vasco da Gama to reach the site.

Public Transportation

The brand-new Oriente train station, a futuristic-looking building designed by Spanish architect Santiago Calatrava, offers direct service to other cities in Portugal, as well as to points outside the country. In the same building, there is a subway station from which you can get downtown in a matter of minutes. Many special buses also leave from downtown, and various big hotels provide a shuttle service for their guests.

As far as getting around EXPO 98 itself is concerned, a cable car with 40 compartments runs the entire length of the site at a height of 20 metres, offering lovely views of the pavilions and the Tagus.

 Practical Information

Aside from the numerous information counters on the site, there is an information office for tourists:

Parque EXPO 98: 37 Avenida Marechal Gomes da Costa, 1800 Lisboa, ☎ 831 98 98, ≈ 837 00 32.
Information on the Internet: **www.expo98.pt**

You can also contact the **ICEP tourist office** (see p 45).

Schedule

The fair grounds are open every day from May 22, 1998 to September 30, 1998, from 9am to 3am. The activities are divided up into two distinct periods: **EXPO-Day,** from 9am to 8pm, devoted to touring the pavilions, and **EXPO-Night,** from 8pm to 3am, devoted to various shows and concerts. The myriad bars and restaurants on the site are also open during the latter period.

Admission

Note that EXPO-Day tickets are also valid for EXPO-Night events.

Pre-EXPO (advance ticket sales from November 22, 1997 to April 21, 1998):

Three days	10,000 ESC
Children ages five to 14 and adults 65 and over	5,000 ESC
Three months, EXPO-Day (May 22 to August 21)	45,000 ESC
Children ages five to 14 and adults 65 and over	22,500 ESC
Three months, EXPO-Night (May 22 to August 21)	22,500 ESC

EXPO (tickets sold from April 22, 1998 to September 30, 1998):

One EXPO-Day	5,000 ESC
Adults 65 and over	2,500 ESC
One EXPO-Night	2,000 ESC
Three days	12,500 ESC
Children ages five to 14 and adults 65 and over	6,250 ESC
Three months, EXPO-Day (May 33 to August 21)	
Adults 65 and over	50,000 ESC
Three months, EXPO-Night	25,000 ESC
	25,000 ESC

Exploring

Covering nearly 60 hectares, EXPO 98 stretches all around the former Cais dos Olivais, once the site of a refinery. In addition to this clever use of the area, a 330-hectare urban development plan is scheduled to be executed until the year 2010. It will include the construction of numerous residential buildings, a

Vasco Da Gama

Vasco da Gama was born in Sines in 1469. Virtually nothing is known about his childhood, and it was as a sailor in King João II's fleet that he first distinguished himself. Under the reign of Manuel I, Vasco da Gama, then an admiral, was entrusted with four ships with which to seek out a route to India. During his two-year voyage, nearly a third of his men perished. In November 1497, after a brief stay in the Canary Islands, he reached the Cape of Good Hope (formerly known as the Cape of Storms), which had been discovered by Portuguese navigator Bartolomeu Dias in 1488. He started exploring the eastern shores of Africa, then decided to venture farther east and discovered Calicut in May 1498. The Arabs had known about this small Indian port, reputed for its spices and its calico, since the 7th century. The famous poet Luís de Camões accompanied da Gama on this voyage. His experiences inspired him to write an epic poem entitled *Os Lusíadas* (*The Lusiads*), which immortalized the era of great discoveries. When Vasco da Gama returned to Lisbon in 1499, he received a hero's welcome and was ennobled and given a generous annuity by the king. Despite his discovery, it wasn't until his second voyage, in 1502 and 1503, that Portuguese trading posts were established in India. During this second expedition, he also founded trading posts in Mozambique. After returning to Portugal laden with riches, he was named viceroy of India. He set out on a third voyage in 1524, but died of illness a few months after arriving in Cochin.

railway station, a subway station and several hotels. As far as the EXPO 98 site itself is concerned, no fewer than eight pavilions, each devoted to a different marine theme, have been built. A 10-hectare stretch of water and a five-kilometre riverside platform also grace the area now. Remarkably enough, all the buildings on the site will be equipped with fibre-optic telephone lines and a pneumatic garbage disposal system. On either side of the site, there are two imposing towers from which visitors can enjoy lovely panoramic views of EXPO 98 and the Tagus. The first, on the south side, is called GALP and has a terrace 70 metres from the ground, while the second, known as Vasco da Gama, has a terrace 100 metres up and a panoramic restaurant 80 metres from the ground.

The Portuguese National Pavilion

Designed by the celebrated Portuguese architect Alvaro de Siza Vieira, who has executed a number of prestigious projects, the Portuguese pavilion is devoted to the era of great discoveries and to the important role Portugal played in European expansion of the 15th and 16th centuries. The architect erected the building near the big pool, so that it would be reflected in the water, thus evoking the omnipresent link between Portugal and the sea. It includes a Ceremonial Square, a vast covered space with a huge concrete roof that is unusual in that it is concave. The official cermonies will be held here. After the EXPO, this pavilion will become an institutional headquarters.

The Oceanarium

This pavilion houses the largest aquarium in Europe, containing as many as 25,000 specimens of about 300 different species. It was designed by the American architect Peter Chermayeff. The building also has an adjoining space for temporary exhibitions. With its undulating glass surfaces imitating ocean waves and its roof supported by steel poles and cables evoking the masts and riggings of a sailboat, the building is reminiscent of a tall ship.

Three major themes are covered here:

• The ocean, a link between the different peoples of the world;

• Life and the diversity of its forms, from the infinitesimal to the biggest;

• The responsibility of human beings in the preservation of the oceans as a resource for humanity.

In the middle of the building, there is a huge pool, which serves as the main aquarium and represents the ocean. Its capacity is equal to that of four Olympic-sized swimming pools. This pool can be observed on two stories; you can walk all around it and admire the teeming marine animal life within through its thick, transparent walls—sharks, rays, tuna, schools of sardines and a thousand and one other species. The four corners of the building contain other, smaller pools devoted to the aquatic animal life from various parts of the world. These aquariums can also be examined on two floors. One contains magnificent tropical species from such exotic places as Mozambique and Madagascar. The other aquariums are home to marine animal life from the rocky coast of the Pacific Ocean, from the shores of the Azores and from the Antarctic Ocean. For the last, a veritable expedition had to be mounted to find seals and penguins. While the seals come from Alaska, finding penguins required a good share of both patience and cunning in regard to international laws. It is actually against the law to capture penguins, so in November 1996, a team of American scientists collected a number of penguin eggs in Tierra del Fuego (Chile) and brought them to the laboratory at the Cincinnati Zoo (USA), where they were put in incubators. Shortly after the eggs hatched, 15 to 20 baby penguins "requested" permission to emigrate to Portugal; they now have Portuguese citizenship!

The Knowledge of the Seas Pavilion

Devoted to the many scientific discoveries that have been made about the sea, this pavilion has a central section that looks like the deck of a ship.

The four themes addressed here are:

• The discovery of navigation and instruments that made it possible to travel to new continents;

• Humanity's gradual exploration of the underwater world and technological advances that will enable us to go farther than ever before;

• The exploitation of the ocean, from saltworks to the fishing industry and from laying underwater cables to extracting underwater deposits;

• The ocean, a factor in the progress of humanity.

This facility will continue to be an oceanography museum after EXPO 98.

The Pavilion of the Future

This pavilion is dedicated to the future of the ocean and its status on the planet. Its design is based on the proportion between the sea and dry land, with three quarters of the building covered in glass, representing the ocean. Portuguese designers created the remarkable interior. A big, multimedia show complete with holograms is presented here, enabling the public to learn about the most recent discoveries that have been made with the help of new technology. A general overview of the health of the ocean is also provided.

The Utopia Pavilion

Every day, a variety of multimedia shows on myths and legends about the ocean are presented in this large amphitheatre. Here, visitors can meet the famous Jules Vernes, unravel the mysteries of Atlantis and even see Moby Dick. Created by the Canadian company Rozon (already internationally renowned for their Just for Laughs festival), the shows last 24 minutes and are put on five or six times daily. The amphitheatre, which seats 12,000, will be used as a multi-purpose theatre for conventions, shows and sporting events after the EXPO.

The International Pavilions

The large section of the site assigned to participating countries is separated into two zones, each containing a series of pavilions: the North International Area, with room for up to 130 delegations, and the South International Area, with space for 60 others.

Stretching along the shores of the Tagus, the North International Area will become the Association of Portuguese Industry's new Lisbon Exhibition Centre *(Feira Internacional de Lisboa)* after EXPO 98. One hundred countries are represented in its six futuristic-looking pavilions. Other foreign delegations can be found in the Southern International Zone, near the sailing harbour.

The various countries' exhibition spaces were granted to them free of charge by the organizing committee, thus enabling poorer countries to participate fully in EXPO 98.

Companies and Organizations Areas

This pavilion is occupied by various organizations and private companies, who display their products here.

The Water Gardens

As indicated by their name, these purely ornamental gardens are dedicated to water. All sorts of fountains can be admired here. In the centre of the gardens, in the Jules Verne Auditorium, visitors can take in various shows organized by participating countries.

The Garcia de Orta Gardens

Laid out in front of the six pavilions in the Northern International Zone, the Garcia de Orta Gardens feature luxuriant vegetation and beautiful landscaping. The purpose of these gardens is to show the public the wide variety of plants brought back over the centuries by Portuguese navigators, species that are now found all over Europe.

The Nautical Exhibition

The Nautical Exhibition not only has room for up to 600 boats, but is also a pleasant spot where all sorts of bars and restaurants with outdoor seating beckon visitors to kick back and relax. During the EXPO, ships from various countries and of all different sizes will drop anchor here, making for an interesting spectacle. In addition to traditional Portuguese vessels (*moliceiras* from Aveiro, *barcos rabelos* from the Douro valley, *fragatas* from the Tagus and the famous *caravelas*, the queens of Portuguese seafaring), visitors will see icebreakers, oceanographical research boats, historic ships and even hydroplanes. Aficionados will be delighted to find the *Polarstern*, a German scientific vessel designed for research in the polar seas; the *Fryken*, a Swedish boat converted into a floating museum; the *James Clark Ross*, a British boat used for research in Antarctica, and many other ships from countries as varied as Russia, Belgium and Finland.

One of the activities planned by the organizing committee is the EXPO 98 Regatta, a rally during which 40 yachts will sail around the world. The event will wind up at the sailing harbour on the eve of the opening of EXPO 98.

Fair-goers are in for a real treat between July 25 and August 3, 1998, when no fewer than 120 participants in the Cutty Sark Tall Ships' Race will put in at Lisbon. In Portugal, this race will be known as the Grande Regate Internacional Vasco da Gama Memorial-Lisboa 98.

OUTDOORS

Because of the urban complexity of Lisbon, where alleys, dead ends and stairways intersect to form an inextricable webbing, Portugal's capital doesn't lend itself at all to outdoor activities. It's practically impossible to get around on a bicycle since there are many steep slopes; also, although there are many parks, jogging is awkward because they're small. And finally, despite Lisbon's location right on the majestic Tagus, a number of industries all along the shoreline and the frequent passage of big cargo ships on the river make it undesirable to engage in water activities. So, if you are in search of some sporting activities, you should go to one of the many fitness clubs, mostly located in downtown hotels or get outside of the city centre and take advantage of the beaches, golf courses and natural parks.

  PARKS AND BEACHES

Tour K: Parque Florestal de Monsanto

In the north part of the capital, the **Parque Florestal Monsanto** *(access from Bairro Alto da Serafina, from Rossio bus 2 or Praça Comércio bus 13, Serafina stop; access from Cruz das*

...tdoors

...as, from Rossio bus 11, Cruz Oliveiras stop) stretches ... a number of hills and covers close to one fifth of the ...face of the municipality of Lisbon. Reforested and turned ...to a park between 1938 and 1942, this gigantic recreation area now houses a few ministerial and military buildings, a number of private sports clubs, a tall radio antenna and many belvederes including the **Miradouro de Monsanto** *(Estrada da Bela Vista, accessible on foot or by car only)*, which has a restaurant (see p 241). It's a pleasant park to go for a walk in or to have a picnic in. However, despite the many paths, unfortunately they are not marked, which means you are left to adventure aimlessly. Exploring the area in the early evening is not recommended as certain areas are known to be frequented by prostitutes and shady characters.

Tour L: Estoril to Cascais

Estoril

Today, Estoril is a slightly out-of-fashion resort with old prestigious hotels and mansions that bear witness to a rather wild era. Its beach, **Tamariz**, separated from the village by railroad tracks that run along the coast, is rather small but there is a large swimming pool *(closed Sep to Apr)* facing the sea.

Around Estoril

The modest, medium-sized beach called **Praia da Carcavelos** *(8 km from Estoril)* is known for its surfing. There are many shops specializing in surfing equipment, as well as a number of bars and cafés.

Cascais

Less than 30 kilometres from the capital and easy to reach, Cascais is besieged by day-trippers year-round, turning it into one of the country's busiest resorts. Today, restaurants, shops, discotheques and game parlours reverberate day and night, attracting many young people in search of weekend fun. For those who enjoy a lively scene and constant crowds, Cascais is a dream come true. As for its rather small beach, show up early to claim your spot and be prepared to elbow your way in! Even if prices here are more reasonable than in Estoril, Cascais remains a rather expensive beach resort.

Around Cascais

Once outside the town of Cascais, a beautiful **scenic highway**, the N247, follows the coast toward Praia do Guincho. This section of the Costa do Estoril is the most interesting part, for it remains in a fairly wild and unspoiled state. Two beaches where it is pleasant to linger are the **Praia do Guincho ★** and, right next to it, **Praia da Galé**. Praia do Guincho is the more popular, famous for sailboarding and surfing. Moreover, it has a broad stretch of white sand lined on one side by dramatic, jagged cliffs and on the other by green hills. The relative lack of crowds at this spot is explained by a rough sea that makes bathing more dangerous than elsewhere. Casual swimmers will prefer the beach beside it, the Praia da Galé, which is less impressive but is washed by much calmer waters.

Tour M: Queluz to Sintra

Around Sintra

Located within the bounds of the Serra de Sintra (see p 151), the **Parque da Pena ★★** *(Tue to Sun 10am to 4:30pm, closed Mon)* has many hiking trails which will enable you to explore some extraordinarily rich and diversified flora. From the temperate to the subtropical, the park has no fewer than 3,000 different species of trees, from firs to palms and including cork oaks and arbutus. Moreover, the many exuberantly designed palaces surrounding the park have transformed the region into a veritable fairyland. Those who enjoy romantic walks will be especially receptive to the charm of this area. Even in rainy weather, nature reveals its many wonders. The mists that waft from the neighbouring forests form a landscape imbued with an almost hallucinatory mystery.

Stretched over a vast manor, **Parque de Monserrate ★★** *(200 ESC; 10am to 4:45pm in the winter, until 5:45pm in the summer)* is worth a visit to admire its especially diverse flora. Everything here is an object of wonder, whether it be tree ferns from New Zealand, the powerfully scented eucalyptus, the African palms, the giant cedars, or simply the generous cork oaks. This wonder is well described by Lord Byron in his tale *Childe Harold's Pilgrimage*, which places his cherished Eden in this spot.

Tour N: Setúbal and Surroundings

Praia da Figueirinha and Praia de Galapos *(16 km from Setúbal)* are two pretty little white-sand beaches that will interest anyone who seeks isolation and calm. Hidden at the end of a bay, they have no services but do offer the advantage of being far less crowded than their western neighbours, Portinho da Arrábida and Sesimbra.

A beautiful **scenic highway ★** and an abrupt descent ending in a cul-de-sac lead to **Praia do Portinho da Arrábida ★** *(18 km from Setúbal)*, a beautiful **beach** nestled in a bay where you can swim to your heart's content. Some services are available here, including a restaurant at the edge of the beach. Before heading for the water, remember theft is an unfortunate reality in this region and that you should exercise caution and leave NOTHING in your vehicle.

Like Cascais, **Costa da Caparica** *(from Marquês Pombal or Metro Palhavã bus 75; single ticket 1 Dia-Praia 480 ESC or family ticket for four passengers 1,440 ESC)* is a popular tourist spot on weekends. Because it's close and easy to reach, this area is regularly invaded by people from Lisbon in search of a beach and a suntanning session. However, unlike the other beaches, the Costa da Caparica has **beaches ★** which stretch out over many kilometres, and most of the coastline has been left in its natural state due to a part of it being classified as a protected zone. In the summer, a little train takes passengers along almost ten kilometres of the coast. Whereas many families go to the beaches close to the village of Caparica, nudists and gays (17th, 18th and 19th stops) often frequent the beaches that are further away. The bus trip from the capital is all the more enjoyable because the bus crosses the impressive Ponte 25 de Abril (bridge) from which you can get a superb view of the Tagus and Lisbon.

HIKING

Tour L: Queluz to Sintra

In the Serra de Sintra, the **Parque da Pena** ★★ *(Tue to Sun 10am to 4:30pm, closed Mon)* has many hiking trails which will enable you to explore some extraordinarily rich and diversified flora. Among the easily accessible hikes, we suggest the one going to the Palácio da Pena by the "gate to the lakes", one of the most magical. To do this, take the Estrada da Pena leaving Sintra Vila, following the signs to the palace. You will find the **Portão dos Lagos** about halfway up, on the right of the highway, near a parking area. This is where the trail begins so park your vehicle here. After passing the entry gate, take the trail running alongside the water on the left. Three small lakes follow, each lined with flourishing vegetation. You can contemplate magnificent tree ferns originating in Australia and New Zealand. Continue your walk along the main road until you come to the first intersection, where you turn left; at the next crossroads, go left again. The entrance to the castle is at the end. Allow one to two hours to reach it. Those who enjoy **panoramic views** ★ should take the trail on the right, located at the second intersection after the lakes. This leads to the **Cruz Alta**, at an altitude of 530 metres, from where you can observe the Serra da Sintra as well as the Pena palace, perched on its rock and standing out from distant plains. Allow about two hours to get there.

If you are interested in longer walks with many viewpoints, take the trail leading to the Palácio da Pena, passing through the beautiful site of the **Castelo dos Mouros** ★★ *(free admission; every day 10am to 4:30pm, see p 159)*. To get there, from the centre of Sintra Vila take Rua Visconde de Monserrate, which later becomes Rua Bernardim Ribeiro. After passing a curve in the street, a stairway located on your right leads directly to the Igreja da Santa Maria, which faces the forest administration buildings of the Serra da Sintra. From there, just next to the buildings, a long, winding trail leads to the ruins of the dos Mouros castle, from where you can enjoy several **panoramic views** ★ of the village of Sintra. Continue climbing, the path joins the main road, the Estrada da Pena, leading to the Pena palace. You then have two choices: left on the Estrada da Pena leads directly to the palace, or to the right leads to the Portão dos Lagos below, from where you can reach the Pena palace by way of narrow trails (see the previous tour). If you opt for this second route, allow for a complete afternoon leaving from Sintra Vila.

Tour M: Setúbal and Surroundings

Located between Setúbal and Sesimbra, the **Serra da Arrábida** ★ is an immense nature park covering nearly 10,800 hectares (more than 26,000 acres). Besides superb beaches, the park has several trails allowing you to observe magnificently verdant and hilly scenery set against an azure blue sea. Four paths have been cleared by the management of the Parque Natural da Arrábida to allow visitors to explore the beauty of the local flora. The length of the proposed tours varies between 5 and 15 kilometres, each presenting a different level of difficulty. You will find an excellent little guide *(free; Guia de Percursos Pedestres Arrábida / Sado; at press time this was available in Portuguese only)* giving precise details of these four hikes, available at the Posto de Turismo da Região de Setúbal *(Largo Corpo Santo)*, in the centre of Setúbal.

 GOLF

Just as in the Algarve, golf has become a much appreciated sporting specialty here, and the Costa de Lisboa ranks second among the regions in terms of the number of golf courses. No fewer than six courses lie between the coast and the Serra de Sintra; there are three south of Lisbon, two of which are near Setúbal. Those listed below are interesting, either for the courses themselves or for their exceptional surroundings.

Tour K: Estoril to Cascais

Besides being located less than two kilometres north of the town of Estoril, the **Estoril Palácio Golf Club** has the advantage of offering a nine-hole course in a very scenic setting. To the south is a fine view of the coast, and to the north is the verdant Serra de Sintra, thus bringing sea and mountain together on one course.

Information and reservations: Estoril Palácio Golf Club / Clube de Golfe do Estoril, 2765 Estoril, ☎ 1-468 01 76, ⇌ 1-468 27 96.

Tour L: Queluz to Sintra

Set at the foot of the southern flank of the Serra de Sintra, in a protected zone, the **Caesar Park Penha Longa** will delight lovers of rugged scenery; hills and granite boulders make its two courses (nine and 18 holes) varied and pleasant to play. A former monastery located in the centre of the complex provides an added touch.

Penha Longa Golf, Lagoa Azul, Linhó, 2710 Sintra, ☎ 1-924 03 20, ⇌ 1-924 03 88.

Tour M: Setúbal and Surroundings

A fine 18-hole course set partly in a pine-scented nature reserve, less than a half-hour from the pulsating capital, awaits you at the **Clube de Campo de Portugal-Aroeira**. This is a protected area, and you can enjoy a setting bereft of high buildings, and the pleasure of exploring several kilometres of fine beaches protected by impressive cliffs.

Clube de Campo de Portugal, Herdade de Aroeira, Fonte da Telha, 2825 Monte de Caparica, ☎ 1-226 32 44, ⇌ 1-226 13 58.

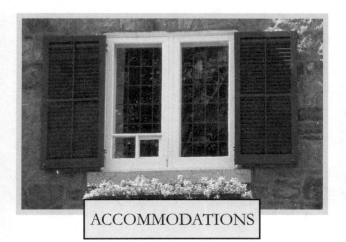

ACCOMMODATIONS

This chapter comprises a selection of the best accommodations in every budget range and category. The prices quoted were current at press time, and of course are subject to change at any time. Except where otherwise indicated, all the prices are for double occupancy. Establishments' complete addresses are included to simplify the task of making reservations from your home. **Breakfast is always included in the room rate, unless otherwise specified.**

The price of making a telephone call from a hotel room in Portugal is very high. It can cost as much as seven dollars per minute to call Canada! It is therefore preferable to use your own telephone company's direct access number (see p 71), so that you will be billed at home instead of in Portugal.

TOUR A: THE ROSSIO AND THE BAIXA

Set up on the fourth floor of a building with no elevator and a dilapidated stairwell, the **Pensão Pension Galicia** *(3,500 ESC sb, 5,000 ESC ps; Rua do Crucifixo no. 50, 4th floor, 1100 Lisboa, ☎ 342 84 30)* appears to be a large apartment where several modestly furnished rooms have been set up. The place is not luxurious, and its rooms are simple but quite decent.

186 Accommodations

> ## Places that stand out
>
> **For business travellers**: Hotel Orion (p 197), Suite Hotel Dom Rodrigo (p 193).
>
> **For history buffs**: Pousada Dona Maria I (p 204), Palácio de Seteais (p 206), Pousada de Palmela (p 210), Pousada de São Filipe (p 209).
>
> **For luxury**: Hotel da Lapa (p 200), the Ritz (p 194), Hotel York House (p 199), Quinta da Capela (p 207), As Janelas Verdes (p 200).
>
> **For a warm welcome**: Pensão Aljubarrota (p 186), Pensão Londres (p 189), Pensão-Residencial Gerês (p 187), Residencial Dom Sancho I (p 196).
>
> **For the best value**: Pensão Aljubarrota (p 186), Pensão Nossa Senhora do Rosario (p 195).
>
> **For the best nightlife**: Casa de São Mamede (p 189).
>
> **For the best views**: Pensão Ninho das Águias (p 188), Albergaria Senhora do Monte (p 188), Hotel da Lapa (p 200), Quinta do Patrício (p 209).
>
> **For romantic atmosphere**: Quinta da Capela (p 207), Hotel York House (p 199), Palácio de Seteais (p 206, 247), Quinta do Patrício (p 209), Casa da Pérgola (p 203).
>
> **For the best swimming pools**: Hotel Orion (p 197), Hotel da Lapa (p 200).
>
> **For the most beautiful gardens**: Hotel da Lapa (p 200), Quinta da Capela (p 207), Palácio de Seteais (p 206, 247).
>
> **For *azulejo* admirers**: Pousada de São Filipe (p 209, 248), Casa de São Mamede (p 189).

Considering the particularly reasonable prices, this is a bargain for budget travellers.

On the 4th floor of a building, the small **Pensão Aljubarrota** *(6,400 ESC sb, 7,900 ESC ps; Rua da Assunção no. 53, 4th* *floor, 1100 Lisboa, ☎ 346 01 12)* is a most charming place, more like a bed & breakfast than a simple boarding house, and the boss, of Italian origin, spares no effort to put you at ease. Friendliness and courtesy here recall the warmth of the Mediterranean. Though comfort proves limited (badly soundproofed rooms, four floors to climb and no elevator), the charm of the place quickly compensates for the few inconveniences. Lovely antique reproductions grace the little rooms, some of which have balconies. Breakfast is taken in this cordial and relaxed atmosphere, surrounded by pretty decorative items and with a view out over the balcony (with large open windows, weather permitting). Ah! sweet Italy, but... are we truly in Lisbon? What is more, a "special" price can be negotiated for extended stays. The entrance, which is hard to find, is between the Rua Augusta and Correiros, between the two show windows of the big *zapatos* store (shoe store). Those who like the B&B formula should definitely consider this place!

Hotel Americano *(7,000 ESC ps, 8,000 ESC pb; Rua 1° Dezembro no. 73, 1200 Lisboa, ☎ 347 49 76, ⇌ 347 49 79)*. An uninviting lobby and prices a bit too high for the quality of the surroundings, but a convenient location in the heart of the neighbourhood. Relatively comfortable, decent-looking rooms.

Slightly set back from the Rossio, on a quiet little street, the **Pensão-Residencial Gerês** *(7,000 ESC sb, 8,500 ESC ps; no bkfst, tv; Calçada do Garcia no. 6, 1st and 2nd floors, 1100 Lisboa, ☎ 881 04 97, ⇌ 888 20 06)* has 24 modestly furnished rooms. Despite the fact that rooms are badly soundproofed and their decor limited to the bare essentials, the pleasant family atmosphere combined with the cleanliness of the establishment makes it a good choice.

Residencial-Albergaria Insulana *(8,000 to 9,500 ESC; pb, tv; Rua da Assunção no. 52, 1100 Lisboa, ☎ 342 76 25)*. Not only does this comfortable 32-room hotel have the advantage of being centrally located, it is also situated on a quiet street.

Hotel Internacional *(9,500-10,000 ESC; pb, tv; Rua da Betesga no. 3, 2nd floor, 1100 Lisboa, ☎ 346 64 01, ⇌ 347 86 35)*. Old-fashioned furnishings but prime location. In an old building at the corner of Rua Augusta, a pedestrian street, it lies a short distance from the local shopping streets and major tourist attractions. Ask for one of the rooms facing the back, which are a bit dark, but sheltered from the noise of the square. Good value for your money.

Hotel Metrópole *(19,800 ESC; pb, ps, tv; Praça Dom Pedro IV, Rossio, 1100 Lisboa, ☎ 346 91 64 or 346 91 65, ≠ 346 91 66)* is one of a chain of beautiful hotels owned by the Almeida family. An old establishment restored in 1993, it has a great deal of character. The limited number of rooms (36), all of which are tastefully decorated, makes for a warm, personal atmosphere. Ask for one facing onto the square, with a view of the Rossio and the Castelo. Good value for this category of hotel.

TOUR B: THE CASTELO AND THE ALFAMA

Pensão Ninho das Águias *(7,500 ESC sb; 8,500 pb; no bkfst; Costa do Castelo no. 74, 1100 Lisboa, ☎ 886 70 08)*. Connected to the walls of the Castelo. Most noteworthy for its romantic setting and lovely, verdant terrace, which offers a view of Lisbon (only a few rooms have a view of the city). This place is somewhat inconvenient, due to its distance from the downtown area and the steep spiral staircase leading to the reception area. Very average level of comfort and inhospitable service. Expensive but enchanting.

TOUR C: GRAÇA AND EAST LISBON

Despite its somewhat depressing exterior and impersonal entrance hall, the **Albergaria Senhora do Monte** *(17,000 ESC, 22,000 ESC with terrace; pb, tv; Calçada do Monte no. 39, 1100 Lisboa, ☎ 886 60 02, ≠ 887 77 83)* has 24 pleasant, modern rooms. If you can fit it into your budget, ask for a room with a terrace so you can savour the pleasure of sitting outside at night when the Castelo is illuminated and the city is all aglitter, offering a real feast for the eyes. This magnificent panorama can also be enjoyed from the outdoor bar *(every day 4pm to 1am)* on the top floor. The only drawback is that the place is far from downtown, so guests have to get about by

TOUR D: THE CHIADO AND THE BAIRRO ALTO

Pensão Globo *(4,500 ESC no bkfst; Rua do Teixeira no. 37, 1200 Lisboa, ☎ 346 22 79)*. With its lovely little, recently repainted façade, this modest guesthouse is perfect for those with limited budgets. Very basic level of comfort (shared shower facilities), but located on one of the few quiet streets in the area. Well-kept rooms and very hospitable service.

Pensão Londres *(6,200 ESC sb, 8,000 ESC ps; Rua Dom Pedro V no. 53, 2nd floor, 1200 Lisboa, ☎ 346 22 03 or 346 55 23, ≠ 346 56 82)*. Set up in a former residence, this guesthouse offers very simply furnished but well-kept rooms with private or shared baths. Pleasant decor. Considering its favourable location, in the very heart of Bairro Alto, this place offers good value for your money.

The friendly, attentive staff at the charming **Residencial Casa de São Mamede** *(11,000 ESC; pb, tv; Rua da Escola Politécnica no. 159, 1200 Lisboa, ☎ 396 31 66 or 396 27 57, ≠ 395 18 96)* make this a very pleasant place to stay. Breakfast is served in a lovely room decorated with *azulejos*. The furnishings are a bit outdated, but nothing is lacking. There is only one minor drawback: you must reserve a long time in advance, due to the limited number of rooms. Furthermore, it is imperative that you request a room at the back, since the place faces onto a very noisy street.

Facing onto a pedestrian street, the **Hotel Borges** *(10,500 ESC; pb; Rua Garrett no. 108, 1200 Lisboa, ☎ 346 19 51, ≠ 342 66 17)* offers quiet rooms. The furnishings and the facilities in general are beginning to look a bit dated, however. Central location.

Príncipe Real *(16,500 to 19,500 ESC; pb, tv, ℜ; Rua da Alegria no. 53, 1200 Lisboa, ☎ 346 01 16, ≠ 342 21 04)*. A good choice for visitors seeking a homey atmosphere and some peace and quiet. Pretty, inviting little rooms, each decorated in a different way. The top-floor dining room offers a lovely view.

The warm welcome and quality service make this a good place to keep in mind.

TOUR E: THE RATO AND AMOREIRAS

Amazónia Hotéis *(15,750 to 16,700 ESC; pb, ℝ, ≈, tv; Travessa Fábrica dos Pentes nos. 12-20, 1200 Lisboa, ☎ 387 70 06 or 387 83 21, ≈ 387 90 90)*. Despite its impersonal looking exterior, this large hotel will be particularly appreciated by those seeking peace and quiet. Outside the town centre, in a relatively quiet neighbourhood, the establishment boasts comfortable, modern rooms. The decor of the rooms and common areas is pleasing though nondescript. Assets include small balconies gracing certain rooms as well as an outdoor swimming pool.

TOUR F: MARQUÊS DE POMBAL, SALDANHA AND NORTH LISBON

Pousada de Juventude *(2,350 ESC dormitory, 5,700 ESC double; no bkfst; Rua Andrade Corvo no. 46, 1050 Lisboa, ☎ 353 26 96, ≈ 353 75 41, Picoas metro or bus #91, Picoas stop)*. Well established in Europe and in North America, youth hostels attract a great number of young budget travellers. This kind of accommodation, though worthwhile in some respects, can nonetheless surprise and, as is the case here, thoroughly disappoint. Indeed, Lisbon's youth hostel proves to be fairly unkept, and the rooms commonplace. As far as the dormitory is concerned, besides its lack of cleanliness, noise caused by the constant comings and goings of travellers makes getting any rest here rather difficult. The high fees asked for the storing of luggage, and the minuscule lockers in which it is stored are two additional drawbacks. Lastly, the reception is none too friendly. The only advantage to staying here is that you are virtually guaranteed to come into contact with other travellers. All things considered, given the high prices being asked here, the backpacking set will do better at a *pensão* or *residencial*, both of which abound in the capital. For a few more escudos, you can find more comfortable accommodation while having the option of storing luggage at the reception at no additional cost.

For inexpensive accommodation, head to the **Residencial Vila Nova** *(3,500 to 4,000 ESC sb, 4,500 to 5,500 ESC ps; no bkfst, tv; Avenida Duque de Loulé no. 111, 3rd floor, 1050 Lisboa, ☎ 353 48 60 or 354 08 38)*, situated right above the offices of the Portuguese Communist Party. This simple *residencial* is in no way connected to the party, however, except for being on neighbourly terms. The few rooms are rather badly soundproofed but always clean. Those at the rear of the building are relatively quiet. Rudimentary but economical.

Of the three hotels on this street, the **Residencial Avenida Parque** *(7,000 ESC; pb, tv; Avenida Sidónio Pais no. 6, 1000 Lisboa, ☎ 353 21 81, ⇌ 353 21 85)* proves to be the best bet. In a quiet setting, opposite the park, this *residencial* offers large, simply equipped rooms. The furniture as well as the common areas look outdated, however, and could use serious freshening up. A smile from the staff when you check in wouldn't hurt either. These few annoyances are soon forgiven, however, given the very affordable prices for such a place.

A member of the Arcantis chain, the **Residencial Avenida Alameda** 's *(7,000 to 9,000 ESC; pb, tv; Avenida Sidónio Pais no. 4, 1000 Lisboa, ☎ 353 21 86, ⇌ 352 67 03)* rooms are plain, square, all painted white, and sparsely decorated. Its location, right next to the park and close to the metro, is its only redeeming feature.

Hotel Flamingo *(12,000 ESC; pb, tv, ℝ; Rua Castilho no. 41, 1250 Lisboa, ☎ 386 21 91, ⇌ 386 12 16)*. Small, modern and nondescript hotel with 39 rooms. As the hotel's name suggests, the decor here is pretty kitschy and renovations would be advisable.

Compared to the modern and rather cold façade, the room furnishings of the **Hotel Excelsior** *(12,500 ESC; pb, tv; Rua Rodrigues Sampaio no. 172, 1100 Lisboa, ☎ 353 71 51 or 352 40 37, ⇌ 357 87 79)* seem straight out of the fifties, and the decor outdated. Not to mention, the use of tinted windows makes the rooms dark and gloomy. Despite all this, they are decently equipped and adequately maintained. The establishment's proximity to Parque Eduardo VII, a pretty expanse of green not too far from downtown, is also a plus.

Hotel Miraparque *(13,000 ESC; pb, tv, ℜ, ℝ; Avenida Sidónio Pais no. 12, 1050 Lisboa, ☎ 352 42 86, ≠ 357 89 20)*. This rather conventional-looking hotel has about one hundred rooms, with a decor that is austere and devoid of any particular style. The choicest rooms are those situated in the front of the building, overlooking Parque Eduardo VII and the elegant Pavilhão dos Desportos.

Though a little far from downtown, near the Gulbenkian Foundation, the **Hotel Dom Manuel I** *(14,500 ESC; pb, tv; Avenida Duque de Avila no. 189, 1050 Lisboa, ☎ 357 61 60, ≠ 357 69 85)* offers good service in a pleasant and quiet environment. The decor of the rooms and common areas is polished and tasteful. Good value.

Facing a lovely little public garden planted with trees, the **Hotel Dom Carlos** *(15,500 ESC; pb, tv; Avenida Duque de Loulé no. 121, 1050 Lisboa, ☎ 353 90 71, ≠ 352 07 28)* has small, opulently decorated rooms, each equipped with a marbled bathroom. Much like at the Hotel Excelsior, however, the use of tinted windows prevents guests from taking full advantage of the view of the statuesque trees bordering the square – an inconvenience made all the more unpleasant by the fact that these are double windows (installed to block out the noise from the busy avenues nearby) and are difficult to open. These drawbacks are soon compensated, however, by the hotel's proximity to Parque Eduardo VII, where guests can enjoy the pleasures of both the outdoors and city life.

Despite its unappealing exterior, **Hotel Fénix** *(16,500 to 20,500 ESC; pb, tv, ℜ; Praça Marquês de Pombal no. 8, 1200 Lisboa, ☎ 386 21 21, ≠ 386 01 31)* has attractively renovated rooms. The windows in the rooms facing the street are double-glazed so that guests can enjoy an interesting view of bustling Praça Marquês de Pombal without having to put up with the noise. Good service. A bit on the expensive side.

A member of the Best Western chain, the **Hotel Rex** *(18,000 ESC; pb, ℜ, ℝ, tv; Rua Castilho no. 169, 1070 Lisboa, ☎ 388 21 61, ≠ 388 75 81, www.rex.pt)* is a modern building devoid of character, with small rooms and standard nondescript decor. Despite recent renovations (1996), these rooms remain boring, even somewhat old-fashioned. Given the high rates, this place offers very average value for the price, despite its desirable location, facing Parque Eduardo VII.

An integral part of the Hotéis Tivoli, the **Suite Hotel Dom Rodrigo** *(19,500 to 25,000 ESC; no bkfst, pb, K, ℝ, tv, ≈; Rua Rodrigo da Fonseca nos. 44-50, 1200 Lisboa, ☎ 386 38 00, ≠ 386 30 00)* is, along with the Orion (see p 197), one of the few hotels in the capital to offer the apartment-hotel option. The Portuguese chain offers three kinds of accommodation here, that is nine studios, 39 suites (with separate bedroom) and nine penthouses, all equipped with modern, tasteful furniture. The suites and studios located on the 7th floor and in the front of the building each have a little terrace that is pleasant, though lacks any particular view. For those who so desire, room service is provided every day at no extra charge. A further advantage is the swimming pool that, though small, is quite delightful.

Another giant in the hotel industry, the **Holiday Inn Lisboa** *(21,000 ESC; no bkfst, pb, ≈, ⊙, ℜ, ℝ, tv; Avenida António José de Almeida no. 28-A, 1000 Lisboa, ☎ 793 52 22 or 793 60 18, ≠ 793 66 72)* is, unfortunately, not noted for its decor. Indeed, the reception area looks more like an airport waiting room than the lobby of a four star hotel. The decor and furnishings of the rooms, though decent, also demonstrate a lack of originality. That breakfast is not included in the price of the room is also surprising, particularly since the rates are rather high for a hotel so far from the downtown area. Its only assets when compared to its competitors in the same category is a rooftop outdoor swimming pool (too small, unfortunately) as well as an exercise room (also accessible to non-clients: 1,500 ESC/visit).

With its futuristic lines, **The Méridien** *(33,500 to 45,000 ESC; no bkfst, pb, ℜ, ℝ, △, tv; Rua Castilho no. 149, 1070 Lisboa, ☎ 383 09 00 or 383 04 00, ≠ 383 32 31)* ranks as one of the most modern hotels in Lisbon in terms of exterior architecture. The renowned chain's Lisbon link offers comfortable cubic rooms, with a standard, rather unoriginal decor. Though the rooms have no balconies, some offer a pleasant view of Parque Eduardo VII. On the whole, the design of the common areas, with the exception of the lobby furnishings, is not always in the best of taste. In fact it is quite tacky, especially in the restaurant, La Brasserie des Amis. Moreover, the lack of

194 Accommodations

facilities (no exercise room or swimming pool) is regrettable as is the the fact that breakfast is not included in the already high rates. To its credit, the hotel boasts non-smoking floors and a fine location, opposite Parque Eduardo VII.

True to its international reputation, the **Ritz** hotel *(38,000 to 46,000 ESC; no bkfst, pb, ℜ, ℝ, ⊙, tv; Rua Rodrigo da Fonseca no. 88, 1093 Lisboa, ☎ 383 20 20, ⇋ 383 17 83)* offers luxury and quality – to those who can afford it, of course. Though the Ritz occupies a building singularly lacking in originality, the interior is in keeping with what one would expect from such a hotel. Be sure to note the very beautiful tapestries in the purest Art Deco style, in the ground floor lounge, true marvels for enthusiasts of this style. The suites, for their part, boast opulent and refined furnishings, and some are decorated with superb antique reproductions. To fully experience such luxury, request a room on the upper floors and overlooking the park as these offer a lovely view of the city. Bar, restaurants, a conference room, lounges and exercise room (on the small side) are but a few of the amenities offered to the clientele. Moreover, an entire floor is reserved for non-smokers. In such an epicurean establishment, the absence of a swimming pool, always useful in a major capital city, is unfortunate, however.

Sheraton and Towers Lisboa *(32,000 to 38,000 ESC; no bkfst, pb, ≈, ℜ, tv, ⊙, △; Rua Latino Coelho no. 1, 1069 Lisboa, ☎ 357 57 57, ⇋ 354 71 64)*. You'd have to be very picky not to like this place, given all its amenities. The swimming pool and gym are particularly popular with guests (and are open to the general public), although both are a bit too small. The rooms on the upper floors (the Towers) are more luxuriously decorated and offer a view of Parque Eduardo VII in the distance (of course, the prices are higher as well). The hotel also has a very pleasant terrace with a bar and a panoramic view.

TOUR G: RESTAURADORES AND LIBERDADE

 Pensão Imperial *(3,500 ESC and 4,500 ESC; ps, no bkfst; Praça dos Restauradores no. 78, 1200 Lisboa, enter through the optometrist's shop; ☎ 342 01 66)*. On the fourth floor of a building with no elevator. Modest, but well-kept and well-located. A few rooms offer a view of the square, but most are at the back, where it is quieter. Guests receive a warm welcome. An excellent choice in this category. Given the limited number of rooms, it is best to make reservations.

Facing the Nossa Senhora da Pena church, the **Pensão Nossa Senharo do Rosario** *(4,000 ESC sb, 5,000 ESC ps; no bkfst, tv; Calçada de Sant'Ana no. 198, 1st floor, 1100 Lisboa, ☎ 885 36 50)* used to welcome penniless young girls. Today, the very convivial proprietor welcomes visitors with the same devotion – for a fee, of course. Simply decorated but particularly well-kept, this guesthouse provides decent accommodation for relatively little money. Those who really want to meet the people can opt for one of the front rooms, where they will be awakened by the din of the busy street below. The rooms at the rear of the building, for their part, offer a pleasant view of the Graça district. Breakfast is served for the modest sum of 350 ESC. A bargain for travellers on tight budgets!

Residencial Florescente *(4,500 ESC sb, 8,000 ESC pb; no bkfst; Rua Portas de Santo Antão no. 99, 1150 Lisboa, ☎ 346 35 17 or 342 66 09, ⇋ 342 77 33)*. The best thing about this place is that it has a large number of rooms at low to moderate prices. Well-kept and comfortable. Decent value for the price.

Residencial Restauradores *(6,000 ESC; no bkfst, pb; Praça dos Resauradores no. 13, 1200 Lisboa, 4th floor, elevator, ☎ 347 56 60 or 347 56 61)*. Centrally located, with about thirty rooms (reservations recommended during the high season). The place is well-maintained and has a modest but decent decor. Friendly, multilingual staff. Reasonable prices.

The **Pensão Residencial 13 da Sorte** *(6,500 ESC; no bkfst, pb; Rua do Salitre no. 13, 1200 Lisboa, ☎ 353 97 46, ☎ and ⇋ 353 18 51)* boasts twenty-four clean and modestly but pleasantly decorated rooms. This guesthouse's central location and affordable rates make it a good choice in the capital.

Pensão Residencial Monumental *(6,500 ESC; no bkfst, pb, tv; Rua da Glória no. 21, 1250 Lisboa, ☎ 346 98 07, ⇋ 343 02 13)*. Small guesthouse with modest, sombre rooms lacking any charm, but well-kept and rented out at very affordable rates. A good choice for travellers on tight budgets.

Accommodations

🛎️ Set up on the 3rd floor of a stylish building on the elegant Avenida da Liberdade, the **Residencial Dom Sancho I** *(7,000 to 9,000 ESC; no bkfst, pb, tv; Avenida da Liberdade no. 202, 3rd floor, 1200 Lisboa, ☎ 354 86 48)* offers a few pleasantly decorated and immaculate rooms with Portuguese-style furniture. For a pleasant view, request a room with a balcony overlooking the avenue. Hospitable reception.

Residência Roma *(9,000 ESC; pb, tv; Travessa da Glória no. 22A, 1200 Lisboa, ☎ and ≈ 346 05 57)*. Clean and comfortable, but somewhat plain. Twenty-four hour bar service.

Right next to the *elevador da Glória*, on a small, narrow street without charm, the **Suíço Atlántico** *(9,500 ESC; pb, tv; Rua da Glória nos. 3-19, 1250 Lisboa, ☎ 346 17 13, ≈ 346 90 13)* houses sombre rooms virtually lacking any decor. This establishment's only redeeming feature is its central location, right next to the Praça dos Restauradores and a few steps from the Rossio.

Though its exterior is lacking in charm and its interior appears rather antiquated, the **Hotel Jorge V** *(10,750 ESC; pb, tv; Rua Mouzinho da Silveira no. 3, 1250 Lisboa, ☎ 356 25 25, ≈ 315 03 19)* has the advantage of being situated on a quiet, tree-lined street. Request one of the front rooms – for they have little balconies, a welcome treat in warm weather. Those on the top floor offer an interesting view of the city. Lovers of Art Deco will appreciate the interesting armchairs right next to the bar.

Occupying a building with a rather impersonal façade on the corner of two noisy streets, the **Hotel Presidente** *(12,000 ESC; pb, tv; Rua Alexandre Herculano no. 13, 1150 Lisboa, ☎ 353 95 01, ≈ 352 02 72)* has an original lobby. From the sitting room set up in a corner on the mezzanine, you'll gaze down upon a snack bar with designer furniture, while a huge modern painting adds a cheerful note to the place, otherwise devoted to studied sparsity. A flight of stairs flanked by a large geometric and streamlined wall, the whole in polished stone, leads to the bar. Unfortunately, with regard to the rooms, the spirit of creativity is sadly lacking here where the simple decor is bereft of any style or interesting views. Despite this, the hotel does boast a comfortable setting and better value for your money than that offered by its close competitors.

The **Hotel Veneza** *(16,800 ESC; pb, tv; Avenida da Liberdade no. 189, 1250 Lisboa, ☎ 352 26 18 or 352 67 00, ⇌ 352 66 78)* is located in a very beautiful bourgeois residence *(palecete)* with a Neo-Moorish façade, an excellent choice for this category of hotel. An elegant staircase with attractive ironwork, the whole surmounted by a magnificent glass cupola as well as elaborate mouldings here and there are worth a visit in and of themselves. The only false note in this beautiful setting is the decor of the entrance hall, the reception hall and bar. In truth, the large brightly-coloured paintings by Pedro Luiz-Gomes, hanging in the stairs of the lobby, though pleasing, seem somewhat out of place here. Moreover, not only is the bar and reception hall's cold and modern arrangement of questionable taste, but constitutes another unfortunate clash of styles. The furnishings and decor of the rooms, also modern, prove attractive and tasteful. Hospitable service.

Housed in what was formerly the Teatro Eden, whose lovely Art-Deco façade has been skilfully preserved, the **Orion** *(17,500 ESC double, 24,600 ESC quadruple; no bkfst, pb, ≈, ℜ, ℝ, K, tv; Praça dos Restauradores nos. 18-24, 1250 Lisboa, ☎ 321 66 00, ⇌ 321 66 66)* apartment-hotel is a particularly interesting choice. The apartment-hotel formula proves ideal for business travellers, for families with young children or for those planning an extended stay. In addition to its ideal location, facing the lovely Praça dos Restauradores and in close proximity to various means of transport (metro and train right nearby), the Orion offers charmingly furnished studios and apartments. While the studios are each equipped with a comfortable sofa bed, the apartments have a separate bedroom. A child-size bed (for those under 10 years of age) is also available upon request, free of charge. A work corner is arranged near the window, and a table and chairs means you can eat comfortably in the studio. All studios and apartments have fully-equipped kitchenettes, including a microwave oven and dishwasher. The lovely marbled bathrooms, for their part, are all supplied with hair dryers. Housekeeping service is provided once a week. For those who so desire, room service is available on a daily basis (600 ESC/day for studios or 800 ESC/day for apartments); breakfast service is also available for 1,000 ESC. Though all rooms are accessible to the physically handicapped, three among them (studios) have been especially fitted out for such guests. Another advantage is the pleasant terrace on the top floor, offering a panoramic view of the *Castelo*, the Baixa and Avenida Restauradores. Finally, as an added treat, guests will find a superb swimming pool and a snack bar, the whole surrounded by a magnificent panorama. Whether for a business stay or holiday, this establishment offers excellent value.

Hotel Avenida Palace *(21,000 to 24,000 ESC; pb, ℝ, tv; Rua 1° Dezembro no. 123, 1200 Lisboa, ☎ 346 01 51, ⇌ 342 28 84)*. Dating from the Edwardian era, this comfortable hotel has retained much of its charm and refined atmosphere, it will appeal to particularly discerning travellers. The elaborate decor includes stucco, crystal chandeliers and a beautiful marble stairwell. Ask for one of the rooms on the fourth or fifth floor, overlooking the train station, for these offer an interesting view of the Castelo and the lovely station. Attentive service. Beautiful, but expensive. At press time, the hotel was temporarily closed due to work being carried out on the metro.

More modest in size than its "big sister" next door (see Tívoli Lisboa below), the **Tívoli Jardim** *(23,500 to 26,500 ESC; pb, ≈, ℜ, ℝ, tv; Rua Júlio César Machado no. 7, 1200 Lisboa, ☎ 353 99 71, ⇌ 355 65 66)* offers all the advantages of a world-class hotel. A large rooftop terrace, free access to the swimming pool (small, but located in a pleasant garden) and its neighbour's tennis court, constitute only a few of the amenities offered to the clientele. The rooms' decor and furnishings are modern and rather nondescript. Renting a room at the rear of the building is preferable, for the front looks out on a large parking lot.

The **Lisboa Plaza** hotel *(25,500 to 35,600 ESC; pb, ℜ, ℝ, tv; Travessa do Salitre, 1200 Lisboa, ☎ 346 39 22, ⇌ 347 16 30)* doesn't look like much from the outside; the refined decor of its entrance hall, consisting of a marble floor, antique furniture and curios combined with elegant fabrics, is the distinguishing feature of this luxurious establishment. Be sure to check out the lounge, where the bar and wallpaper pleasantly recall the splendours of Art Nouveau. With regard to its 106 small rooms (with the exception of the 12 suites), their decor is markedly simpler and, though tasteful, somewhat lacking in character. Also, the few amenities offered (no swimming pool or exercise room) constitutes another disadvantage, though compensated by the hotel's central location.

Facing the elegant Avenida da Liberdade, the **Tívoli Lisboa** hotel *(26,500 to 33,000 ESC; pb, ≈, ℜ, ℝ, tv; Avenida da Liberdade no. 185, 1250 Lisboa, ☎ 353 01 81 or 314 11 01, ≠ 357 94 61)* has 329 small but nicely appointed rooms. Those on the top floors, overlooking the *Avenida*, offer an interesting view. In addition to its location, close to downtown, the hotel has various amenities, such as a tennis court and a small swimming pool in a lovely garden. What is more, a terrace restaurant has been set up on the building's top floor, affording a lovely panoramic view of the city.

Hotel Sofitel *(35,000 ESC; no bkfst, pb, ℜ, ℝ, tv; Avenida da Liberdade nos. 123-125, 1250 Lisboa, ☎ 342 92 02, ≠ 342 92 22)*. Some 170 rooms, four of which are suites, all equipped with functional and neutrally-painted furniture, a rather mundane restaurant and bar, the whole impeccably clean. Efficiency reigns supreme in this establishment of the celebrated French chain, and business people will feel at ease here: in fact, a large conference room accommodating up to 300 people is intended for their use. Staying in this four-star hotel necessitates having a hefty bank account, however, particularly since breakfast (2,500 ESC) is not included in the (somewhat excessive) price of the room.

TOUR H: SANTA CATARINA AND CAIS DO SODRÉ

Pensão Residencial Santa Catarina *(8,500 to 9,200 ESC; pb; Rua Dr. Luís de Almeida e Albuquerque no. 6, 1200 Lisboa, ☎ 346 61 06, ≠ 347 72 27)*. Noteworthy chiefly for its peaceful location. Pleasant surroundings, but rather expensive considering the lack of services.

TOUR I: ESTRÊLA AND LAPA

🐚 A former monastery, the **Hotel York House** *(23,500 to 26,500 ESC; pb, ℜ, tv; Rua das Janelas Verdes no. 32, 1200 Lisboa, ☎ 396 24 35 or 396 27 85 , ≠ 397 27 93)*, like its neighbour (see As Janelas Verdas below), is one of those rare hotels that has successfully managed to combine charm with comfort. It is worth describing how you get into the hotel: after passing through the entrance, which is decorated with scores of *azulejos*, you have to climb a long flight of stairs flanked by massive pink walls covered with luxuriant greenery; at the top, you will find yourself on a beautiful patio adorned with plants. In fine weather, you can enjoy a meal or simply sip a refreshment beneath the tall palm trees (see p 238). Next door, the luxurious and more intimate hotel bar, with its wood panelling, is also a pleasant place to have a coffee or a drink, although the prices are quite high. The rooms, for their part, are tastefully decorated with Portuguese furniture, fabrics in warm colours, gleaming wood floors and antique *azulejos*, many featuring naive motifs. Unfortunately, the rooms facing the street are somewhat noisy despite the double-glazed windows. The only other drawback is that the employees at the reception seem a little stiff. A charming place nonetheless. Good value for the price.

The beautifully furnished **As Janelas Verdes** *(26,000 to 28,000 ESC; pb, tv; Rua das Janelas Verdas no. 47, 1200 Lisboa, ☎ 396 81 43, ≈ 396 81 44)* occupies a sumptuous former residence, whose charm has been artfully preserved. Its 17 rooms are extremely comfortable, and breakfast is served on a romantic, verdant patio.

The **Hotel da Lapa** *(35,000 to 47,500 ESC; no bkfst, pb, ≈, ℜ, tv; Rua do Pau da Bandeira no. 4, 1200 Lisboa, ☎ 395 00 05 or 395 00 06, ≈ 395 06 05)*, set in a pretty and open part of town with embassies and the like for neighbours, is probably Lisbon's loveliest hotel in this category. The building is a former palace to which a wing has been added, and architects have wisely preserved some of the original features. These include a splendid banquet hall (on the second floor) richly adorned with stucco and imitation marble, and bathed in light filtered through period stained-glass windows. The luxurious ground floor, all decorated with marble, opens onto a vast inner garden with a big swimming pool and an adjacent bar. The landscaping, complemented by a magnificent fountain decorated with *azulejos*, makes this place a true haven of peace. Each of the charming rooms is decorated differently and equipped with all the conveniences. From your balcony, you can enjoy a direct view of the verdant inner garden. If you're looking for real luxury, opt for one of the suites, from which you can see the Tagus and the Ponte 25 de Abril in the distance. And finally, if you'll only settle for the acme of perfection, there's room #701, a presidential suite with access to a little turret offering a 360° view of Lisbon. Of course, the suites are all equipped with a whirlpool and other such sophisticated amenities! To top it all off, the place has shops, conference rooms, a private underground parking lot and an elegant restaurant (see p 238). Expensive but oh, how elegant! Very good value for the price.

TOUR J: ALCÂNTARA, SANTO AMARO AND BELÉM

Located steps away from the Mosteiro dos Jerónimos, the **Pensão Residencial Setubalense** *(5,000 ESC; pb, tv; Rua de Belém no. 28, 1300 Lisboa,* ☎ *363 66 39 or 364 87 60,* ⇌ *362 13 72)* rents out clean rooms at moderate prices. Although the common areas are pleasant, the decor of the rooms is a bit depressing. Very good value for your money.

The **Hotel da Torre** *(13,500 to 14,700 ESC; pb, tv; Rua dos Jerónimos no. 8, 1400 Lisboa,* ☎ *363 62 62 or 363 73 32,* ⇌ *364 59 95)*, also near the monastery, has 50 comfortable rooms. Tasteful decor, hospitable staff. A good choice.

TOUR K: PARQUE FLORESTAL DE MONSANTO

Camping Site: **Campismo Municipal de Lisboa**, Câmara Municipal de Lisboa, Estrada da Circunvalação, 1400 Lisboa, ☎ 760 20 61 or 760 20 62, ⇌ 760 74 74.

TOUR L: ESTORIL TO CASCAIS

Estoril

Graced with a charming garden, the **Pensão Smart** *(7,000 ESC; pb; Rua Maestro Lacerda no. 6, 2765 Estoril,* ☎ *1-468 21 64)* is a good hotel with reasonable rates. Its few rooms are impeccably-kept, and a few of these afford a pleasant view.

Hotel Inglaterra *(11,550 to 18,800 ESC; pb, tv, ≈; Rua do Porto no. 1, 2765 Estoril, ☎ 1-468 44 61, ≠ 1-468 21 08)*. Situated right next to the park and close to the casino, this former bourgeois residence converted into a hotel has 50 comfortably and tastefully arranged rooms. Opt for one of the upstairs rooms, as these offer a beautiful view. Like most establishments in Estoril, however, this one is rather pricey considering the few services offered.

A good part of the hotels that stretch along the coast look modern, impersonal and uninteresting. Among the few remaining *belle époque* buildings, the **Hotel Palácio Estoril** *(22,000 to 35,000 ESC; pb, tv, ≈, △, ⊙; Rua do Parque, 2765 Estoril, ☎ 1-468 04 00, ≠ 1-468 48 67)* is worthy of mention for its pleasant setting, both inside and outside. Its 162 rooms have classic furnishings, all in good taste, and the interesting lighting brings out the warm decor. The bathrooms are especially big, decked out in fine marble and well equipped. On the ground floor, the hotel has several lounges, most of them tastefully appointed. The Austrian-style lounge with its piano, as well as the games room adorned with oriental rugs and exotic wood panelling, are worth a visit. The elegant breakfast room, with fine antique marble, is also worthy of mention. A plentiful breakfast buffet is served there. Finally, a big pool, open year-round and surrounded by a perfectly manicured English lawn, renders this spot very pleasant. A bit expensive.

Oeiras *(20 km from Estoril)*

Youth Hostel: **Pousada de Juventude Catalazete** *(1,700 ESC dormitory, no bkfst, 4,100 ESC double, bkfst incl.)*, Estrada Marginal, next to the INATEL building, 2780 Peiras, ☎ and ≠ 1-443 06 38.

Cascais

Close to the Cascais train station, **Residencial Palma** *(7,000 ESC sb, 11,000 pb; tv; Avenida Valbom nos. 13-15, 2750 Cascais, ☎ 1-483 77 97, ≠ 1-483 79 22)* deserves a mention as much for its charming rooms as for its pleasant surroundings: there is a small, lovely flowering garden.

Casa da Pérgola *(10,000 ESC sb, 14,000 to 18,000 ESC pb; closed Oct to mid-Mar; Avenida Valbom no. 13, 2750 Cascais, ☎ 1-484 00 40, ≠ 1-483 47 91)*. Located in the centre of town, this little six-room hotel is worth considering both for its relatively affordable prices and for its slightly old-fashioned charm. Its *azulejos*, flower garden, and old knickknacks and furniture will please the most romantic visitors. Friendly and professional service.

Set by the seaside, the **Hotel Albatroz** *(35,500 to 43,000 ESC; pb, tv, ≈, ℜ; Rua Frederico Arouca no. 100, 2750 Cascais, ☎ 1-483 28 21, ≠ 1-484 48 27)* has two distinct buildings, now set around a single terrace overlooking the cliffs. The older part, formerly a resort for the nobility, still has some rooms decorated in the old style, as well as a restaurant and a bar with panoramic views. Most of the rooms and a small luxury shopping gallery are located in the new building. Rooms are appointed with modern furniture, and most have balconies with sea views. On the broad terrace, a small saltwater pool as well as many lounge chairs will delight sunbathers and idlers. The only regret is the singular lack of greenery.

Praia do Guincho *(8 km from Cascais)*

Camping: **Campismo do Guincho / Orbitur,** at Areia, 2750 Cascais, ☎ 1-487 21 67 or 487 04 50, ≠ 1-487 21 67.

The designers of the **Hotel do Guincho** *(26,000 to 34,000 ESC; pb, tv, ℜ; 9 km west of Cascais, Estrada do Guincho, 2750 Cascais, ☎ 1-487 04 91, ≠ 1-487 04 31)* did a good job of blending the crudeness of a former military building with the elegance and comfort required today for any quality hotel establishment. Although it looks modern from the outside, this hotel was built from the ruins of a fortress. While some elements in the common areas recall its distant past (doors with semi-circular arches, a stairway and walls in crudely cut stone), the atmosphere has been rendered warmer by luxurious carpets and classy furniture. The guest rooms are set in the former vaulted cells, linked around a central courtyard still equipped with its well. Some of them have a small enclosed gallery with views of the coast. The magnificent meeting room, with its fully medieval appearance, and the congenial restaurant, with its panoramic view of the sea, are worth a glance for their decor.

TOUR M: QUELUZ TO SINTRA

Queluz

The latest in a prestigious line, the **Pousada Dona Maria I** *(29,600 ESC; pb, tv, ℜ; facing the Palácio de Queluz, 2745 Queluz, ☎ 1-435 61 58 or 435 61 72, ≠ 1-435 61 89)* is just as spectacular as its cousins. Facing the splendid Palácio de Queluz (see p 149), the *pousada* is set up in a building that was to have been part of a vast grouping of buildings next to the palace. French invasions and the flight of the Court to Brazil was, however, to change the course of things. As such, besides the lack of an identical building to complete the central square, the original blueprints do not indicate a tower. The present clock tower was added to the existing building after the fact. To this day, historians still ponder the reason for the addition; what is known is that the clock started running on the very day Dona Maria II was born, that is July 28th, 1819. Designed as an outbuilding to the palace, the present building served mainly to accommodate the great number of servants assigned to the Court. Today, it consists of 24 rooms and two suites, all comfortably and luxuriously furnished. The clever arrangement of the premises as well as the preservation of various period elements, such as the small theatre's balcony and the impressive clock mechanism, add still more cachet to the place. Its ideal location, close to all the sights (Lisbon, Sintra, Cascais, Estoril, etc.) as well as the magnificent palace gardens make this *pousada* a perfect place to combine the pleasures of discovery with those of luxury and comfort.

Sintra

Youth Hostel: **Pousada da Juventude** *(1,600 ESC dormitory, 4,100 ESC double; no bkfst)*, Santa Eufémia, 2710 Sintra, ☎ and ≠ 924 12 10.

Tour M: Queluz to Sintra 205

Two hundred metres from the Sintra train station, the **Casa de Hóspedes Adelaide** *(3,500 ESC; sb, ps, no bkfst; Avenida Guilherme Gomes Fernandes no. 11, 1st floor, 2710 Sintra, ☎ 923 08 73)* will especially appeal to travellers seeking low-priced accommodation. In this guesthouse, there are several rather austerely furnished, but always clean, rooms. Only a few among them have a private shower, however. The friendly reception will further your appreciation of this place's simple charm.

Located just across from the Sintra train station, the small **Residencial Monte da Lua** *(7,500 ESC; no bkfst, pb; Avenida Miguel Bombarda; 2710 Sintra, ☎ and ≈ 924 10 29)* has only seven rooms, each pleasantly but simply decorated and above all very well kept. The mood here is distinctly family oriented. A few rooms have a lovely view of the surrounding mountains, with the ocean in the distance. Bearing in mind the few low-priced accommodations in Sintra, this establishment offers good value.

In a beautiful large residence, rather sparingly decorated, lies the **Pensão-Residêncial Sintra** *(12,000 ESC; pb, ≈; Travessa dos Avelares 12, Calçada de São Pedro, 2710 São Pedro de Sintra, ☎ 1-923 07 38)*. Despite its respectable size, this guesthouse has only 10 rooms, and this makes it preferable to reserve far in advance. Its pretty terrace, with views of verdant hills, as well as its garden and pool, will delight those who seek space and open air.

The best reason to stay at the **Hotel Central** *(14,000 ESC; pb, tv; Praça da República no. 35, ☎ 923 09 63 or 923 00 63)*, which looks rather antiquated but has a great deal of cachet, is its location right in the middle of the village next to the Palácio Nacional da Sintra. Its lovely breakfast room is certainly worth a look even if you aren't staying here. In fact the staff is so aloof to guests that it is quite easy to roam about this hotel. You may well have to wait a while at the reception before someone appears to serve you! Fairly expensive, but central.

A ten-minute walk from downtown Sintra, in the quaint little village of São Pedro de Sintra, is the **Estalagem Solar dos Mouros** *(15,500 ESC; pb, tv; Calçada São Pedro no. 64, São Pedro da Sintra, 2710 Sintra, ☎ 923 02 64, ☎ and*

≈ *923 32 16)*, a modest hotel with a family atmosphere. Its seven rooms are exceptionally well-kept but very plainly decorated, and a pleasant veranda acts as a breakfast room. Given the services offered, the rates are a bit high, a disadvantage compensated for in part by the warm welcome.

Tívoli Sintra *(19,000 to 21,300 ESC; pb, ≈, ℜ; Praça da República, behind the Palácio Nacional; 2710 Sintra, ☎ 923 35 05, ≈ 923 15 72)*. Though this hotel boasts a decent interior decor, the presence of such a modern building so close to the magnificent Palácio Nacional is indeed regrettable – a mistake that is all the more unfortunate as it the only such building in the area. Indeed, this is a truly deplorable example of tourist development showing little concern for the setting, an example of an administration with little respect for the city's heritage. If this clash of the centuries does not bother you, however, you will find 75 comfortably equipped rooms, most benefitting from a small terrace with a pleasant view.

Seteais *(2 km from Sintra)*

Less than two kilometres from Sintra, the **Hotel Palácio de Seteais** *(Nov to Mar 27,000 to 29,000 ESC, Apr to Oct 40,000 to 43,000 ESC; pb, ℜ, ≈; Rua Barbosa Bocage nos. 8-10, Seteais, 2710 Sintra, ☎ 1-923 32 00 or 923 42 77, ≈ 1-923 42 77)* is set in a magnificent palace (see p 157) dating from the 19th century. Its 30 rooms are appointed with beautiful period furniture and offer a level of comfort worthy of the best hotels. Walking through its common areas, you can observe elegant frescoes as well as a great number of knickknacks and antique tapestries. In front of the buildings is a majestic esplanade which is enticing for a walk, while in back, a terrace looks out over beautiful French-style gardens, and offer a truly romantic and panoramic view of the surrounding countryside. For those seeking refinement and luxury, this is an unforgettable experience.

Várzea de Sintra *(4 km from Sintra)*

Four kilometres from Sintra, the **Pátio do Saloio** *(9,500 ESC; pb, tv, ℜ; Rua Padre Amaro Teixeira de Azevedo no. 14,*

Várzea de Sintra, ☎ 924 15 20, ☎ and ≈ 924 15 12) is a small guesthouse run by a friendly Belgian couple. This quaint country house has nine simply but very tastefully decorated rooms. The proprietors are, in fact, seasoned decorators: the living room as well as the very beautiful Bistrobar Opera Prima (see p 245), located in downtown Sintra, are two beautiful examples of their work. Finally, why not give into temptation and try the fine cuisine offered at the restaurant of the same name, at the same location (see p 247)? Excellent value.

Monserrate

Built in 1773 on the site of the former residence of the Duke of Cadaval, the **Quinta da Capela** *(21,000 to 24,000 ESC; pb, ≈, △, ☉; along the N375, to the right of the old road going from Sintra to Colares, shortly before the Palácio de Monserrate; 2710 Sintra, ☎ 1-929 01 70, ≈ 1-929 34 25)* is one of those spots that leaves you with a certain sense of nostalgia. Set within the Serra da Sintra (see p 151), this property is humble and noble at the same time, and is literally overrun by exuberant vegetation. As you descend the little cobbled road leading to the *quinta*, you are surrounded by a silence that is disturbed only by the rustling of the leaves in the wind and by the songs of birds. The powerfully aromatic flora reminds us of their African and South American origins. In rainy weather, mists spread from the neighbouring forests and form scenery that is even more beautiful and hallucinatory. Will visitors find the Eden so splendidly described by Lord Byron?

The main building, rather modest-looking from the outside, has seven rooms decorated with exceptionally refined furniture and knick-knacks. Whether it be the elegant lounge, the breakfast room or simply the corridors, good taste is evident throughout. Facing the building, a superb French-style garden entices the visitor to stroll, as two white swans in a little pond keep a jealous watch over their surroundings. Going to the end of the garden, you can admire a pretty little Manueline chapel (Nossa Senhora da Piedade), the only survivor of the 1755 catastrophe, which destroyed the rest of the property. Located just below the main building is an annex containing three fully appointed cottage apartments with a terrace bathed in greenery. Here also, meticulous decoration turns rooms, lounges and kitchens into objects of wonder. Finally, to fully enjoy this dream place, a sauna and a pool as well as an exercise room have been provided for the pleasure of guests. One of the best quality-to-price ratios in the area.

Praia Grande *(11 km from Sintra)*

Camping: **Campismo Amistad**, Praia Grande, 2710 Colares, ☎ 1-929 05 81 or 929 18 34.

Almornos *(17 kilometres away)*

Camping Site: **Clube de Campismo de Lisboa**, in Almornos, near the N117, 1675 Caneças, ☎ 1-962 39 60, ⇆ 1-962 37 60.

TOUR N: SETÚBAL AND SURROUNDINGS

Setúbal

Camping: **A Toca do Pai Lopes**, Câmara Municipal de Setúbal, 2900 Setúbal, ☎ 65-52 24 75 or 53 25 78.

Located on a pedestrian street, the **Residencial Bocage** *(6,000 ESC; pb; Rua de São Cristóvão no. 14, 2900 Setúbal, ☎ 65-215 98, ⇆ 65-218 09)* has 39 rooms that, though well-kept, have no particular charm. A good place for those with limited budgets.

Set in the heart of the historical centre, the **Residencial Setubalense** *(7,000 to 9,000 ESC; pb, tv; Rua Major Afonso Pala no. 17, 2nd floor, 2900 Setúbal, ☎ 65-52 57 90, ⇆ 65-52 57 89)* has 24 rooms offering modern furnishings, comfort and good taste. One of the best quality-to-price ratios in its category.

Attractive because of its façade and its location in the heart of town, on a pretty little tree-shaded square, the **Albergaria Solaris** *(10,000 ESC; pb, tv; Praça Marquês de Pombal no. 12, 2900 Setúbal, ☎ 65-52 21 89, ⇆ 65-52 20 70)* will suit those for whom comfort and the purely functional take precedence over everything else. Spanking clean and adorned with modern furniture, this hotel has a bar, a conference room, a TV room, etc., in short just about everything. This is not, however, a spot for romantics or lovers of squeaky doors!

Hidden in the Serra da Arrábida, near the Castelo de São Felipe, the **Quinta do Patrício** *(9,000 to 13,000 ESC; pb, ps, K, ≈; at the western end of Avenida Luísa Todi; follow at first the signs on the left for the Pousada de São Filipe, Estrada do Castelo de São Filipe, 2900 Setúbal, ☎ and ≈ 65-338 17)* is a rural property established in a beautiful setting. It includes a charming main residence with rooms equipped with various modern conveniences. Close by, a secondary residence as well as a charming windmill have been turned into well-appointed apartments. Whichever you choose, all rooms are carefully decorated with delicate rural taste. Besides a particularly warm welcome, you can enjoy a natural setting, suitable for taking many walks.

Overlooking the town of Setúbal, the **Pousada de São Filipe** *(29,600 ESC with view, 26,600 ESC without; pb, tv; go west along Avenida Luísa Todi and, at the end, turn right and then immediately to the left to reach Rua de São Filipe, which will lead you directly to the fortress, Rua de São Filipe, 2900 Setúbal, ☎ 65-52 38 44 or 52 49 87, ≈ 65-53 25 38)* is set in the central building of a former fortress dating from 1590 (see p 162), built by order of Felipe II of Spain to keep watch over the coast and the town below. You can take a room in the very building that served as a residence for the governor of that period. The entrance to the *pousada* lies through a long vaulted corridor with several fortified gates, and it is sure to impress. Atop the stairway, a magnificent terrace with a panoramic view of the Tróia peninsula awaits you. The comfortably appointed rooms are tastefully decorated and offer sea views. You can also keep watch over the coast, which these days has been overwhelmed by tall buildings. Some of the rooms are set in the former dungeon of the fortress, a dungeon whose comfort today would surprise the former governor!

Palmela *(8 km from Setúbal)*

Opened in 1979 in an ancient 15th-century monastery, the **Pousada de Palmela** *(29,600 ESC; pb, tv, ℜ; atop the village of Palmela, 2950 Palmela, ☎ 1-235 12 26 or 235 13 95, ≠ 1-233 04 40)* was the saving grace of this beautiful but long abandoned historical site (see p 164). At the entrance, your attention will be drawn to the imposing dimensions of the vaulted halls and of the galleries surrounding the cloister. Several comfortable lounges as well as a particularly convivial bar have been set up here. After walking along a series of broad corridors where the coolness of the stone contrasts pleasantly with the thick carpeting covering the ground, you will reach one of the 26 rooms. It is through a small door that you enter your cell, which has been transformed into a cosy room. Besides the knick-knacks and beautiful Portuguese-style furniture, from the southwest wing you can enjoy a grandiose view of the surrounding valleys and the distant sea. In the morning, breakfast awaits you in one of the galleries facing the cloister; the atmosphere is very monastic.

RESTAURANTS

This chapter is an assembly of the best restaurants in every budget range. Each listing includes the restaurant's telephone number, so making reservations is a breeze. **The prices listed apply to a meal for one person, not including drinks, but including tax and service** (see the pricing chart, p 212). In any case, prices listed on menus in Lisbon are always net, including tax and service.

Note that it is common practice to serve appetizers (*acepipes*) at the beginning of a meal. These are not free; you will be required to pay for what you have eaten.

Cheese in Portugal is very expensive, although, like *queijo da serra* (mountain cheese), delicious. Be aware that the actual price of your meal might differ from that listed on the menu depending on where you are seated, on the terrace or in the dining room. Generally, posted prices are for meals served in the *salão* (dining room); other rates (higher ones, of course!) are applied to meals served on the *esplanada* or *balcão* (terrace).

Inexpensive restaurants often offer half-portions (*meia dose*) for about 30% less than the price of a full portion. Since servings are generous, a *meia dose* is often sufficient.

Caldeirada (Fish Stew)

Serves 6

500 g of dogfish	4 garlic bulbs
10 large sardines	1 red pepper
400 g of ray	1 green pepper
500 g of small squid	2 small chili peppers
500 g of grey sea bream	1 bunch of flat parsley
500 g of potatoes	2 bay leaves
6 tbsp. olive oil	1 tbsp.. paprika
1/4 L dry white wine	salt and pepper

Peal and wash the potatoes. Slice them coarsely. Peal the garlic and the onions. Cut them into fine slices. Clean the fish, removing the heads and fins, and cut them into large sections. Clean and prepare the squid. Mince the tomatoes and the peppers.

In a casserole dish or terrine, heat the oil. Gently fry the onions and the garlic. Add the chopped parsley, then the tomatoes, peppers, bay leaves and chili peppers. Reduce.

Add, without mixing the squid, then the different fish in layers alternating with layers of potato. Lay the sardines on top. Dust with paprika, and sprinkle with the white wine and an equal volume of water. Add salt and pepper, reduce the heat, cover and let cook without mixing.

Reproduced with the permission of Éditions du Laquet.

Restaurant Classification

$	less than 1,600 ESC
$$	1,600 ESC to 3,200 ESC
$$$	3,200 ESC to 5,000 ESC
$$$$	5,000 ESC to 7,000 ESC
$$$$$	more than 7,000 ESC

Places that stand out...

For Romantic Atmosphere:
Atire-te ao Rio, p 247
Casa do Leão, p 219
Cozinha Velha, p 245
Palácio de Seteais, p 206, 247
Ponto Final, p 248
Tagide, p 227
York House, p 238

For Refinement:
Casa da Comida, p 229
Casa Nostra, p 226
Consenso, p 224
Dom Sopas, p 217
Pátio do Saloio, p 247
Pato Baton, p 225

For True Value:
Bachus, p 226
Bistrobar Opera Prima, p 245
Casa do Leão, p 219
Conventual, p 237
Cozinha Velha, p 245
Embaixada, p 238
Frei Contente, p 236
Gambrinus, p 233
Pátio do Saloio, p 247
Sancho, p 232

For Originality:
Hell's Kitchen, p 222
Os Tibetanos, p 231

For Trendiness:
Alcântara Café, p 240
Café no Chiado - Ciber-Café, p 220
California Dream, p 234
Doca do Santo, p 239
Gringo's Café, p 235
Guillaume Tell, p 226
Majong, p 222
Massima Culpa, p 225
Pap'Açôrda, p 225

For Traditional Lisbon:
Café Estadio Silva Seixas, p 228
Cervejaria Lua Dourada, p 217
Confeitaria de Belém, p 240
Palmeira, p 216
Retiro da Mina, p 244

For Decor:
A Brasileira, p 227
Bistrobar Opera Prima, p 245
Casa de Leão, p 219
Casa do Alentejo, p 231
Cervejaria da Trindade, p 222
Consenso, p 224
Cozinha Velha, p 245
Hotel do Guincho, p 244
Pastelaria São Roque, p 228
Pastelaria Versailles, p 230
Restaurante do Museu, p 220
Tacho Real, p 247
Tavares Rico, p 227

For the Exotic:
Cantinha da Paz, p 234
Furusato, p 242
Novo Bonsai, p 226
Tropical Brasil, p 243
Xêlê Bananas, p 237

Restaurants by Type of Cuisine

Portuguese
Adega das Caves, p 246
Adega do Teixeira, p 223
Bachus, p 226
Bizzaro, p 225
Café de Paris, p 246
Casa do Leão, p 219
Casa do Alentejo, p 231
Cervejaria Lua Dourada, p 217
Cervejaria da Trindade, p 222
Conventual, p 237
Cozinha Velha, p 245
Flor do Duque, p 221
Flor des Estrêla, p 236
Gambrinus, p 233
Já Sei!, p 239
Martinho da Arcada, p 218
Monte Verde, p 241
Os Doze, p 243
Palácio de Seteais, p 247
Palmeira, p 216
Panorâmico de Monsanto, p 241
Pap'Açorda, p 225
Pato Baton, p 225
Ponto Final, p 248
Pousada de Palmela, p 249
Pousada de São Filipe, p 248
Restaurante Regional de Sintra, p 246
Retiro da Mina, p 244
Sancho, p 232
Securas, p 224
Serra da Estrêla, p 229
Solar dos Presuntos, p 232
Tacho Real, p 247
Tagide, p 227
Tavares Rico, p 227

Mexican
Casa México, p 236
Gringo's Café, p 235

Brazlian
Atira-te ao Rio, p 247
Tropical Brasil, p 243

Middle Eastern
Ali-a-Papa, p 222
Pedro das Arábias, p 223

Japanese
Furusato, p 242
Novo Bonsai, p 226

Italian
Casa Nostra, p 226
Lucullus Restaurante, p 243
Massima Culpa, p 225
Pizzeria Mama Rosa, p 223

Indian
O Natraj, p 228

Asian
Majong, p 222

Chinese
Huá Li Tou, p 222
Xi Hu, p 239

African
Cantinha da Paz, p 234
Costa do Castelo, p 219
Ideal de São Bento, p 234

Belgian
Bistrobar Opera Prima, p 245
Chez Degroote, p 221

French
Bec Fin, p 243
Frei Contente, p 236
Pátio do Saloio, p 247

Swiss
Guillaume Tell, p 226

Fast Food
Bibikas, p 231
Esplanada da Avenida-Café Lisboa, p 231
Estrada Velha Bar, p 246
Music Bar, p 243
O Antigo Ferrador, p 220
O Golfinho, p 243
O Pelourinho, p 246
Palmeira, p 216
Pão Pão Queijo Queijo, p 239
Pub Eduardo VII, p 230
Tavares Self Service, p 227

Spanish
Siesta Brava, p 237
Tapas-Bar El Gordo, p 224

Éclectique
A Commenda, p 239
Alcântara Café, p 240
Arameiro, p 231
Café no Chiado, p 220
Cais da Ribeira, p 234
California Dream, p 234
Casa da Comida, p 229
Cervejaria O 10, p 248
Charcuteria Francesa, p 221
Consenso, p 224
Doca do Santo, p 239
Dom Sopas, p 217
Embaixada, p 238
Four Season Grill, p 242
Hell's Kitchen, p 222
Janela do Bairro, p 224
Mercado Original, p 229
O Tacão Pequeno, p 225
O Primeiro da Conceição Velha, p 216
O Farnel, p 216
O Capuchinho, p 221
Palácio del Rei, p 244
Pastelaria Apolo XI, p 235
Poeta na Bicha, p 223
Porta Branca, p 226
Restaurante de Rua em Rua, p 223
Restaurante do Museu, p 220
Tasca a Latina, p 246
Umpuntocinco, p 238
Xêlê Bananas, p 237
York House, p 238
Zutzu, p 238

Fish and Seafood
Cervejaria A Berlenga, p 217
Hotel do Guincho p 244
O Leão da Estrêla, p 235
O Cardador, p 248
Solar dos Bicos, p 218
Solmar, p 232
Xico's Bar Restaurante, p 237

Steak and Ribs
Assóporco, p 236
Brasserie de l'Entrecôte, p 222
El Último Tango, p 224
Foxtrot, p 236
Grill 20, p 232
Picanha, p 235

Vegetarian
O Sol, p 221
Os Tibetanos, p 231
Yin-Yan, p 217

Hamburgers
Abracadabra, p 216
Rage Bar Pub, p 242

TOUR A: THE ROSSIO AND THE BAIXA

Strolling along Baixa's main pedestrian mall, Rua Augusta, you will cross Rua de São Nicolau, which is also reserved for pedestrians. On São Nicolau there is a row of small snack bars with patios right on the street. They all serve essentially the same food, mostly simple sandwiches at reasonable prices. Among them, **Campesina** has the advantage of offering a few daily specials, like *feijoada* and *leitão* (suckling pig). This area is a perpetually crowded tourist spot.

If you crave a hamburger, head to **Abracadabra** *($; every day 9am to 2am; Praça Rossio no. 65, beside Telecom, or Rua 1º Dezembro nos. 102-108)* for a traditional hamburger-fries-pop combo (600 ESC). As well as unbeatable prices (compare 650 ESC at McDonald's), Abracadabra offers much more pleasant surroundings and the opportunity to contribute to the development of an independent local business. They also serve quiche, slices of home-made pizza (265 ESC) and traditional pastries. There's a non-smoking room on the main floor of the building. A good place to grab a quick bite.

O Farnel *($; Rua dos Fanqueiros nos. 51-53, at Rua de São Julião)*. This restaurant-café, with its rather flashy decor of mirrors, copper and pink granite cheerfully mixed together, is a good place to stop during your exploration of Baixa. You can get a simple *bica* with a pastry or, if you're in the mood, try one of the daily specials such as meat kebabs or egg hamburgers. Unpretentious, fast and reasonably priced.

With its pretty entranceway, a harmonious blend of *azulejos* and stone arches, the **O Primeiro da Conceição Velha** restaurant-cafeteria *($; Tue to Sat 8:30am to 5:45pm; Rua da Alfândega no. 108, 2nd floor, ☎ 886 60 36)* deserves a visit. The attractive little dining room is richly decorated with flower motifs. A number of different dishes are offered, such as *vol-au-vent* (900 ESC) and spinach pie served with a refreshing salad, and there are daily specials at 800 ESC and up. A pleasant change from the other restaurants in the area.

 Whether to quench your thirst, eat a *petisco*, or enjoy a typical Portuguese dish, the **Palmeira** restaurant *($, Mon to Fri*

11am to 8pm; Rua do Crucifixo no. 69, ☎ 342 83 72) hits the spot. As you enter you'll notice many large wine casks behind a big counter, which is particularly busy in the late afternoon. For a modest 40 ESC, you can enjoy a glass of red or white wine, or a mix the two, in the company of local workers. If you get a little hungry during your wine-tasting session you can always have a *pastéi de bacalhau* (100 ESC) or a fish sandwich for as little as 170 ESC. For the comfort of a table go to the arched room at the back, where simple but tasty Portuguese meals are served for 950 ESC. Tourist menu for 1,500 ESC.

The unpretentious and very popular **Restaurante Cervejaria Lua Dourada** *($; Rua dos Arameiros no. 21, at the corner of Rua dos Bacalhoeiros)* serves traditional Portuguese cuisine at reasonable prices.

Located above a large grocery store, the buffet-style vegetarian restaurant **Yin-Yan** *($, Mon to Fri 10am to 8:30pm; Rua dos Correeiros no. 14, 2nd floor, ☎ 342 65 51)* offers macrobiotic meals in the sparest of environments. Unfortunately, the chilly atmosphere is not very inviting, which is all the more regrettable since opposite the restaurant is an interesting little grocery store (see p 270). Nonetheless, don't miss dropping by for one of their delicious daily specials (about 1,500 ESC).

The **Cervejaria A Berlenga** *($$; Rua Barros Queiros nos. 29-35, ☎ 342 27 03)* is an authentic Portuguese tavern-restaurant, whose specialty is fish and seafood *(açorda de Marisco, arroz de Marisco)*. Simple but pleasant decor. Good game dishes during the hunting season.

Dom Sopas *($$; Mon to Fri noon to 2am, Sat 7pm to 2am; Rua da Madalena no. 50)*. As you may have already guessed, this restaurant's trademarks are high-quality, rich, creamy soups: *sopa de cacão* (cocoa soup), *sopa de peixe a Dom Sopas* (fish soup), and *sopa de alho a moda de Évora* (garlic soup) among others. Soups cost around 1,000 to 1,500 ESC. Of course, the great classic Portuguese dishes are also on the menu, and a tourist menu is available for 3,000 ESC. The owner is none other than painter Eduardo Alves, so it goes without saying that the decor is meticulous and makes maximum use of this modest semi-basement's potential.

Eating at **Martinho da Arcada** *($$$; Mon to Sat noon to 3pm and 7pm to 10pm; Praça do Comércio no. 3, ☎ 887 92 59)* is a bit like following in Fernando Pessõa's footsteps. According to some people, the famous Portuguese writer composed some of his poems here. From the lovely covered terrace, the view of elegant Praça do Comercio could definitely be a source of poetic inspiration. It's the food, however, that is most important: don't miss the savoury suckling pig or the *cabrito a padeira*. Tourist menu for 1,600 ESC.

At the end of a row of fish and seafood restaurants, **Solar dos Bicos** *($$, Tue to Sun noon to 10:30pm; Rua dos Bacalhoeiros no. 8A, ☎ 886 94 47)*, two steps from the Casa dos Bicos, offers essentially the same fare as its competitors but deserves special mention for its lush, leafy terrace.

Cafés and Tearooms

If you're looking for an authentic Lisbon pastry shop, head to the **Confeitaria Nacional** *(at the corner of Praça da Figueira and Rua dos Correiros)*, where the Portuguese like to go after a tiring day of shopping. Sparsely decorated, with only a few mirrors on its cream-coloured walls, this place attracts a mature clientele, who come here for a *bica* and one of a large assortment of home-made desserts. Old-fashioned, but positively charming. Friendly service.

Known throughout Lisbon, **Café Nicola** *(Rua 1° Dezembro nos. 10-14, ☎ 342 91 72)* is not only a famous café once frequented by the Portuguese poet Bocage, it is also now a brand of coffee distributed to every region of Portugal. At press time, some sections of the establishment on the Rossio were closed; hopefully its beautiful Art-Nouveau façade will be preserved. The business is actually in a phase of major expansion and renovation of its cafés. In its new establishments, called **Nicola Gourmet**, you can buy coffee beans from all over the world, or, like in the original café, simply sip an excellent *bica* and nibble a *pastéi*.

As indicated on the shop, the **Casa Chimeza** *(Rua Aurea nos. 274-278, also known as Rua do Ouro, or "Gold Street")* has been serving delicious pastries since 1866. The main draw here is the large selection and reasonable prices, since the uninspiring decor does not do justice to the pretty façade. Those who would like to bring home an edible souvenir of Portugal can buy excellent coffee here.

What better way to top off a spiritual visit to the *Sé* than with a sinfully sweet pleasure! Two steps from the cathedral, the **Pastelaria Flor da Sé** *(Sun to Fri until 8pm; Largo Santo António da Sé nos. 9-11,* ☎ *887 57 42)* offers all sorts of sweet temptations in sparse surroundings (at least there's no TV!). There are a few sandwiches on the menu and a daily special for the modest sum of 600 ESC.

TOUR B: THE CASTELO AND THE ALFAMA

The bar-restaurant **Costa do Castelo** *($$; Tue to Sun 3pm to 2am; at the corner of Costa do Castelo and Travessa de Chão do Loureiro)* serves Mozambican dishes *(the kitchen opens at 8pm)* and has a terrace with a pretty view of the city. This is a pleasant place to come in the afternoon; stop by and quench your thirst after visiting the Castelo (see p 97).

 The **Casa do Leão** *($$$$$; every day 12:30pm to 3:30pm and 7:30pm to 8:30pm; Castelo de São Jorge,* ☎ *887 59 62)* boasts a prestigious location within the walls of the Castelo, in a magnificent vaulted room in what was once the commanding officer's residence. Impeccably laid tables and mouthwatering Portuguese dishes with a slight French influence make for an extremely pleasant meal. The restaurant is run by the ENATUR, which manages the country-wide network of *pousadas*.

Cafés and Tearooms

Located right beside the decorative arts museum, **Bar Cerca Moura** *(every day 10am to 2pm; Largo das Portas do Sol no. 4,* ☎ *887 48 59)* has a large terrace from which the view includes the periodic passing of amusing tram 28 and, in the distance, the radiant dome of Igreja-Panteão de Santa Engrácia. The interior is interesting too: the decor highlights the small room perfectly and is enhanced by a tastefully lit part of the old city wall. There are also a few Art-Deco-style tables and chairs. A place that is definitely worth stopping at for a *bica* or a *cerveja*. Snacks available.

TOUR C: GRAÇA AND EAST LISBON

Right beside a tiny abandoned church, on a small tree-shade square, the *casa do pasto* **O Antigo Ferrador** *($; Rua do Jardim do Tabaco nos. 6-8)* is a simple neighbourhood restaurant that offers Portuguese daily specials. Its location near the Museu Militar and the Panteão de Santa Engrácia make it an agreeable place to have a meal or to simply enjoy a drink on the little terrace. Popular with local young people.

During your visit to the Museu Nacional do Azulejo, stop for lunch at the **Restaurante do Museu** *($; Tue 2pm to 5:30pm, Wed to Sun 10am to 5:30pm; Rua da Madre de Deus no. 4, ☎ 814 77 90)*, in the museum building. In the unique setting of the old convent's kitchen, covered with extraordinary *azulejos* with images of rabbits, hams, pheasants, pig-heads, fish, etc., you can sample delicious stuffed savory crepes and refreshing salads. There's also a large, elegant terrace. The only disappointment in this enchanting setting is the slow service but it's quickly forgotten since the people are so friendly. Daily specials for 1,200 ESC and 1,400 ESC.

Cafés and Tearooms

The **Café Papasom** *(Largo da Graça)*, frequented mostly by young locals, is a pleasant, but loud, place to have a coffee with a *pastéi* or a simple sandwich. Except for the attractive little tablecloths, the furnishings are vaguely Scandinavian in style.

TOUR D: THE CHIADO AND THE BAIRRO ALTO

Away from the very touristy Largo do Chiado area, in the centre of a theatre neighbourhood, **Café no Chiado** *($; every day 11am to 2pm; Largo do Picadeiro nos. 10-12)* is a place worth investigating. If you are seeking a bit of peace and quiet, its lovely terrace is ideal, or you can sit in the old dining room

Tour D: The Chiado and the Bairro Alto 221

with its vaulted ceilings and modern furniture. The menu consists of various good, but fairly predictable, Portuguese dishes. You can escape the confines of Europe and connect with the rest of the world at a **cyber café** upstairs from the restaurant (see p 228).

Located in an old delicatessen, the **Charcuteria Francesa** restaurant *($; Mon to Sat 8am to 7pm; Rua Dom Pedro V nos. 54-56)* offers daily specials to take out or eat in (half-portions available for 550 ESC) and an agreeable setting. You can eat at one of the winsome tables in the main room and observe the activity at the counter or watch the world go by on the street through the large window. There is also a more intimate back room decorated with rich woodwork. This is a pleasant, unpretentious spot frequented by business people at lunch and students in the afternoon.

In an agreeable room with vaulted ceilings, the owner of **Chez Degroote** *($; Mon to Sat noon to 2am; Rua Duques de Bragança no. 5, ☎ 347 28 39)* invites you to discover the pleasures of Belgian cuisine from his native country. In addition to these, there are a few Portuguese dishes, in honour of his friendly Portuguese wife. *Meia dosa* (half-portions) are available for 600 ESC and up. A great deal!

Visitors on a tight budget can head to **O Capuchinho** *($; Rua da Rosa no. 71, ☎ 342 4797)*, which serves tasty *feijoadas* and other simply prepared dishes.

Although it doesn't look very inviting, the macrobiotic restaurant **O Sol** *($; closed Sat for lunch and all-day Sun; Calçada do Duque 21-23, ☎ 347 35 44)* serves good vegetarian cuisine. It lies halfway up Calçada do Duque, which leads up to the Chiado like a giant staircase. Its small terrace, located in the middle of the pedestrian mall, offers a pleasant view of the lower part of the city.

On the same street, the small **Restaurante Flor do Duque** *($; Calçada do Duque no. 1)* is also a good spot for something reasonably priced. In a simple but pleasant environment, you can have a calamari, fish or meat dish for 1,000 ESC. If you don't have a big appetite, *petiscos* are also offered.

Whether it be for *tajine* seasoned with merguez sausage, or chicken couscous with almonds and currants, the **Ali-a-Papa** restaurant *($$; every day until 11pm; Rua da Atalaia no. 95, ☎ 347 21 16)* deserves of a visit. On weekends it's often full to capacity; if you can't find a seat, try Pedro das Arábias (see below), where similar dishes are served.

The menu at the **Brasserie de L'Entrecôte** *($$; Mon to Sat 12:30pm to 3pm and 8pm to midnight, Sun to 11pm; Rua do Alecrim nos. 117-121, ☎ 342 83 43)* lists salads, steaks and fries (all you can eat). The place is modeled after a Parisian brasserie, but the decor is somewhat stark. Elegant clientele, including many businesspeople. Extremely popular; reservations recommended. Tourist menu at 2,450 ESC.

If you like lively places, make sure to go to the **Cervejaria da Trindade** *($$; every day until 2am; Rua da Trindade 20C, ☎ 342 35 06)*, where you can enjoy good Portuguese cuisine in a congenial atmosphere, surrounded by both tourists and locals. The restaurant has three rooms, which are all connected but decorated in different ways. In the first one, you'll find lovely *azulejos* painted with Masonic symbols. In the second, you can dine beneath beautifully restored vaults, which serve as reminders that this was once a monastery. The last, with its numerous candlesticks, will appeal to those seeking a cozy atmosphere. The menu consists mainly of fish and meat dishes, and there is a daily special starting at 680 ESC.

With *falafel*, Creole salmon, chili, *papacom*, etc., **Hell's Kitchen** *($$; Tue to Sun 7pm to 1am; Rua da Atalaia no. 176, ☎ 342 28 22)* serves truly international cuisine. In this pleasant and relaxed atmosphere, let yourself succumb to the temptations of intermingling flavours.

The very popular **Huá Li Tou** *($$; Rua da Misericórdia 93)* serves reasonably priced Chinese food. Nondescript decor.

Chinese food with an Indian touch isn't the only thing out of the ordinary at **Majong** *($$; every day 7pm to 11pm; Rua da Atalaia no. 3, ☎ 342 10 39)*. The decor, or lack it, also draws your attention. Actually, they have chosen to go completely minimalist: modern wood tables of no particular style stand next to bare walls of roughly applied plaster. As if to reinforce this "unfinished" look, concrete-coloured flooring was installed.

Tour D: The Chiado and the Bairro Alto 223

Despite all this, subtle lighting exudes a certain warmth and exotic plants brighten the atmosphere, making for a very comfortable evening.

Pedro das Arábias *($$; every day until 11pm; Rua da Atalaia no. 70, ☎ 346 84 94)* is steeped in the warm atmosphere and aromatic spices of the Middle East. Dressed in a jellaba, the young owner serves savoury couscous or *tajines* on attractive regional dishware. Try lamb with prunes and almonds, *tagine de borrego com ameixas e amendoas*, an absolute delight! As for the decor, it will transport you to exotic lands on a musical wave of Arab rhythms. A great spot!

In a small, arched dining room, warmly decorated in earthy colours, with Portuguese music in the background, the owner of the **Poeta na Bicha** restaurant *($$; every day 7:30pm to midnight; Travessa do Água da Flor no. 36, ☎ 342 59 24)* greets you with a smile. There are various Portuguese specialties on the menu, including delicious *açorda* which is worth the trip in itself. Combining culinary pleasure with art, there are a number of paintings on the walls and a brief presentation of the works on display is inserted in the menu. Although there are some original ideas on the menu, some dishes combine incongruous ingredients. The copious portion of mustard turkey is served with French fries (alas, frozen) and rice.

Oh how we love our pizza! Two steps from Largo Trindade Coelho, **Pizzeria Mama Rosa** *($$; Mon to Fri 12:30pm to 3pm and 7:30pm to 1am, Sat 7:30pm to midnight; Rua Grémio Lusitano no. 14, ☎ 346 53 50)* offers a wide variety of pizza made with love in a genuine Italian setting. Small tables with checkered tablecloths, terracotta dishes, rows of wine bottles and ... the smiling *mama*, all evoke Italy's *joie de vivre*.

If you're looking for a quiet spot in the bustling Bairro Alto, head to the **Restaurante Adega do Teixeira** *($$; Rua do Teixeira 39)* for some traditional Portuguese cuisine. The place has an attractive terrace as well.

For a simple meal and some local colour, try the **Restaurante de Rua em Rua** *($$; Rua São Boaventura no. 51)*, which serves home-style cuisine in a small, nondescript dining room. The set menu starts at 1,750 ESC.

The **Restaurante Janela do Bairro** *($$; closed Wed; Rua do Teixeira no. 1, ☎ 347 14 88)* has a pleasant decor and a lively atmosphere. Standard Portuguese cuisine.

Right next door to Restaurante O Sol, a cute restaurant by the name of **Securas** *($$; Calçada do Duque no. 27, ☎ 342 85 14)* serves home-style Portuguese cuisine on little wooden tables. Simple but good.

As its name suggests, the **Tapas-Bar El Gordo** *($$; closed Sun; Rua São Boaventura nos. 16-18, ☎ 342 42 66)* offers an assortment of little snacks. It also has an excellent wine list. Decorated with warm colours and frequented by a trendy clientele, this is an altogether pleasant place to be.

Established in the heart of the house that is the birthplace of the Marquês de Pombal, **Consenso** *($$$; Mon to Fri 12:30pm to 3pm and 8pm to 11:30pm, Sat 8pm to 12:30am; Rua da Academia das Ciências nos. 1-1A, ☎ 343 13 13, 346 86 11 or 343 13 11)* offers three successive dining rooms with earth, fire and water as their respective themes. The small entrance room, nicely fixed up as a bar, represents the theme of air with its futuristic and spare furnishings. Parts of the old walls and stone archways have been uncovered in each of the dining rooms. The room dedicated to water is of particular interest because of its stucco walls on which rococo-style medallions mimic the movement of waves. There is no direct lighting: light shoots up from the floor, rebounds a few times on the stone edges of the walls, then lands lightly on the frescoes and the stucco ceilings. The floors are particularly well conceived: perimeters in frosted glass for lighting, and a combination of three kinds of wood and marble tiles. As for the food, although the menu is simple, it demonstrates no lack of imagination: tarragon and oregano monkfish, *linguado com bananas fritas*, Portuguese steak with Roquefort sauce, etc.. Each dish is presented as a work of art decorated with a few leaves and sometimes even flowers – all edible, we've been assured. The service is efficient and friendly, and the ambient music is pleasant. This spot is not to be missed! The only drawback is the limited selection on the affordable tourist menu (2,500 ESC). Reservations are recommended.

For meat lovers hungry for steaks, grilled or rare, what better than an Argentinian restaurant. **El Ultimo Tango** *($$$; Mon to*

Ilhas douradas of the Igreja da Madra de Deus at the Museu do Azulejo. (Camâra Municipal de

The Pousada Dona Maria I boasts comfortable rooms and an exceptional setting. (ENATU

Sat 7:30pm to 11pm; Rua Diário de Noticias no. 62, ☎ 342 03 41) has a lively atmosphere and an inviting decor under attractive stone arches. Busy on weekends.

Imagine a large dining room in velvety colours, the floor covered in little cobblestones like a street, and modern furniture: this is **Massima Culpa** *($$$; every day until 11pm; Rua da Atalaia nos. 35-37, ☎ 342 01 21)*, unfortunately called a "spaghetti house". Pasta in all its forms, served with various sauces, is the specialty here. This restaurant is enchanting if you appreciate modern decor and "high society". The relatively high prices and the cold ambiance are the only shortcomings in this posh establishment.

Fashionable Lisboans get together at **Pap'Açorda** *($$$; closed Sun; Rua da Atalaia os. 57-59, ring bell to enter, ☎ 346 48 11)*, whose two adjoining rooms have been decorated with great care. The first room is spacious, with soft colours and lovely crystal chandeliers, while the second will appeal to those with a taste for contemporary design. Make sure to try the *açorda*, the house specialty, a mixture of bread, oil, coriander and various other ingredients, such as seafood, all generously seasoned with garlic; it's truly delicious. The menu also includes a good selection of traditional dishes. Very pleasant but a bit noisy. Reservations a must.

The **Pato Baton** restaurant *($$$; Tue to Sun; Travessa Fiéis dos Deus no. 28, ☎ 342 63 72)* provides a calm contrast to nearby, lively Rua da Atalaia with its plush decor of pastel colours and modern furniture. With Brazilian or jazz music in the background, this is the perfect spot for a pleasant, intimate evening. The cuisine is excellent, although unoriginal; it includes many typical Portuguese dishes, enhanced by more elaborate presentations.

The **Restaurante Bizzaro** *($$$; every day; Rua da Atalaia nos. 131-133, ☎ 347 18 99)* offers the usual meat and fish dishes. Make sure to try the *peixe espada* (swordfish), which is served in generous portions. For dessert, the *doce de amêndoa* is an interesting taste treat for almond-lovers. Friendly service.

Located steps away from the São Pedro de Alcântara lookout, the little **Restaurante O Tacão Pequeno** *($$$; Travessa da Cara* no. 3A, ☎ 347 28 48) is a good choice for those in search of a lively atmosphere (especially at night).

At the **Restaurante Novo Bonsai** *($$$; closed all-day Sun and Mon for lunch; Rua da Rosa nos. 244-248, ☎ 346 25 15)*, you can dine on Japanese cuisine in an authentic Japanese setting.

Right nearby, on the same street, the **Restaurante Porta Branca** *($$$; closed Sun and all of July; Rua do Teixeira no. 55, ☎ 347 92 57)* has a large, inviting dining room. Your money will be well spent.

Trout *salteboco alla romania* and *fettucine al vongole* are just two of the dishes that conjure up images of warmhearted Italy at the **Casa Nostra** restaurant *($$$$; Tue to Fri 12:30pm to 3pm and 8pm to 11pm, Sat 8pm to 11pm; Travessa do Poço da Cidade no. 60, ☎ 342 59 31)*, where, in a predominantly pistachio-green decor, you can enjoy the finest of Italian meals, accompanied by a bottle of excellent Chianti or *orvieto*. Chic, expensive and very popular. Reservations recommended.

Dark-wood parquet floors, richly coloured walls, gold fixtures and tasteful lighting all combine to create an attractive modern interior at **Guillaume Tell** *($$$$; Tue to Sun 8pm to 2am; Rua da Barroca no. 70, ☎ 342 85 88)*, a Swiss restaurant established in the lively Bairro Alto area. That famous staple of Swiss cuisine, cheese fondue (meat is also available for dedicated carnivores), is served at little tables lit by candles. In staying true to tradition, expect to pay 4,000 ESC per fondue. But why dwell on such material things at the end of a meal? Instead, try a delicious mango mousse, the crowning element of a wonderful meal in such lovely surroundings.

The **Restaurante Bachus** *($$$$; closed Sat lunch and Sun; Largo da Trindade no. 9, ☎ 342 28 28 or 342 12 60)* specializes in fish and seafood. This two-floor temple of gastronomy will appeal to those who appreciate top-notch classic cuisine. To pique your appetite, start off with an appetizer of little eels seasoned with garlic. For the main course, perhaps the *calmar a Chiado*, served with shrimp (a house specialty) or the succulent sea perch with *cataplana*, both treats for the palate. As far as dessert is concerned, the orange and coconut pie takes the prize. Before heading upstairs into the 1950s decor, take the time to have a liqueur (a glass of port, of course!) on the cozy ground floor, which is adorned with lots of woodwork (see p 256). You can have a light meal at the bar for about 5,000 ESC.

As well as a beautiful view of the old city and the Tagus, **Restaurante Tagide** *($$$$$; closed Sat noon and Sun; Largo da Academia Nacional de Belas Artes nos. 18-20, ☎ 342 07 20 or 346 05 70)* offers diners an elegant setting. In the rich-coloured dining room decorated with *azulejos* various fish and seafood dishes are served. The menu, however, is not terribly original and the price of the tourist menu (7,000 ESC) is expensive in relation to its quality. Reservations recommended.

The **Restaurante Tavares Rico** *($$$$$; closed all-day Sat and Sun for lunch; Rua da Misericórdia 37, ☎ 342 11 12 or 347 09 05)* is decorated with stucco, mirrors and crystal chandeliers, all set off by gilding fit for a palace. In these extremely "rich" surroundings, you can dine on dishes as varied as stuffed octopus and delicious steak tartare with whiskey. Carefully prepared international cuisine. The prices are high, but so is the quality. Reservations recommended. If you're on a tighter budget or in a hurry, there is also fast food service upstairs at **Tavares Self Service** *($-$$; same hours, 2nd floor, entrance at the right side of the building, ☎ 342 89 42)*. The lack of decoration and cold neon lights are uninviting. The contrast is particularly striking to those who have had the opportunity to admire the decor of Tavares Rico. The only advantages are the moderate prices and the interesting formula of assorted "mini-dishes" (four choices for 700 ESC or seven for 1,000 ESC).

Cafés and Tearooms

Known throughout the Chiado, the café **A Brasileira** *(every day until 2am; Rua Garrett NO. 120, at Largo do Chiado)* is one of those places that has become a "victim of its success". Its turn-of-the-century decor features stucco, woodwork and mirrors, and paintings by Portuguese artists. In front of the café, stands a statue of the celebrated writer Fernando Pessôa, a reminder that once upon a time he and other noted intellectuals used to frequent the place. Nowadays, A Brasileira attracts a lot of tourists, and its prices tend to exceed its reputation. Foreign visitors are bound to be disappointed by the small selection of pastries. Apathetic service.

Ciber-Chiado *(Mon 11am to 7pm, Tue to Fri 11am to 1pm, Sat 7pm to 1am; Largo do Picadeiro nos. 10-12)*, upstairs from Café no Chiado (see p 220), is the place to connect with the world and "surf" to your heart's delight. In addition to comfortable chairs, there is a small library set up like an opulent living room. The only unfortunate aspect of this very pleasant setting is the high cost of "web crawling": 600 ESC for a mandatory six-month subscription fee and 900 ESC per hour of internet use (30 min, 500 ESC; 15 min, 300 ESC).

The **Café O Paço do Principe** *(every day until midnight; Praça do Principe Real)*, located in a pleasant little park, is a perfect place for a *bica* and a pastry in peace. Light meals are also served on the terrace (traditional menu).

Café Estadio Silva Seixas *(every day until 2am; Rua São Pedro de Alcântara no. 11, a few steps from the elevador)*. Make sure to stop here for a *bica* in the evening, when the place is packed with regulars, Lisboans of all ages who are deeply attached to the age-old tradition of frequenting cafés. The decor is beautiful, particularly the ceiling. Although the fluorescent lighting spoils the atmosphere a bit, it probably also helps keep the place from becoming too popular and trendy.

Sudden hunger pangs in Bairro Alto provide an excellent opportunity to visit the majestically decorated **Pastelaria São Roque** *(every day 7am to 7pm; Rua Dom Pedro V, at Rua da Rosa)*. In a small oval room with stuccoed ceiling and walls, pink marble columns, a large gold chandelier and Art-Nouveau-motif *azulejos*, you can sample delicious egg pastries or the daily special served between noon and 3pm.

TOUR E: THE RATO AND AMOREIRAS

In 1497, Vasco da Gama discovered the passage to India and brought the riches and flavours of a thousand-year-old civilization back to the western world. These same flavours emanate from the **O Natraj** restaurant *($; noon to 3pm and 7pm to 10pm; Rua do Sol ao Rato no. 52, ☎ 388 06 30)*, and the

Tour E: The Rato and Amoreiras

delicious dish *cabrito com coco e amêndoas* is just one example. Budget for between 950 and 1,250 ESC per dish.

The **Restaurante Serra da Estrêla** *($$; closed Sun; located on the upper floor of the Amoreiras shopping centre, ☎ 383 37 39)* is a great place to have a bite to eat after browsing through the shops. It specializes in cuisine from the Beíras region, in the northern part of the country, and has excellent deli products and a good selection of fine cheeses. The tapas platter, made up of an assortment of specialties and served with a glass of house wine, is a real feast. The little tables, laid out in a rustic fashion with handcrafted dishes, make for an unusual setting that breaks out of the monotonous shopping centre mold.

 The **Casa da Comida** *($$$$$; closed Sat for lunch and all day Sun; Travessas da Amoreiras no. 1, ☎ 388 53 76)* is one of those places where connoisseurs of fine cuisine simply have to go during their stay in the capital. After piquing your appetite with a glass of port and some unusual little snacks, you will be guided into a pleasant dining room that wraps its way around a garden. As its menu indicates, the Casa da Comida is eager to introduce guests to its culinary "works of art". *Piballes* (young eels), shrimp cocktail with kiwis and Portuguese-style *escargots* are just a few of the appetizers available. You can also share the excellent *Mariscada Casa da Comida* (seafood soup with shrimp and rock lobster). The main dishes are attractively presented and served in copious portions. You can opt for meat, seafood (rock lobster *gratinée* with champagne), or one of a good selection of fish dishes. During pheasant season, make sure to try the pheasant *Convento de Alcântara*, served with a fairly sweet port sauce and chicken liver pâté on warm toast. What a treat! The excellent desserts are very much in the Portuguese tradition, and thus egg-based. Opulent surroundings and impeccable service make for an extremely pleasant evening. Reservations recommended.

TOUR F: MARQUÊS DE POMBAL, SALDANHA AND NORTH LISBON

After visiting the Parque Eduardo VII, drop by **Mercado Original** *($; Mon to Fri 9am to 6:30pm; Rua Joaquim António Aguiar no. 62, ☎ 385 23 53)* for refreshing salads, the house specialty, served in an agreeable spring-like atmosphere. There are various sandwiches on the menu for between 400 and 500 ESC.

The **Pub Eduardo VII** *($$; every day 10am to 10:30pm; Rua Castilho no. 149, ☎ 383 09 00)* in the Meridien Hotel is a pleasant place to dine. The attractive modern decor features natural wood, and there is a lovely view of the park from the terrace. There is a striking selection of sandwiches on the menu (400 to 800 ESC). Of generous proportions and served with a small salad, these are ideal alternatives to the rather expensive Portuguese dishes.

Cafés and Tearooms

Galeto *(every day 8am to 3am; Avenida da República no. 14, ☎ 354 44 44)* wouldn't even stand out in the United States, with its counters and vinyl covered stools. More of a luncheonette than a restaurant, it serves coffee and pastries at all hours. In the rather upper-middle-class neighbourhood of Saldanha (right near the subway station), however, it is a curiosity, almost mocking the 19th-century café across the street. The service is friendly but the menu is very ordinary. It's a shame that you can't eat on the charming terrace, with its wood floor and unbleached canvas parasols – we would have stayed for more than one drink.

Also two steps away from the Saldanha subway station, the **Pastelaria Versailles** *(every day 7:30am to 10pm; tables reserved for meals between noon and 3pm during the week; Avenida da República no. 15A, at the Saldanha subway exit, ☎ 355 53 44)* offers excellent pastries in an attractive, turn-of-the-century decor, which, unfortunately, is a bit spoiled by the orange-coloured tablecloths and cold neon lighting under crystal chandeliers. Try a *bagaço*, a *bolo de chila* or a *toucinho do céu*. At lunchtime they serve some interesting items in their daily specials such as prawn salad and cream of garlic. A distinguished clientele dines amid trompe-l'oeil porphyry columns under a stucco ceiling.

TOUR G: RESTAURADORES AND LIBERDADE

A little restaurant located on a little street, the **Restaurante Arameiro** *($; closed Sat for dinner and all day Sun; Travessa de Santo Antão nos. 19-21)* serves a wide assortment of light dishes (salads, soups, etc.). The perfect place for a snack. A 2,200 ESC full menu is also available.

In the heart of Parque Mayer, a strange complex of old theatres, the tiny restaurant **Bibikas** *($; Parque Mayer, Rua 5, at Rua 2, ☎ 346 60 00)* is a good spot for an inexpensive meal. With soups for 200 ESC and sandwiches between 250 and 400 ESC, this restaurant certainly will satisfy budget travellers.

For health food enthusiasts, **Os Tibetanos** *($; Mon to Sat noon to 2:30pm and 7:30pm to 10pm; Rua do Salitre no. 117, ☎ 314 20 38)*, a Tibetan vegetarian restaurant with a very creative menu, is a must! Dine in the pleasant garden or in the pretty dining room decorated with various Tibetan objects. Try the delicious crepes stuffed with cabbage, carrots and tofu, the amazing ginger cauliflower, or the curry seitan with aromatic basmati rice. To drink, although excellent wines are available for traditionalists, why not discover the unusual flavour of Tibetan *chá*, a type of tea with a milky, slightly salty taste. For the grand finale, try the heavenly chocolate pie, the light cheesecake or a refreshing cup of mangoes and cream. For further exploration of Tibetan culture, there's a small bookstore in the entrance to the restaurant and a Buddhist teaching centre on the second floor.

The **Casa do Alentejo** *($$; closed Mon; Rua das Portas de Santo Antão no. 58, ☎ 346 92 31)*, a private club, is a sumptuous residence with a Moorish-style decor (see p 124); part of it is open to the public. If you walk up the majestic staircase to the second floor, you will find a pleasant restaurant set up in a large room decorated with lovely *azulejos*. You can dine with club members on the daily special or on one of an assortment of traditional Portuguese dishes. Simple, nourishing food.

The **Esplanada da Avenida-Café Lisboa** *($$; every day until 2am; Avenida da Liberdade no. 122, on the right side as you* *head towards Marquês de Pombal)*, located on busy Avenida da Liberdade, is most suitable for a quick, simple lunch (traditional menu). You can eat in a little pavilion surrounded by greenery or on the terrace (assuming you enjoy the bustling atmosphere of the street).

Despite its location in an unappealing neighbourhood, the **Grill 20** restaurant *($$; Rua da Palma no. 208B, ☎ 888 49 88)* deserves a visit for its delicious veal steaks and copious fondues. Indeed, meat is highlighted here as the house specialty. Excellent dishes are served on a small terrace, away from the noise of Rua da Palma, and in a lovely dining room, where modern woodwork and matte chrome elements combine to create attractive results.

The **Restaurante Solmar** *($$; Rua das Portas de Santo Antão nos. 106-108, ☎ 342 33 71)* specializes in fish and seafood. This place will appeal especially to visitors with a taste for the 1950s. The decor, which looks a bit like a stage set, is worth seeing: a large glassed-in room where a giant grouping of *azulejos* is displayed like a movie screen, a high ceiling supported by massive columns and a mezzanine with curvy lines. Somewhat touristy.

For an intimate evening or a business luncheon, **Sancho** *($$$; Mon to Sat; Travessa da Glória nos. 8-16, ☎ 346 97 80)* is a sure bet. Dark woodwork, pewter dishes on the walls, an imposing fireplace with *talha dourada* candlesticks on its mantle, and heavy velvet curtains covering multi-paned windows are all evocative of an old-time inn. The only drawback is the annoying neon lighting behind some of the windows. In this rather sombre decor the great classics of Portuguese cuisine are served in a formal manner, much to the satisfaction of a bourgeois clientele.

Beside the picturesque Elevador da Lavra, the **Solar dos Presuntos** *($$$; Mon to Sat, noon to 3pm and 7pm to 10:30pm; Rua das Portas de Santo Antão no. 150, ☎ 342 42 53 or 347 29 55)* proposes Portuguese specialties such as rice and prawn dishes and meals prepared in the Monção style. A good selection of Portuguese wines and straightforward traditional food.

Gambrinus *($$$$$; every day until 2am; Rua das Portas de Santo Antão no. 23, ☎ 342 14 66)*. A classic. Portuguese cuisine with top billing going to fish and seafood. Highly reputed for its excellent wine list. Expensive but a favourite with gourmets.

Cafés and Tearooms

Confeitaria Marquês Pombal *(every day 7am to 11pm; Avenida da Liberdade no. 244)* is a large, tidy, lively establishment with counter service of attractive pastries and *bica*. At lunch and supper, light meals are served at tables. This is an oasis in this generally deserted, uninviting section of Avenida da Liberdade.

Health food enthusiasts will not want to miss the **Os Tibetanos** restaurant-tearoom *($; Mon to Sat noon to 2:30pm and 7:30pm to 10pm; Rua do Salitre no. 117, ☎ 314 20 38)*. Light cheesecake and heavenly chocolate pie are some of the sheer delights served in the pretty dining room decorated with various Tibetan objects or in the pleasant garden. Of course classic *bica* is on the menu, as well as aromatic teas and coffees. If you're feeling adventurous, come back and try the restaurant's savoury vegetarian dishes (see p 231). There is a small bookstore at the entrance and, for your spiritual nourishment, a Buddhist teaching centre upstairs.

At **Pastelaria Snack-Bar Veneza** *($; every day 7:30 am to 10pm; Avenida da Liberdade no. 63)*, on long Avenida da Liberdade, enticing pastries await in a large, attractively decorated dining room. Daily specials (around 700 ESC) and a tourist menu (1,500 ESC) are offered. Agreeable and unpretentious.

Coffees, pastries, salads, hamburgers and even omelettes can be found on the menu of the **Café Snack-Bar Pastelaria Zante** *($; Rua da Palma no. 265)*, all at very reasonable prices. The only interesting thing in terms of the building's decor is the Art Deco façade.

TOUR H: SANTA CATARINA AND CAIS DO SODRÉ

For a Cape Verdean meal accompanied by island music, the small **Ideal de São Bento** restaurant-café *($; Rua dos Poiais de São Bento no. 108)* is a pleasant spot. You must be attentive, however, because there is neither a menu outside nor a sign indicating the establishment. It is much-frequented by the Cape Verdean community and, from time to time, musicians play informally. The daily special costs between 700 to 900 ESC.

The Santa Fé-style **California Dream** restaurant-bar *($$; Tue to Fri noon to 11pm, Sun 7pm to 11pm; Cais do Sodré no. 42, ☎ 346 79 54)* is sure to please those looking for an atmosphere that is both relaxed and refined. Under big ceiling fans, they offer California-style food, accompanied by jazz music. There is a nightclub in the basement of the building if you want to stretch out a weekend evening.

Do you feel an intense *saudade* for the islands? Don't miss weekends at the **Cantinha da Paz** restaurant *($$$; Tue to Thu 8pm to 11pm, Fri to Sun 7pm to midnight with live music; Rua do Poço dos Negros no. 64, ☎ 60 86 38)*, where various singers improvise languorous Cape Verde melodies in the style of Cesaria Evora. Cape Verde cuisine is a pleasure to discover. *Feijoada de pedra*, with sweet potatoes, *bife de atum com cebola* or *caril de gamas* – everything is delicious. For dessert, ask for the *bedinca*, a rich coconut pudding with cinnamon. Ah, what a lovely trip to the islands of "the barefoot diva"!

The **Cais da Ribeira** *($$$$; Wed to Fri noon to 3pm and 7pm to 10:30pm, Tue and Sat 7pm to 10:30pm; Cais do Sodré, behind the train station for Cascais, ☎ 342 36 11 or 347 66 53)*, not to be confused with its next-door neighbour (the Cais do Sodré restaurant), deserves mention for its generous fish dishes and its romantic view of the Tagus. Here, shrimp from Mozambique, oysters, salmon and, of course, *bacalhau* will entice seafood lovers, while wild boar with clams, calf liver with bacon and *tournedos* with raisins are other interesting choices. Tourist menu for 4,500 ESC. For a fascinating view, choose the upstairs dining room, decorated with exposed ceiling beams.

Cafés and Tearooms

Under the watchful eye of the sea demon *Adamastor*, so well described in Camões' *The Lusiads*, high on his pedestal, the terrace of the **O Miradouro** *(Miradouro de Santa Catarina, Rua Santa Catarina, at the end of Rua Marechal Saldanha)* invites you to lounge. It's a pleasant spot to have a beer or coffee and a pastry, and, as a bonus, you can enjoy a panoramic view of Ponte 25 de Abril.

TOUR I: ESTRÊLA AND LAPA

Gringo's Café *($; every day until 1am; Avenida 24 de Julho no. 116, ☎ 396 09 11)*. Corona beer and *chili con carne* in a friendly, American-southwest setting. Mainly for fans of Tex-Mex cuisine. Young clientele.

The pink and green **Pastelaria Apolo XI** *($; open until 7pm; closed Sun; at the corner of Rua de Santos-o-Velho and Rua das Janelas Verdes)* serves excellent daily specials at unbeatable prices. You can have *bifinho* (a small filet of pork) with rice and salad for 500 ESC - 800 ESC if you have a beer, coffee and dessert as well. What a bargain! Friendly service and a neighbourhood atmosphere. The best place in the area for a quick bite to eat.

O Leão da Estrêla *($$; every day until 2am; Calçada da Estrêla no. 203, ☎ 396 98 87)*. A pleasant restaurant whose dining room is decorated with *azulejos*. The house specialty is seafood.

The **Picanha** *($$; Mon to Sat until 1am, closed Sun; Rua das Janelas Verdes no. 96, ☎ 397 65 96)*, located opposite the Museu de Arte Antiga, serves one-dish meals made up of *picanha* (marinated, grilled meat) with mango sauce, *farofa* or *chimichurri*, plus potatoes, rice, salad and beans. There is enough food to satisfy even the heartiest of appetites. If your stomach is a bottomless pit, however, you can top off your meal with a piece of cheesecake or apple pie for dessert. A pretty stone portal leads into the dining room, which is decorated with *azulejos*.

If you like ribs, the **Restaurante Assóporco** *($$; Mon to Sat until midnight; Rua das Janelas Verdes no. 102, ☎ 395 18 00 or 397 65 96)* is a must. This is an inviting place with a contemporary decor, where you can eat an unlimited amount of ribs (the only item on the menu), along with a variety of sauces and a salad. If meat does not tempt you, you can create a vegetarian meal by combining some of the tasty appetizers. Simple but positively delicious. For dessert, there's cheesecake and *tiramisú*. Young clientele. Enthusiastic and very friendly staff.

Located alongside the Basilica da Estrêla, the **Restaurante Flor des Estrêla** *($$; Rua João de Deus no. 60)* serves home-style Portuguese cuisine. Pleasant dining room decorated with *azulejos*. Very popular with Lisboans.

In the basement of this building, located on the major artery Avenida Dom Carlos, inundated with bright colours, **Casa México** *($$$; Tue to Sun 12:30pm to 3pm and 8pm to 11:30pm; Avenida Dom Carlos I no. 140, small and poorly indicated entrance, to the right of Café Republica, ☎ 396 55 00)* will make your palate zing with its spicy dishes. After a giant *margarita*, don't hesitate to tackle the excellent *fajitas*, as only Mexicans know how to make! Colonial decor, ceiling fan, colourful furniture, tropical music and staff dressed in Mexican fashion – every aspect of this place is reminiscent of the warmth of that faraway country, but...are we really still in Lisbon? The prices and excessively fast service remind us that indeed we are!

If you have a sudden craving for steak in the wee hours of the morning, you can go to the **Foxtrot** *($$$; every day until 2am; Travessa de Santa Teresa no. 28, ☎ 395 26 97)*, which serves food in its attractively decorated bar.

French cuisine is always a pleasure, and the affable head waiter at the **Frei Contente** restaurant *($$$; Mon to Fri noon to 3pm and 7pm to 10:30pm, Sat 3pm to 10:30pm; Rua de São Marçal no. 94, ☎ 347 59 22)* can be proud to be one of its worthy representatives. Agen prune rabbit, champagne duck and Alsatian sauerkraut are only a few samples from the menu. There are two or three traditional Portuguese dishes offered and some exotic creations such as shrimp curry. The rustic decor is complemented by pretty, summery fifties-style dishware. A particularly likeable place!

At **Siesta Brava** *($$$; Tue to Sun 12:30pm to 1am; Rua Manuel Bernardos no. 5A, ☎ 397 63 90)*, Spanish-Portuguese collaboration produces wonderful results. *Cabrito e leitão assado* and pork kebabs go well with *gaspacho andaluza*, *paella valenciana* and *tortilla*. Portuguese or Spanish cuisine? It's up to you to choose! Classic cooking in a very plain environment.

There are several good restaurants around Praça das Flores, a quiet square shaded by trees and located just a short distance from the busy Bairro Alto. One of these is **Xêlê Bananas** *($$$; closed Sat for lunch and all day Sun; Praça das Flores no. 29, ring bell to enter, ☎ 395 25 14 or 395 25 15)*, just the place for visitors looking for a change from the usual *bacalhau*. This place strives to be innovative, an effort that is to be applauded here in Portugal, where tradition can become tiring. The menu lists original dishes made up of a tasty blend of fruit, meat and fish and served in generous portions. The chef seems to be particularly fond of sauces, some of which are a bit too sweet. Guests dine in a slightly kitschy tropical setting featuring banana trees and walls painted to look like the jungle. Friendly staff and cosmopolitan clientele. A good place to keep in mind.

Xico's Bar Restaurante *($$$; Mon to Fri until 1am, closed Sat for lunch and all day Sun; Calçada da Estrêla no. 3, ☎ 60 10 22)*, located opposite the Palácio da Assembleia Nacional, has an inviting Santa Fe-style decor and serves delicious dishes like fettucine with shrimp sauce. Very popular with the political set.

Being close to parliament, the **Restaurante Conventual** *($$$$; closed Sat lunch and Sun; Praça das Flores no. 45, ☎ 60 91 96 or 60 92 46)* is regularly frequented by Portuguese politicians. This refined setting, whose decor is mainly comprised of wood sculptures from an ancient convent and religious objects, is the site of one of the most renowned restaurants in Portugal. Don't expect revolutionary cuisine here; they serve the Portuguese classics, elaborately prepared, such as *pato com champagne e pimenta rosa*. In this temple of gastronomy, only the limited choice of the tourist menu is a disappointment: the ubiquitous *bacalhau a bras* or *carne de porco alentejana* for no less than 5,000 ESC! Reservations recommended.

Restaurante Embaixada *($$$$$; every day; Rua do Pau da Bandeira no. 4, ☎ 395 00 05 or 395 00 06)*, in the prestigious Hotel da Lapa (see p 200), will appeal to visitors seeking a sophisticated ambiance, as well as those looking for good international cuisine. The buffet-style brunch is particularly worthwhile, as it enables you to sample a variety of dishes for a reasonable sum. Good assortment of desserts.

Restaurante York House *($$$$; every day; Rua das Janelas Verdes no. 32, ☎ 396 25 44 or 396 24 35)*. High-quality, traditional cuisine served in sophisticated surroundings. The menu lists vegetarian fettucine, duck cutlet pan-fried with grapes, roast chicken with rosemary, pig's feet with coriander sauce, etc. Simply reading it over will make your mouth water. When the weather is fine, you can enjoy your meal on the hotel patio (see p 199). Expensive, but what a setting! Reservations recommended.

The **Restaurante Zutzu** *($$$$; closed Sat for lunch and all day Sun; Rua Nova da Peidade no. 99, ☎ 397 94 46)* serves *nouvelle cuisine* — fish carpaccio with colourful lettuce, game with coriander and lamb with mustard, to name just a few of the dishes on the menu. The main dining room, shaped like a half-moon, makes for an unusual setting. The greyish hues are a bit cold, but give the place a contemporary feel. A good place to keep in mind.

For the perfect intimate evening, the **Umpuntocinco** restaurant *($$$$; Mon to Fri 12:30pm to 3pm and 7:30pm to 10:30pm; Rua Marcos Portugal no. 5)* offers tables illuminated by candlelight, comfortable cushioned chairs, subdued lighting and warm woodwork decor, all of it two steps away from lovely Praça das Flores. A very fine trout stuffed with shrimp and ham and an excellent chicken with Roquefort sauce are two specialties. Ideal for an elegant evening.

TOUR J: ALCÂNTARA, SANTO AMARO AND BELÉM

Rua Vieira Portuense, near the Mosteiro dos Jerónimos, has become extremely popular with tourists. It is crowded with all kinds of restaurants and bistros, and although none of these places are particularly noteworthy, you won't have any trouble finding somewhere to eat.

The **Pão Pão Queijo Queijo** *($; every day 7am to 11pm; Rua de Belém no. 124)*, located right near Mosteiro dos Jerónimos, is a good place to get an inexpensive meal. The menu is primarily comprised of sandwiches for 400 ESC (including vegetarian), pita *shoarma* and salads (unfortunately served in plastic containers with plastic utensils!). Whether on the terrace or inside, be patient since this is a popular place with tourists and is always crowded. Simple, unpretentious and economical!

Established right on the Santo Amaro wharf, next to old warehouses now serving as discotheques, restaurants and night clubs, the **Doca do Santo** restaurant *($$; Tue to Sun noon to 3am; Doca de Santo Amaro, ☎ 396 35 22)* features a large terrace dappled with parasols. While heavy ropes are a pleasant reminder of life on the sea, the presence of palm trees contrasts unpleasantly with the environment. Inside there is a large, glass-enclosed dining room with an elegant metal V-shaped counter. The menu mainly consists of quiches, salads, sandwiches and *petiscos* served until the wee hours of the morning.

For a nice change, the **Restaurante Xi Hu** *($$; every day 10am to 10:30pm; Rua de Belém nos. 95-99, ☎ 362 33 22)*, serves most classic Chinese dishes, in a setting that is... Chinese, of course! An excellent, very friendly spot. Tourist menu for 1,800 ESC.

Located close to the Padrão dos Descobrimentos monument, the restaurant **Já Sei!** *($$$; Mon to Sat 12:30pm to 3:30pm and 7:30pm to 10:30pm, Sun 12:30pm to 3:30pm; Avenida Brasília no. 202, ☎ 301 59 69)* offers good, plain and simple, Portuguese fare. The only special feature is an interesting view of the Tagus and the south shore, visible from a covered terrace. Reservations recommended.

For those most interested in designer decor, the **A Commenda** restaurant *($$$$; Mon to Sat 12:30pm to 3pm and 7:30pm to 10:30pm, Sun 11am to 3:30pm; in the Centro Cultural de Belém, Praça do Império, ☎ 301 96 06)* is perfect. It is located in the brand-new Centro Cultural de Belém, a veritable labyrinth built with the support of the European Economic Community. Despite the acceptable quality of the food and service that aspires to sophistication, there is a total lack of originality and creativity in the choice of dishes. Brunch every Sunday. Mostly a place to see and be seen.

Already a veritable institution in Lisbon, the **Alcântara Café** *($$$$$; every day 8pm to 1am; Rua Maria Luísa Holstein no. 15, formerly Rua Primeira Particular, ☎ 363 71 76)* is a must for visitors seeking out Lisbon's trendiest spots. It's a restaurant, bar, discotheque and art gallery, all in one giant space, which Antonio Pinto has transformed into a temple of contemporary design. After spending many years in Belgium, where he designed two beautiful restaurants, La Quincaillerie (Brussels) and the Parkus (Ghent), Pinto returned to his native country and succeeded in making the most of this old building, which was once a printing-house and a garage. The decor? Well, in the main room, you'll find immense painted steel beams (although partly false, you can't tell), cleverly decorated columns, a lot of hanging fans to emphasize the height of the place, and to top it all off, a copy of the *Winged Victory of Samothrace* perched in the centre of a metal bar. At the back of the room, right beside a metal footbridge leading to the discotheque, is a boudoir lit with crystal chandeliers and decorated with red velvet furniture, forming a striking but attractive contrast with the rest of the decor. The cuisine is original, too, although somewhat expensive. This is actually one of the rare places in Lisbon that serves steak tartare. This place is an absolute must if you're looking to see and be seen!

Cafés and Tearooms

During your visit to the Mosteiro dos Jerónimos, make sure to stop in at the **Antiga Confeitaria de Belém** *(every day until 11pm; Rua de Belém nos. 84-88)*, the best-known pastry shop in the area. This worthy establishment was founded in 1837. The entrance hall is furnished with nothing but a large counter and glass-doored cabinets, which completely cover the walls and are filled with old bottles of port. The only decoration is some stucco on the ceiling. The whole place is cream-coloured, and has taken on a patina with time (and with the help of cigarette smoke). It definitely has a certain charm about it.

Tour J: Alcântara, Santo Amaro and Belém 241

Next, there is a series of little rooms decorated with — you guessed it — *azulejos*, and filled with a motley crowd of students, neighbourhood residents and tourists awaiting their turn to sample the famous *Pastel de Belém*, a type of flan sprinkled with your choice of cinnamon or powdered sugar. A specialty of Belém, the *Pastel* is supposedly served nowhere else in Lisbon. Whether that's true or not, these particular *Pastels* are well worth the trip, and the house *bica* tops off this small indulgence splendidly. Sandwiches are also sold.

As its name indicates, the **Cafetaria do Museu da Marinha** *(Tue to Sun 10am to 5pm; Praça do Império)* is the marine museum's cafeteria. What makes this place interesting is not so much its menu, which is fairly limited (a few sandwiches at 400 ESC, beer for 200 ESC or coffee), but its terrace, which is very pleasant for lounging and admiring the marvellous west entrance of Mosteiro dos Jerónimos (see p 138).

TOUR K: PARQUE FLORESTAL DE MONSANTO

Restaurante Monte Verde *($$; Parque Florestal de Monsanto, Cruz das Oliveiras stop of bus # 23, or, by car, the first exit from the A5 highway in the direction of Estoril or Cascais, ☎ 363 03 38)* is a good spot for a refreshing drink before heading off to the park or for a meal after returning. On its comfortable, shady terrace imbued with the scent of pines, standard Portuguese dishes are served. If you're not very hungry you will be satisfied with the *petiscos* which are served to everyone. With a cool beer, they make a pleasant little meal.

In a circular, fifties-style building, the **Panorâmico de Monsanto** restaurant *($$$; Mon to Sat noon to 3:30 and 7pm to 11pm, Sun noon to 3:30pm; Estrada da Bela Vista, right beside the Miradouro de Monsanto, ☎ 778 17 63 or 778 17 66)* is a pleasant place to stop for a meal during an exploration of Parque Florestal de Monsanto. Its large, somewhat old-looking dining room resembles a cafeteria. Traditional Portuguese dishes are served before a view of Lisbon in the distance.

TOUR L: ESTORIL TO CASCAIS

Estoril

To satisfy bouts of hunger, the **Rage Bar Pub** *($; Rua de Olivença)* serves good hamburgers in unpretentious surroundings.

For a change from Portuguese cuisine, **Furusato** restaurant *($$$$; Wed to Sun 12:30pm to 2:30pm and 7:30pm to 10:30pm, closed Tue afternoon and all day Mon; Praia Tamariz; to get there, cross the railway at the former station and go along the seaside until the western end of the beach, ☎ 1-468 44 30)* offers excellent Japanese food. Do not miss the experience of the *teppan yaki* table: seated before a long counter covered with cooking grills, you can savour meat, fish, rice and vegetables sauteed before your eyes by the expert hands of Japanese cooks. Many other dishes such as *sushi* (raw fish wrapped in rice), *sukiyaki* (thin slices of beef accompanied by vegetables and sauteed in soya sauce), *sashimi* (slices of raw fish), or delicious *tempura* (marinated and fried fish and vegetables) are also worthy of consideration. An elegant setting, fine sea views and very friendly service add to the quality of this original spot. Full-course meals starting at 5,500 ESC.

Traditionalists will not want to miss the **Four Season Grill** *($$$$; Rua do Parque, ☎ 1-468 04 00)*, the opulent restaurant attached to the Hotel Palácio Estoril. Comfortably set around a small dance floor, you will be lulled by music from another era, performed live; customers sometimes waltz a few steps. The 1970s-style curtains and carpets, form an outmoded decor that could use some serious freshening-up. Classic cuisine is served here, with few surprises but good quality. Among the dishes worthy of mention, the venison with chestnuts and the *suprême* of hake with saffron are recommended. As well, the veal liver with avocado and the chicken with shrimp are excellent. Despite a worn setting and disturbingly slow service, this restaurant will be appreciated by lovers of good traditional cuisine. Meals starting at 3,500 ESC.

Cascais

Music Bar *($; every day 11am to 2am; Largo da Praia da Rainha)*. Well situated facing the sea, this little bar and restaurant has a pleasant terrace frequented by a young, local crowd. Sandwiches are available starting at 200 ESC, as are various salads, including tuna salad for 400 ESC. Ideal for a light meal.

Pizzas, hamburgers, or the daily menu starting at 800 ESC await you at the **O Golfinho** restaurant *($; every day 11am to 2am; Rua Sebastião José Carvalho de Melo no. 5)*. Besides its pleasant decor, this establishment has the advantage of being located in the town's most interesting tourist district.

For good classic Portuguese cuisine, head to **Os Doze** *($$; Thu to Mon noon to 10:30pm, closed Tue evening and Wed; Rua Frederico Arouca)*, where whitewashed walls and stone arches form a warm decor. Very popular with a Portuguese clientele.

If a Brazilian evening tempts you, **Restaurante Tropical Brasil** *($$; take the Beco dos Inválidos, located just left of the fire station and right of the town hall, then turn left at the first small street to reach the small square where the restaurant is located)* will satisfy you with its *feijoada* or its *tutu à mineria*. Count on spending between 900 and 1,450 ESC for the daily special. Atmosphere guaranteed.

If you are in the mood for some French cuisine, head to the **Bec Fin** *($$$; closed in Jan; near the Câmara Municipal, Beco Torto no. 1, ☎ 1-484 42 96)*, where you can savour tasty little items while enjoying the pleasant terrace.

Lucullus Restaurante *($$$$; Rua da Palmeira no. 6, ☎ 484 47 09)* offers you an excellent choice of Italian dishes (*fettucine Alfredo, osso buco all Fiorentino*, etc.) in a very congenial setting. If you have the chance, choose the terrace in back, for the setting is especially pleasing.

Cafés and Tearooms

Pasteleria Parrisol *(Rua Frederico Arouca 21)*. A pretty pastry shop offering a vast selection.

Praia do Guincho

The designers of the **Hotel do Guincho** *($$$$; 8 km west of Cascais Estrada do Guincho, ☎ 1-487 04 91)* has done a great job of blending the crudeness of a former military building with the elegance and comfort required today for a hotel of this calibre. Although it looks modern on the outside, this hotel and restaurant was actually designed starting from the ruins of a fortress. While some elements, including the entrance, recall its distant past (doors with semi-circular arches, a stairway and walls in crudely cut stone), the atmosphere has been warmed by luxurious carpets and classy furniture. The dining room offers a panoramic view of the sea and has a pleasant foyer. During your visit, be sure to take a peak at the beautiful conference room, as medieval-looking as can be. Specializing in seafood and fish.

 TOUR M: QUELUZ TO SINTRA

Queluz

The **Retiro da Mina** restaurant *($$; Wed to Mon; Avenida da República no. 10, ☎ 435 29 78)* has a faithful following of Portuguese families who flock to it in great numbers for traditional Portuguese fare at very reasonable prices. For 1,900 ESC diners are served good home-made soup, a savory *açorda de marisco* or *pato ao forno com arroz*, accompanied by a *vinho da casa* (in general an excellent *vinho verde*). To finish in fine style, dessert and coffee are also served. A real deal! Amiable and unpretentious.

In its county-style decor replete with exposed beams and *azulejos*, the **Restaurante Palácio del Rei** *($$; Mon to Sat; Largo Mousinho de Albuquerque nos. 1-4, ☎ 435 06 74)* offers a meat, fish or fowl tourist menu for 2,750 ESC. *Arroz de* *mariscos* and *pato no forno* are just a couple of the Portuguese specialties on the menu.

🍽️ Occupying the west wing of the old Palácio de Queluz, right in the palace's former kitchens, the **Cozinha Velha** restaurant *($$$-$$$$; in the west wing of the Palácio de Queluz, ☎ 435 02 32)* is faithful to the reputation of the Pousadas de Portugal chain. In addition to the fine cuisine included in the regular menu, the restaurant offers of a three-course meal *($$$$$)* of more elaborate dishes such as *cataplana de lombinhos de porco com amêijoas e camarão* (fried pork loin with shrimp and clams) and *cabrito frito com migas de grelos* (goat meat served with fried bread and broccoli), which proves rather expensive. As for the setting, there is a pleasant, modern little terrace, and the impressive enormous old central fireplace, supported by eight columns and adjoining marble table.

Cafés and Tearooms

In the prestigious palace of Queluz, the *cafetaria-bar* **Pitada Daqui Pitada Dali** *(Wed to Mon 9:30am to 6pm; Palácio Nacional de Queluz)* is a good spot for coffee before your visit. Various daily specials are served for 1,200 ESC.

Sintra

🍽️ The friendly Belgian owners of **Bistrobar Opera Prima** *($; every day 9am to midnight; Rua Consiglieri Pedroso no. 2A, ☎ 924 45 18)* greet guests with the smile and kindness characteristic of their culture. As they are also decorators, they have made the most of the two basement rooms, one of which is equipped with a bar, that make up the restaurant. Stone walls and warm colours in the first room create the perfect setting for an intimate evening, while the second room, with its highly original, bright decor, is ideal for lunch. In addition to large mirrors adorned with Art-Nouveau designs, you will discover amusing twisted metal decorations here and there and an attractive painting, under a vault, recalling Moorish Portugal. As for the cuisine, Nele Duportail prepares a tasty *prato económico* (about 750 ESC) with the rich aromas of Belgium, accompanied by delicious whole-wheat bread (a rare treat in Portugal). A tourist menu is also available for 1,350 ESC. A wonderful place, not to be missed!

Estrada Velha Bar *($; every day, 11am to midnight; Rua Consiglieri Pedroso no. 16)*. This friendly little bar, very popular with young people, offers meals including soup, sandwich and beer starting at 1,200 ESC. Ideal for coping with bouts of hunger. Service with a smile.

The little **O Pelourinho** café and bar *($; next to the palace; Calçada do Pelourinho no. 4)* offers very good light meals and tasteful decor. The absence of television and of fluorescent lighting renders this spot, with its stone arches, all the more pleasant. Friendly, smiling staff.

The little **Adega das Caves** restaurant *($$; Rua da Pendora no. 2, ☎ 1-923 08 48)*, located below the Café de Paris, prepares simple Portuguese dishes such as salads, plates of sardines and pork chops. Simple and unpretentious.

Adjoining the pretty Câmara Municipal, **Restaurante Regional de Sintra** *($$; Mon to Fri 9am to 10:30pm, Sat and Sun noon to 10:30pm; next to the town hall)*, though modest on the outside, has a pretty dining room upstairs where you can enjoy deliciously prepared salmon or rabbit dishes.

In the middle of the small village of São Pedro, near Sintra, the restaurant **Tasca a Latina** *($$; Tue to Thu 8:30pm to 2am; Calçada São Pedro no. 28)* offers an original menu and fairly reasonable prices. Seven-vegetable couscous, seafood curry, Spanish tortillas and vegetarian curry are a few examples to whet your appetite. Youthful atmosphere, colourful decor and a friendly, relaxed welcome await.

In the heart of Sintra, in a building with a beautiful façade of blue *azulejos*, the **Café de Paris** *($$$; every day until midnight; Praça da República no. 32, ☎ 923 23 75)* is decorated in the style of a Paris bistro (of course!). It offers some dishes that are unusual in Portugal, such as a melon and port appetizer, vichyssoise, coriander clams, and grilled halves of rock lobster. This is a busy, lively place, with a view of the palace from an abundantly flowered, covered terrace.

Set in the upper part of town, the **Tacho Real** restaurant *($$$; closed Wed; Rua da Ferreira no. 4, ☎ 1-923 52 77)* has a particularly refined and elegant decor and very friendly service. You will find Portuguese food, somewhat more elaborate than usual, although without surprises.

Seteais

Located less than two kilometres from Sintra, in Seteais, the restaurant of the **Hotel Palácio de Seteais** *($$$$$; every day 12:30pm to 2:30pm and 7:30pm to 9:30pm, Rua Barbosa Bocage no. 10, Seteais, ☎ 1-923 32 00)* offers an excellent four-course meal starting at 6,500 ESC in a truly beautiful setting (see p 157). The chicken braised in Madeira is a delight, as is the pork medallion with dates. The dining room decor, worthy of a palace, includes magnificent frescoes and fine period furniture. Before starting your gourmet evening, however take a little stroll on the terrace with its splendid views of the French-style gardens and of the surrounding countryside.

Várzea de Sintra

 In a small guesthouse run by a friendly Belgian couple, the **Pátio do Saloio** restaurant *($$$$; Thu to Sat 7:30pm to 10:30pm, Sun 11:30 to 3pm; Rua Padre Amaro Teixeira de Azevedo no. 14, Várzea de Sintra, ☎ 924 15 20, ☎ and ⌐ 924 15 12)* will satisfy travelling gourmets. From Chateaubriand to the "three delights" fish dish, the cuisine here is an homage to the flat country. The owners are also seasoned decorators, and the pretty decor is as delectable as are the carefully presented dishes.

TOUR N: SETÚBAL AND SURROUNDINGS

Costa da Caparica

About one kilometre along the Cais do Ginjal, in an out-of-the-way spot, is the Brazilian restaurant **Atira-te ao Rio** *($$; Tue to*

Fri 7pm to midnight, Sat and Sun 4pm to midnight; Cais do Ginjal, ☎ *275 13 80)*, where diners savour *feijoada* and other typical Brazilian dishes. Friendly and unpretentious. Given its distance from downtown, reservations are recommended.

On the banks of the Tagus, beside the Atira-te ao Rio Brazilian restaurant, the **Ponto Final** *($$$; Tue to Sun 12:30pm to 11:30pm; Cais do Ginjal,* ☎ *276 07 43)* serves typical Portuguese fare of no particular interest. Nonetheless, the view from the restaurant's terrace, right on the docks, is simply magnificent. With the Tagus flowing at your feet, you can admire the rolling hills of Lisbon in the distance, lighting up, at nightfall, with fabulous colours. The sunset alone is worth the long walk along the quay (about 1 km).

Setúbal

O Cardador *($$; every day 12:30pm to 3pm and 7:30pm to 10:30pm; near the Praça Marquês de Pombal, behind the Albergaria Solaris)*. Fish and seafood top the menu in this charming restaurant with its pleasant little terrace. Friendly, smiling staff.

Cervejaria O 10 *($$$; Avenida Luísa Todi nos. 420-422,* ☎ *65-52 52 12)*. Although meals are prepared without great originality, this restaurant, unlike many of its competitors, serves meals all day long, without interruption. Its pleasant terrace also enhances this unpretentious but convenient spot.

Overlooking the town of Setúbal, the restaurant of the **Pousada de São Filipe** *($$$; go west along Avenida Luísa Todi to the end, turn right and then immediately to the left to reach Rua de São Filipe, which will lead you directly to the fortress, Rua de São Filipe,* ☎ *65-52 38 44)* is one of the most pleasant spots in Setúbal for a meal. Opening onto a former fortress dating from 1590 (see p 162), its impressive entrance leads through a series of vaulted corridors with several fortified gates. At the top of the stairway, a magnificent terrace with panoramic views of the Tróia peninsula and the sea entices you to linger for a pre-dinner drink. The dining room, although warmly decorated, lacks originality for such an exceptional spot. It is relaxing nonetheless, and fish lovers can enjoy an excellent *caldeirada à Setubalense* as well as excellent *Moscatel* wine, both regional specialties.

Cafés and Tearooms

Café Comm C *(every day 10am to 2am; Avenida Luísa Todi no. 184)*. Jute coffee bags adorn the walls at this friendly little bar: the ideal surroundings in which to sip a coffee or perhaps a delicious *Moscatel* wine, a specialty of the region.

Palmela

Set in the little village of Palmela, the restaurant of the **Pousada de Palmela** *($$$; atop the village of Palmela, ☎ 1-235 12 26)* enjoys the exceptional setting of a former monastery dating from the 15th century (see p 164) teetering atop a steep rock formation. Upon entering, the eye is drawn to the imposing dimensions of the numerous vaulted halls and galleries that surround the cloister. You may have an apperitif in the friendly, comfortable bar before taking your meal in the former refectory of the monastery or, if you prefer, on the elegant terrace around which the cloister stands. Besides the regional specialties, do not miss the excellent regional wine, *Moscatel*.

ENTERTAINMENT

Lisbon is full of entertainment options for all tastes and budgets. Classical music concerts, opera, variety shows – not to mention the innumerable bars and nightclubs that open their doors every night in the Bairro Alto, Alcântara and on the docks of Santo Amaro.

This chapter presents an overview of the variety of nocturnal experiences that is available in Lisbon. For more information on shows and concerts see the section entitled, "Cultural Activities", on p 266.

 TOUR B: THE CASTELO AND THE ALFAMA

Fado

At the **Taverna d'El Red** *($$$; open until 3:30am; Largo de Chafariz de Dentro no. 14/5, at the corner of Rua São Pedro, ☎ 887 67 54)*, you can dine on traditional Portuguese dishes while listening to authentic *fado*.

Clube de Fado *($$$$; Rua São João de Praça nos. 92-94, ☎ 885 27 04)*. Expensive and touristy certainly, but an evening spent listening to fado while comfortably seated at a table laden with Portuguese dishes is worth at least as much as an evening spent at a nightclub with its pricey cover charge and exorbitantly priced drinks.

Bars and Nightclubs

Nostalgic for Brazil? Gather round the bar at the small unpretentious **Pé Sujo** *(Tue to Sun 10pm to 2am; Largo de São Martinho nos. 6-7)*, where you can enjoy *musica ao vivo brasileira* every weekend.

TOUR D: THE CHIADO AND THE BAIRRO ALTO

Fado

Restaurante O Forcado *($$$$; Thu to Tue until 3:30am, closed Wed; Rua da Rosa no. 219, ☎ 346 85 79)* serves up Portuguese cuisine and *fado* until the wee hours of the morning.

Adega do Ribatejo *(every day 7pm to midnight; Rua do Diário de Notícias no. 23)*. Though the decor and horrible neon lighting are particularly uninspired here, visitors can nonetheless enjoy authentic *fado* in a lively ambiance.

Bars and Nightclubs

A good atmosphere and a youthful clientele spell success for **Bar Gráfico's** *(Mon to Sat 10pm to 2am; Travessa do Agua da Flor nos. 40-42)*, which gets so crowded on weekends that people eventually end up spilling out onto the street. It is worth stopping by just to see the decor, which is made up partly of contemporary paintings and contrasts interestingly with the rather old-fashioned neighbourhood.

Nearby, tourists from the world over mingle with young Lisboans at **A Tasca-Tequila Bar** *(every day 9pm to 2am; Travessa da Queimada nos. 13-15)* where both tequila and beer

Tour D: The Chiado and the Bairro Alto 253

seem to flow like water. "Aphrodisiac" cocktails with decidedly evocative names are also proffered here!

Fans of techno music who want to be able to hear themselves talk: **Fremitus** bar *(every day 8pm to 2am; Rua da Atalaia no. 78)* is just the place. The stunning decor features a giant propeller incorporated into the bar, large valves on the walls, imposing metal beams and amusing bar stools mounted on springs (those prone to seasickness or who've had one too many should abstain from using these!); this bar will give you something to write home about. Not to mention, the young and "well-behaved" clientele that seems somewhat out of place in this modern and industrial setting. Relaxed ambiance and reasonable prices.

Did the owner give the **A Capela** *(Sun to Thu 10pm to 2am, Thu and Sat until 4am; Rua da Atalaia no. 49)* its name because of its narrow vaulted rooms, its holy-water basin or simply because it inspires late-night confidences? The unusual decor features mirrors surrounded by gilding set against contrasting sober grey walls. A pleasant place (the moderate prices don't hurt, either), which will appeal mainly to students and fans of English-language music.

As its Portuguese name suggests, the **Portas Largas** *(Rua da Atalaia nos. 101-105)* is distinguished by its large doors making it hard to miss despite the fact that it lacks a sign. Located just opposite the very popular Frágil discotheque (see p 255), this establishment is the ideal early evening meeting place. A mixed gay and straight crowd flocks here, and on weekends, the throng of people is so great that revellers spill out onto the sidewalk. The decor is simple and cozy, with small, plain wooden tables and a few benches scattered throughout. This delightful place is a must for those who wish to discover the Lisbon of Lisboans.

At the tiny **Mezcal** *(every day 8pm to 2am; Travessa do Agua da Flor no. 20)*, you can have all sorts of alcoholic beverages, including tequila, of course. All-ages clientele.

With its modern and colourful decor harmoniously contrasting with the antiquity of the building, **Café Suave** *(every day 9:30pm to 2am; Rua do Diário de Notícias no. 6)* is a particularly delightful place in which to quench your thirst and share your latest secrets, to the sounds of modern hits.

Another great spot for an evening of chatting among friends is the **Cafediário** *(every day 9pm to 2am; Rua do Diário do Notícias no. 3)*. Latin-American tunes, jazz and Brazilian songs from the fifties set the mood. The excellent tropical cocktails here will certainly help loosen your tongue...

After having walked the old streets of the Bairro Alto, you might be surprised to come upon the very modern **Café Targus** *(every day 9pm to 2am; Rua do Diário de Notícias no. 40)*. In a refined decor where the accent is on designer furniture, you can take a load off in one of the lovely (but uncomfortable!) chairs while sipping your choice of the many cocktails offered here. A gilded youth frequents the place, so expect to pay dearly for libations (beer at 500 ESC, spirits at 1,400 ESC).

Another good place to start off an evening to the sounds of retro music is **Páginas Tantas** *(every day 9pm to 2pm; Rua do Diário de Notícias no. 85)*. Lengthy "happy hours", lasting from 9pm to midnight, and a refined and relaxed ambiance are particularly appreciated on this bar-lined street.

In need of a little escape? Internet surfers, head to **Café Webs** *(Rua de Diário de Notícias no. 126)*, where you can "surf" all around the world while sipping a *bica*.

Lisbon already has the "Kremlin" (see p 261), so it was only natural that the **KGB** *(cover charge; Rua de Diário de Notícias no. 122)* should open up as well. This new nightclub is on the famous Rua de Diário de Notícias, the street in the Bairro Alto that seems to hold the record for the greatest number of clubs! After having gotten past the appropriately-clad doorman, you can dance to the latest hits in attractive surroundings, where stone arches dominate the decor.

If you like pub-style bars, you can have a drink or a light meal *(menu starting at 2,800 ESC)* at the **Pedro Quinto Bar-Restaurant** *(Mon to Sat noon to 3am; Rua Pedro V no. 14)*, which is warmly decorated with wine-red wallpaper and softly lit woodwork.

Located inside a former house, in a somewhat dated setting, the **Solar do Vinho do Porto** *(Mon to Fri 10am to 11:45pm, Sat 11am to 10:45pm; Rua de S. Pedro de Alcântara no. 45, entrance to the right once you pass through the portal)* is a port-tasting salon financed and run by the Instituto do Vinho do Porto. Its purpose is to serve as a showcase for the country's port wines, of which it has an impressive selection. The quiet atmosphere is a haven in this busy neighbourhood. Unfortunately, however, there is no one to offer advice or information about the products, and the service is slow and even discourteous at times. Furthermore, although the list of ports is exhaustive, it would seem that some of the wines, especially the moderately-priced ones, are not always available.

What could be more pleasant than sipping a drink in an antique-shop setting? That's what you can do at the **Pavilhão Chines** *(Mon to Sat 2pm to 2am, Sat 6pm to 2am, Sun 9pm to 2am; Rua Dom Pedro V nos. 89-91)*, where glass-doored cabinets full of lead figurines and oriental vases serve as a reminder that the place was once a general store. There is a series of rooms, one of which has a billiard table. The illustrated drink list includes a wide assortment of whiskies and cocktails, though the prices are rather high. The entrance, with its 1920s decor, is perhaps the most interesting room, but it has unfortunately been marred by an unattractive video system. A more varied selection of music would be an improvement as well.

Hip Egyptologists can head to **Keops** *(every day 11pm to 3:30am; Rua da Rosa no. 157)* to admire the giant hieroglyphics adorning the bar. English-language music and a young, super-trendy clientele.

The name Mantel Reis automatically conjures up images of the Bairro Alto for Lisboans. He is now unanimously considered to have ushered in the Portuguese *movida* that became all the rage in this area. About 10 years ago, he opened the truly avant-garde discotheque **Frágil** *(Mon to Sat 10:30pm to 3:30am; Rua da Atalaia nos. 126-128)* in what was then a quiet area, thus transforming the local nightlife. Since that time, the Bairro Alto has become a mecca for nighttime fun-seekers, who still flock to the Frágil. After battling your way inside (arrive early; the doormen can be very selective), you'll find yourself surrounded by a motley crowd (the very young, the very fashionable, gays, etc.). The decor is modified regularly by local artists. The only constant is the big gilded mirror, in which Narcissus himself would never tire of watching himself dance. Guaranteed atmosphere and trendy music.

As its name suggests, the **Céu de Lisboa** *(every day until 11pm)* will transport you into the skies of Lisbon. No, it's not a potent drink, but rather a terrace at the very top of the famous Elevador Santa Justa. If you're in town during the weekend, don't miss the excellent recitals given here *(Sat and Sun 5pm to 10pm)*. The soft music and magnificent view of the hills of Lisbon bathed in late-afternoon light can make even the most blasé tourist fall in love with this city. Be careful, though: climbing up the narrow spiral staircase to the terrace is not recommended if you're subject to dizzy spells. Come early for the concerts, as both seats and space are limited. Light snacks available.

Bar-Restaurante Bachus *(Mon to Fri noon to 2am, Sat 6pm to 2am; Largo da Trindade no. 9, ☎ 342 28 28 or 342 12 60)*. A lovely bar surrounded by woodwork and cabinets full of old bottles, making for a cozy atmosphere. Popular with politicians and artists. People also come here for drinks before heading upstairs to eat (see p 226).

Bar Pintál *(Tue to Sun 10pm to 3:30am; Largo Trindade de Coelho nos. 22-23)*. A large, lovely and well-lit bar popular with Lisbon's gilded youth. Live music (usually Brazilian) from 11:30 on, and exotic cocktails like *doce de mais* and *caipirinha*.

Gay Bars and Nightclubs

The small, elegantly decorated **Bar 106** *(every day 9pm to 2am; Rua de São Marçal no. 106, ring bell to enter)* is one of the most popular places for gay Portuguese men to get together. It attracts a fashionable clientele and gets packed on weekends once midnight strikes. The "happy hour" from 9pm to 11:30pm is a pleasant way to start off an evening.

The **Bricabar** *(every day 10pm to 4am; Rua Cecilio de Sousa no. 82, ring bell to enter)* is a two-level gay bar decorated with a certain degree of elegance: royal blue curtains, contemporary furnishings, strategic lighting. Although popular with Lisbon's young and beautiful people, this big place seems to have a hard time filling up. The music is not only original and interesting, but also not too loud, which is a plus.

Tattoo *(Mon to Sat 8pm to 2am; Rua de São Marçal no. 15, ring bell to enter)* appeals to those who prefer a more mature clientele.

Trumps *(1,000 ESC cover charge, one drink included; Tue to Sun 11pm to 4am; Rua da Imprensa Nacional no. 104-B)* is a large gay discotheque that is also popular with straights. This place is frequented above all by serious party-ers, especially as the night wears on. Friendly ambiance, with some extravagant behaviour here and there, like the Sunday and Wednesday night shows at 2:30am.

Set up on the ground floor of a handsome building, the small **Agua no Bico** *(every day 9pm to 2am; Rua de São Marçal no. 170, ring bell to enter)*, with brightly-coloured walls, is a very pleasant place where you can meet your soul mate or simply have a drink at the large marbled bar. Unfortunately, like many other establishments, this one is equipped with a giant screen, monopolizing clients' attention and thus impeding conversation.

On the outskirts of Bairro Alto, the nightclub **Finalmente** *(every day 11pm to 6am; Rua da Palmeira no. 38, ring bell to enter)* welcomes a gay and lesbian clientele in a simple room, with kitschy decor and a small stage. Every night, at 2:30am, there is a transvestite show, a performance that is faithfully attended by a large, enthusiastic audience. Not to be missed!

Located a few steps from the pretty park in the Praça do Príncipe Real, **Satyros** *(every day 10pm to 6am; Calçada da Patriarcal nos. 6-8, corner Rua da Alegria, ring to enter)* is a small gathering place for gay men, young and old. The decor is a bit on the kitschy side and the music is an enjoyable mix of French, Brazilian, English, American and even Spanish. Drag queens perfrom on weekends (Fri and Sat as of 2:30am). This is a simple and unpretentious spot worth remembering.

Set in the basement of a small building, the **Memorial** *(cover charge; Tue to Sat 10pm to 3:30am, Sun 4:30pm to 8:30pm; Rua Gustavo de Matos Sequeira no. 42, ring bell to enter)* mainly caters to a lesbian clientele. In a vaulted cave decor, a young clientele (20-35 years old) lets loose to the beat of an assortment of music; Brazilian sounds, Portuguese disco and dance beats.

TOUR E: THE RATO AND AMOREIRAS

Located in the basement of a Cape Verde restaurant, the **Pillon II** *(cover charge 2,000 ESC including 2 drinks; Wed to Sun 11pm to 4am; Rua do Sol ao Rato no. 71-A)* restaurant plays African music, notably from Cape Verde. In a decor bordering on kitsch, a variety of musicians appear while "a most respectable" audience dances with abandon to these frenetic rhythms. Proper dress required.

TOUR G: RESTAURADORES AND LIBERDADE

Bars and Nightclubs

Jazz-o-philes should head to the **Hot Clube de Portugal** *(cover charge; Tue to Sat 10pm to 2am; Praça da Alegria no. 39, ☎ 346 73 69 or www.isa.utl.pt/HCP/informations.html)*. In a small room with Spartan decor, located in the basement of an office building, various concerts are staged Thursday to Saturday, from 11pm to 12:30am. Jam sessions are organized on Tuesday and Wednesday nights, with no cover charge.

TOUR H: SANTA CATARINA AND CAIS DO SODRÉ

Bars and Nightclubs

Ó Gilín's Irish Pub *(every day 11am to 2am; Rua dos Remolares nos. 8-10)*. You guessed it, this is the place where Lisbon's English-speaking, beer-guzzling crowd gathers. On weekends, you can listen to *música ao vivo* in a particularly boisterous ambiance, for the beer flows like water here. The establishment serves various Irish specialties and gets particularly crowded on weekends, so be sure to get there early if you want a table. An

Irish brunch is also offered on Sundays as of 11am. Friendly and unpretentious.

On the very street where the delightful *elevador da bica* runs, you will find **WIP** (Work In Progress) *(Wed to Sun 2pm to 2am; Rua da Bica de Duarte Belo nos. 47-49)*, a most original concept. Indeed, here is an establishment that is at once a bar, a hair salon and clothing boutique, no less! In a "futuristic" decor, you can quench your thirst while getting your hair done or picking up a new kit. Friendly and unpretentious.

TOUR I: ESTRÊLA AND LAPA

Fado

The owner of the **Senhor Vinho** *(Mon to Sat 8:30pm to 3:30am; Rua do Meio in Lapa no 18, ☎ 397 26 81)* restaurant sings *fado* in the purest Portuguese tradition. Somewhat expensive, but unforgettable. Reservations recommended.

Bars and Nightclubs

Café Santos *(every day 9:30pm to 2am; Rua de Santos-o-Velho nos. 2-4)* is a very pleasant place in which to start off the evening. On weekends, between 10pm and midnight, a young clientele meets up here for the first drink of the night. Spilling out onto the sidewalk, patrons, with drinks in hand, engage in animated discussions. Functional Scandinavian designer furniture, marble floors and small candle-lit tables make up the greater part of the decor.

The **Foxtrot** *(every day 6pm to 2am; Travessa de Santa Teresa 28, ☎ 395 26 97)*, with its indoor terrace and sumptuous decor, is a delightful place to start off or wind down an evening out. The place has several rooms, one of which contains a variety of games, including pinball, snooker, etc. You can eat here as well (see p 236).

Another good rendezvous to kick off your evening (starting at 10pm here) is the **Pérola** *(Tue to Sun 10pm to 2am; Calçada*

Ribeiro Santos no. 25), with a great location, close to two renowned discos, the Kremlin and the Plateau. Before hitting the livelier nightclubs, a young crowd gathers here amidst the kitsch. A small back room, decorated with comic strips and a few tables, welcomes those craving a little sustenance. Various *petiscos* as well as a daily special are offered as early as 10pm, that is if the cook shows up on time (which is not always a given here, it seems!).

Até Qu'Enfim bar *(every day 10pm to 2am; Rua des Janelas Verdes no. 8)* is the place for *música ao vivo* on weekends. Quench your thirst as you relax on a sofa or at the bar, while listening to somewhat retro rock music.

Another bar on this decidedly hopping street, the ΛΚΛΔΣ ΠΥΚΦS (**AKADE NYKOS**) *(Rua das Janelas Verdes no. 2)* is also a good place in which to get revved up for a night out. Its beautiful red doors lead into a well laid out and harmonious interior with old stone arches and modern furnishings. The music is very loud here.

You can dance the night away to African rhythms at **A Lontra** *(cover charge 2,000 ESC including 4 drinks; every day 11pm to 4am; Rua de São Bento no. 157)*, one of the most well-known African discos in Lisbon. A chic and well-off clientele frequents the place; showing up in "proper" attire – preferably with a well-padded wallet – is therefore a must.

Whether you're starting off or winding down your evening, stop in at **A Ultima Ceia** *(Tue to Sun 8:30pm to 4am; Avenida 24 de Julho no. 96)*, a lovely place nestled at the far end of a verdant courtyard. On the ground floor, you can sample all sorts of cocktails (clearly an activity very much in fashion in Lisbon); simple snacks (*pestiscos* or salad for 600 ESC) are served on the second floor. This is a cosy place, although the music is a bit loud. Friendly staff.

If you're looking to party until the wee hours of the morning, head to the **Café Central** *(every day 10pm to 4am; Avenida 24 de Julho nos. 110-112)*, where you can warm up with a cocktail (large selection, but relatively high prices), then head next door to **Metalúrgica**, a discotheque. Both the bar and the disco have been beautifully decorated by architect Mantel

Graça Dias, who designed the Portuguese pavilion for the World Fair in Seville. Student clientele.

Kapital *(every day 10:30pm to 4am, Fri and Sat until 6am; Avenida 24 de Julho no. 68)*. Spread out over two floors, this large disco attracts a crowd of rock and techno fans. The decor is cold and sterile; upstairs patrons enjoy drinks at the bar, while on the ground floor, a young and wild crowd lets it all out to unbelievably loud music. Expect selective admission and a particularly expensive evening – all drinks cost 1,000 ESC (and they do not accept credit cards!). A place for those who like being where everyone says is the place to be.

Along with the Alcântara Mar, the **Kremlin** *(Tue to Thu midnight to 6am, Fri and Sat midnight to 8am; Escadinhas da Praia no. 5)* was one of the first nightclubs in the capital to remain open into the wee hours of the morning. Large arches make up the bulk of the basement decor of this place, where you can groove to techno, dance and house music, provided of course you made it past the severely guarded entrance, this is the Kremlin after all!

Le Plateau *(Tue to Sat midnight to 6am; Escadinhas da Praia no. 7)* is definitely one of the most fashionable discotheques in the capital. Once again, it is worth coming here just to see the decor, which features columns shaped like upside-down cones and adorned with burning candles, mirrors, gilding and candelabra. Lisbon's decorators seem to draw a lot of inspiration from the splendour of the baroque era. A large map of the Old World makes the place seem even more like a lounge. The well-off clientele includes middle-aged businesspeople and young cruisers: appropriate dress recommended! Varied music on the weekend and rock on Thursday.

TOUR J: ALCÂNTARA, SANTO AMARO AND BELÉM

Bars and Nightclubs

Alcântara

The **Alcântara-Mar** *(Wed to Sun 11:30 until you drop; Rua Maria Luísa Holstein no. 15, formerly Rua Primeira Particular, ☎ 363 71 76)* is part of a complex including a restaurant, bar and art gallery (see p 240). Oddly enough, the discotheque has three entrances, one by way of the footbridge in the Alcântara-Café (mainly for patrons of the restaurant), another on Rua Maria Luísa Holstein (for "guests" and "friends") and the last, for mere mortals, on Rua Cozinha Económica *(1,000 ESC cover charge)*. As the place is very popular, and those permitted to enter are selected very quickly, you are better off arriving fairly early. The decor is amusingly surprising and shows a lot of imagination. It might feature anything from crystal chandeliers to big mirrors and gilded columns. The music is mostly techno, except on Wednesdays (retro night), while the crowd is a fashionable mix of affluent, urbane, and trendy types, both gays and heterosexuals, who come here with the sole intention of letting loose until breakfast time.

The Alcântara-Mar's major competitor is its neighbour, the **Discoteca Benzina** *(Tue to Sun until 4am; Travessa Teixeira Júnior no. 6)*, a gigantic discotheque known for its techno music. A young, motley crowd dances up a storm here until 4am, when the real die-hards head over to the Alcântara to start off the morning. Tuesday is hippie night, and music from the 1970's is featured on Wednesdays. The place gets packed, so get there when it opens *(11:30pm)* to avoid having to wait in line.

The **Discoteca Rock Line** *(every day until 6am; Rua das Fontainhas no. 86)*, located in the same area, caters to a much younger and less fashionable crowd (in Portugal, you only have to be 16 to get into discotheques). As far as the music is concerned, the name says it all: rock.

Tour J: Alcântara, Santo Amaro and Belém 263

The following four nightclubs *(Mon to Sat 8:30pm to 6am)* stand side by side in old warehouses at the port, just southeast of the Avenida Infante Santo viaduct, which transects Avenida Vinte Quatro de Julho in front of the Doca de Alcântara. These four establishments are all good examples of successful efforts to restore the urban heritage and allow visitors to take advantage of the romantic Tagus so close by, in the heart of downtown.

Since its very opening, the **Kings and Queens** has attracted, perhaps due to its name, a young, modern clientele of all sexual orientations. Despite its large space, the candelabras, mirrors, rose windows and other elements borrowed from the Baroque give it a rich and warm atmosphere. A magnificent Art-Deco chandelier disrupts these historical references, as does the techno music, the half-naked dancers atop loudspeakers and the occasional transvestite shows. The place also boasts a terrace.

Things are much more low key next door at the smaller **Indochina**, featuring a very lovely Asian decor of red-lacquered walls, Chinese lamps, wood panels and Buddhas, and a *bacalhau* clientele. This place is not for posers, but rather for those who just feel like having a fun time, letting loose to the exotic sounds of the Flamenco version of *All of my love* or to a medley of Spanish hits. You can take in the scene from the mezzanine or from a table whole seated on comfortable stools. For a little variety, Thursdays are "vintage music" nights, when classical, soul, jungle, salsa and hip hop follow one after the other in an almost-perfect mix.

Each bar has its own crowd, and the **Blues Café**'s is young, professional and conventionally-minded. A large pub with big picture windows giving out on the Tagus, it is an attractive place with brick walls, floors and ceilings of dark wood as well as a billiard table. The clientele and decor go hand in hand with the top-40 commercial music played here, and strobe lighting pulsates throughout the bar on occasion.

Lest you forget that you are at the port, you can take to the open sea at **Dock's Club**, with its maritime decor of bulwarks, metal, pale wood and old colonial-style ceiling fans. Upstairs, delightful couches with Angolan leopard patterns and Cape Verdean palm trees. Little lamps on each table shed subdued lighting, but the house music will soon bring you back to the reality of the docks!

Santo Amaro

Much like the Doca de Alcântara, the old warehouses of the Doca de Santo Amaro *(before the Doca de Alcântara, southeast of the Rua de Cascais viaduct, which crosses Avenida da India and spans over the railway and Avenida Brasilia)* have also been the objects of clever restoration. In fact, bars, discotheques, restaurants and boutiques succeed one another here along the pier, and the marina. Unlike its counterpart (the Doca de Alcântara), however, the long succession of establishments here starts to get repetitive and confers a very commercial and rather artificial quality to the place. The fact of the matter is that competition is fierce here, and every bar, restaurant and nightclub seems to want to play the originality card at any cost (not always very successfully) in order to attract as many clients as possible. Moreover, the music, playing at ear-shattering volume and, spilling out of the various establishments, generates such a racket that this stretch seems more like a permanent fair than it does a strip of nightclubs. By walking the pier from west to east, you will see: the **Café do Ponte**, a bar equipped with a large terrace; the **Santo Amaro Café**, a bar-restaurant where 18 television screens make up most of the decor and where latino music is worshipped; the **Cosmos** discotheque; the very chic (and over-priced) **Tertulia do Tejo** restaurant, featuring regional Portuguese cuisine, for those who like to be seen; the **7 Mares** bar, where several screens broadcast sports programmes and where, on weekends, patrons can listen to *música ao vivo*; the **Havana** bar-restaurant-discotheque, where *salsa, cumbia* and *merengue* are played, and finally, housed in a building slightly set back from the pier, the **Doca de Santo** bar-restaurant (the fist bar in the area) closes out this long list. Of all the establishments mentioned above, the latter is the most original by far. Huge windows and small tables line either side of this long, narrow space, while a very modern, V-shaped bar monopolizes the entire middle section. Two terraces, one of which is covered, pleasantly complement this architecture with refined lines and an airy appearance. The only problem is those palm trees, which just don't fit.

Belém

Cais da Princesa *(every day until 2am during summer; Cais da Princesa, near the Torre de Belém, ☎ 387 14 30)* is a docked boat that has been converted into a bar, where patrons can sip a delicious cocktail on the deck or inside amidst the wonderful nautical decor. Romantic view.

TOUR L: ESTORIL TO CASCAIS

Bars and Nightclubs

Estoril

Danse Pub Alô Alô *(every day 10pm to 4am; Beco Esconso)*. Pool tables, a dance floor and *música ao vivo* every Friday aim to satisfy night owls. In case a hunger attack hits, light meals are also served.

TOUR M: QUELUZ TO SINTRA

Bars and Nightclubs

Queluz

Património Bar *(cover charge 1,000 ESC; Avenida da República nos. 4-8)*. The best thing about this modest, unpretentious bar is its proximity to the magnificent Pousada Dona Maria I. *Música ao vivo* on weekends, with Brazilian rhythms playing in the background.

Sintra

The superb fountain right next door and lovely area make the **Bar Fonte da Pipa** *(4pm to midnight; Rua Fonte da Pipa nos. 11-13)* a pleasant spot for a drink. The old-fashioned decor with a preponderance of wood panelling and cushioned booths, lends itself well to the enjoyment of a nice cold beer.

266   Entertainment

The stone walls and warm tones of the **Bistrobar Opera Prima** *($; 9am to midnight; Rua Consiglieri Pedroso no. 2A)* are conducive to a good tête-à-tête. The staff are very friendly, making this pleasant and refined place worth checking out.

TOUR N: SETÚBAL AND SURROUNDINGS

Bars and Nightclubs

Setúbal

Bar Iguana *(Rua Pereira Cão no. 44)*. A friendly little bar. Musicians every Friday starting at 10pm.

Disco Fabrica *(along the N10-4 toward the west, 300 m after the end of Avenida Luísa Todi)*. This big discotheque set in a former factory will delight night people who can get down and dance into the wee hours of the morning.

A vaulted brick hall, decorated only with a few wrought-iron lamp fixtures and walls of bare stone, is what awaits you at the **Conventual** *(6pm to 2am; Travessa da Anunciada no. 2)*. This bar, assuredly one of the most elegant in Setúbal, tries also to be one of the most original: art exhibitions and concerts are presented here regularly.

CULTURAL ACTIVITIES

The year 1994 was marked by all sorts of cultural activities celebrating Lisbon's role as "Cultural Capital of Europe". During this period, a lot of attention was focused on developing the arts. This energy continues as EXPO 98 approaches, an event that promises to be just as rich on a cultural level. Like other capital cities, Lisbon has excellent theatres, where visitors with adequate knowledge of Portuguese can enjoy all different kinds of entertainment.

Bearing in mind the great number of activities offered each month, we invite you to consult the various publications listed below. These will give you detailed information on current events and schedules as well as rates. Addresses and phone numbers of a few facilities and venues as well as other sources of information are also listed below.

Publications

Agenda Cultural *(www.portugal.hpv.pt/lisboa/agenda)*: Cultural monthly issued by the City of Lisbon. Available free of charge at most tourist or cultural facilities (bookshops, hotels, bistros) or at the head office: Rua de São Pedro de Alcântara 3.

Sete: Weekly information guide of all the goings-on about town (film, theatre, opera, concerts, nightlife, etc.). Available at most newsstands.

Diário de Notícias *(www.dn.pt)*: This widely circulated daily paper publishes a special section every Friday entitled "Programas", detailing all cultural activities taking place in the city.

Público *(www.publico.pt)*: Another national daily, in which you will find "Zap", a section published every Friday dedicated to cultural activities in Lisbon.

JL Jornal de Letras, Artes e Ideias: A particularly interesting newspaper devoted to art and literature *(320 ESC, published every two weeks)*.

Paginas de Lisboa *(www.eunet.pt/Lisboa)*: Information pages featuring cultural activities in the capital.

Film

Most films are presented in the original language with Portuguese subtitles. A few places worth checking out are:

Cinemateca Portuguesa *(Rua Barata Salgueiro no. 39, ☎ 354 65 29)*. Film museum; retrospectives, sometimes featuring English-language films.

Cinema São Jorge *(Avenida da Liberdade 175)*

Cinema Tivoli *(Avenida da Liberdade 188)*

Theatres, Concerts and Shows

One hub of cultural activity in the capital is the **Coliseu dos Recreios** *(between the Travessa Santo Antão and Rua dos Condes, on the right side as you head north up the street, ☎ 346 19 97)*. Numerous concerts (classical and modern), operas, plays and more are presented on a regular basis in its huge hall.

Another particularly lively place is the **Parque Mayer** *(at the entrance of Travessa do Salitre, near Avenida da Liberdade)*, with several theatres, such as the **ABC** *(☎ 343 01 03)* and the **Maria Vitória** *(☎ 346 17 40)*; light comedies and variety shows are presented here.

For those who prefer the great classics of the theatre and opera, the **Teatro Nacional Dona Maria II** *(Praça Dom Pedro IV, ☎ 342 22 10)* and the **Teatro Nacional São Carlos** *(Rua Serpa Pinto 7, ☎ 346 59 14, 795 02 36 or 793 51 31)* are just the places, as long as you speak Portuguese. As for the **Grande Auditório Gulbenkian** *(Avenida de Berna no. 45, ☎ 793 51 31)*, its reputation is firmly established when it comes to concerts. Visitors can also take full advantage of the numerous free concerts presented in churches such as the Sé, the Igreja São Roque and others, all year round.

Finally, the latest among great cultural complexes, is the **Centro Cultural de Belém** *(Praça do Império no. 1, ☎ 361 24 00)*, a huge, modern, soulless building, constructed thanks to the generous support of the European Economic Community. Conferences, shows, concerts and temporary exhibitions are organized here on a regular basis.

SHOPPING

Like most great European cities, Lisbon has its share of well-known retail chains. While window shoppers will lap up the Baixa and the Chiado, specialty shop lovers will enjoy combing the Bairro Alto in search of that special find. Fans of shopping centres will enjoy the futuristic Amoreiras mall.

Stores are generally open from 9am to 1pm and from 3pm to 7pm, Monday to Friday, and from 9am to 1pm on Saturday. Shopping centres are open all day, Monday to Saturday.

 ## TOUR A: THE ROSSIO AND THE BAIXA

The Baixa has become a shopping mecca. You will find all sorts of shops within the rectangle bordered on either side of Rua Aurea (also known as Rua do Ouro) and Rua dos Fanqueiros. Of the many streets in this area, the most pleasant by far is Rua Augusta. A pedestrian mall with fashionable boutiques (selling clothing and leather goods, for the most part), it offers a lovely view of the triumphal arch. Since the street is so popular with tourists, however, the prices are significantly higher here than elsewhere, (for less expensive shopping, head to Restauradores, the Bairro Alto or the Rato).

Groceries

Celeiro Dieta *(Mon to Fri 8:30am to 8pm, Sat 8:30am to 7pm; Rua 1º Dezembro no. 65)*. Macrobiotic food and books on the subject. Not to be confused with the "classic" **Super Celeiro** *(Mon to Fri 8:30am to 8pm, Sat 9am to 6pm; corner of Rua 1º Dezembro and Calçada do Carmo)* located on the same street, which offers a wide choice of food: from pasta and assorted prepared meats to cheese and vegetables.

Set up above a supermarket, the **Yin-Yan** vegetarian self-service restaurant *(Mon to Fri 10am to 8:30pm; Rua dos Correios no. 14, 1st floor, ☎ 342 65 51)* houses a small grocer's, with an old-fashioned decor. You'll find a large selection of cereals, including muesli, as well as pasta, several kinds of lentils and even organic beer.

If you like specialty food shops, make sure to stop by Lisbon's version of the Harrod's food court, **Tavares** *(Rua da Betesga nos. 1A-1B)*. Dried fruit, home-made preserves, deli products, wine, port and all sorts of other treats. Expensive, but how could anyone resist?

The **Manteigaria Silva** *(Mon to Fri 9am to 7pm, Sat 9am to 1pm; Rua Dom Antão de Almada nos. 1C-1D)* is a real find! Your mouth will begin to water as soon as you enter this modest deli-style cheese and prepared-meat shop, which is sure to whet your appetite with its many delicacies! It is all you can do to resist the plump and glistening black and green olives or the sumptuous spread of fine cheeses. What more can we say about this place, teeming with temptations for the palate, except to head there as soon as possible! Excellent and inexpensive.

Located on the east side of Praça da Figueira, the **Mercado da Figueira** *(Mon to Fri 8:30am to 8pm, Sat 8:30am to 7pm; Praça da Figueira no. 10)* is a good place to purchase economically-priced victuals.

Antiques

O Dobrão *(Mon to Fri 10am to 6:30pm; Rua de São Nicolau no. 113, ☎ 346 99 50)*. This charming jeweller's, located on a street corner, offers a very beautiful choice of antique jewellery as well as little curios at relatively reasonable prices. Fans of vintage watches and small antiques, do not hesitate to drop in, if only to feast your eyes!

Music

Valentim de Carvalho *(Mon to Fri 10am to 8:30pm, Sat 10am to 8pm, Sun 10am to 7pm; Praça Dom Pedro IV no. 58)*. Whether shopping for a CD, a magazine or even the latest bestselling novel, you'll find everything you're looking for in this pleasant shop, where customers are always served with a smile. Many works are also available in English.

Discoteca Amália *(Sat until 7:30pm, Rua Aurea/Rua do Ouro no. 272)*. Good selection of Portuguese and Brazilian music.

TOUR B: THE CASTELO AND THE ALFAMA

Groceries

Conserveira da Lisboa *(Rua dos Bacalhoeiros no. 34)*. Canned sardines, canned salmon, canned tuna, canned squid, canned eel, canned mussels, canned shrimp, ... Imagine hundreds of cans piled one atop the other in an turn-of-the-century setting. Now there's something to add to a picnic for a song. A fun place!

Crafts

At **Espace Oikos** *(10am to noon and 2pm to 5pm; Rua Augusto Rosa no. 40)*, a wonderful multicultural centre set up inside some old stables, you can purchase lovely objects (jewellery, masks, fabrics, records, etc.) produced in developing countries. Reasonable prices.

TOUR C: GRAÇA AND EAST LISBON

Antiques

If you have a fondness for antique objects and curios, make sure to go to the **Campo Santa Clara** during your visit to the Panteão de Santa Engrácia. Various secondhand dealers set up all shop around the delightful open market, in the very centre of the little square. With a little patience, you may well find the deal of the century here!

Azulejos

Fans of antique *azulejos* should head to the **Museu Nacional do Azulejo**'s boutique *(Tue 2pm to 6pm, Wed to Sun 10am to 6pm; Rua da Madre de Deus no. 4, ☎ 814 77 47)*, where you can purchase various reproductions of works exhibited at the museum, and at very affordable prices *(azulejos at 2,000 ESC and more)*. Magazines and books on *azulejos* are also available.

Market

The **Feira da Ladra** *(Wed and Sat 7am to 6pm; Campo de Santa Clara; bus #39A from Praça do Comérçio, Estação Santa Apolónia stop; bus #46 from the Rossio, Estação Santa Apolónia stop; bus #12 from Marquês de Pombal, Campo Santa Clara stop)* is a big flea market.

TOUR D: THE CHIADO AND THE BAIRRO ALTO

Before a terrible fire ravaged the neighbourhood in 1988, the Chiado was a shopping mecca, whose major arteries were Rua do Carmo and Rua Garrett. Although the area is still under reconstruction, it is pleasant to stroll about here and admire the

Tour D: The Chiado and Bairro Alto

few surviving shops, most of which are chic and expensive. Local curiosities include the tiny and elegant **Luvaria** *(Rua do Carmo 87A)*, which is probably the smallest glove shop in Europe, but nevertheless boasts a vast selection. The goldsmith's shop **Aliança** *(Rua Garret 50-52)* is also noteworthy for its richly decorated interior.

Crafts

If you appreciate quality handicrafts, make sure to visit the simple **País em Lisboa** boutique *(Mon to Fri noon to 7pm, Sat 2:30pm to 7pm; Rua do Teixeira no. 25, ☎ 342 09 11)*. In lovely surroundings cooled by stone walls and arches, visitors can feast their eyes on jewellery, curios, paintings and clothing from various regions of Portugal. The selected artifacts are of high quality, and the charming proprietress will be glad to show them to you.

Azulejos

Azulejos of all shapes and colours can be found at the **Fabrica Sant'Anna** *(Rua do Alecrim no. 95)*, a two-hundred-year-old Lisbon institution.

If you have a taste for antique *azulejos*, make sure to go to **Solar** *(Rua Dom Pedro V nos. 68-70)*. Vast selection.

Shoppers will find every conceivable pattern at the **Viúva Lamego** boutique *(Mon to Fri 9am to 1pm and 3pm to 7pm, Sat 9am to 1pm; Calçada do Sacremento no. 29, ☎ 346 96 92)*, where the vast choice of styles and colours, which have made this *azulejos* factory in the Sintra region famous, are available. Very pricey but truly beautiful!

Decorative Items and Knick-knacks

For beautiful (but somewhat costly) fabric, head to **Soleiado** *(Largo do Carmo no. 2)*, on pretty Praça do Carmo. The location alone is worth the trip.

If you're yearning for the exotic, stop by **De Natura** *(Rua da Rosa no. 162-A, ☎ 346 60 81)*, a lovely shop that sells decorative objects from Africa, Asia and other parts of the world. Both the merchandise and the setting in which it is displayed will take you to far-off places. Prices are a bit steep, however.

The **Boutique Dirk Otto Hendrik** *(Rua do Século no. 4C)* sells both decorative objects and attractively designed utilitarian articles.

Spera *(Mon to Fri 2pm to 9pm, Sat 5pm to 9pm; Rua da Atalaia no. 64-A)*. Carpets, curios and little furnishings from Africa hold a place of honour in this boutique, which draws its finds from the cradle of humankind. Beautiful and expensive!

Bookstores and Stationer's

Livraria Bertrand *(Rua Garrett no. 73)*. International newspapers and a good selection of books. There is another one in the Amoreiras shopping centre.

A Bibliófila *(Rua da Misericórdia no. 102)*. Slightly old-fashioned, but interesting Portuguese bookstore with many books on art and history, as well as old prints, which can be framed on the premises.

Livraria Britânica *(Mon to Fri 9:30am to 7pm, Sat 9:30am to 1pm; Rua de São Marcal no. 168A)*. An English-language bookstore with a very wide selection.

Groceries

Mercado do Bairro Alto *(Mon and Sat 7am to 2pm; corner of Rua da Atalaia and Rua Boa Hora)*. Local market (fruit, vegetables, etc.).

Fashion

Patine *(Mon to Sat 2pm to midnight; Travessa Água da Flor no. 30, ☎ 347 04 11)*. With techno music playing in the background, this clothing boutique offers creations by young Lisboan designers as well as those of international names such as Gaultier, WXLT, EXTÉ, etc. If you want to make an impression during your nights out in the Bairro Alto, be sure to stop by this very trendy place!

Music

Discoteca do Carmo *(Rua do Carmo no. 63)*. Good record selection (same owner as the Discoteca Amália, in the Baixa).

Art

Visitors will find a good choice of watercolours depicting the city of Lisbon at the **Livraria & Galeria Stuart** *(Rua Nova do Almada nos. 20-22, ☎ 343 21 31)*, and for all budgets, too. As its Portuguese name suggests, books are also available, though most are secondhand.

TOUR E: THE RATO AND AMOREIRAS

Shopping Centres

Those who enjoy wandering through the malls and department stores of Paris, London, Montreal or New York will appreciate the **Amoreiras Shopping Center de Lisboa** *(from Rossio or Praça dos Restauradores bus # 11, Amoreiras stop, or, from Praça dos Restauradores, take the Elevador da Glória then bus #15, Amoreiras stop)* and its futuristic architecture. With its 200 shops, 10 cinemas, 47 restaurants, supermarket, gym and several banks, visitors could spend days on end here.

Decorative Items and Knick-knacks

The **Loja Conceicão Vasco Costa** *(Rua de Escola Politécnica no. 237)*, a lovely shop located in a restored palace, specializes in fine fabrics. The furniture shop next door (same owner) is also very interesting.

TOUR F: MARQUÊS DE POMBAL, SALDANHA AND NORTH LISBON

Bookstores and Stationer's

From novels and travel guides to books on the city's architecture and history, you will find everything you've always wanted to know about Lisbon at **Livraria Municipal** *(Mon to Fri 10am to 7pm, Sat 10am to 1pm; Avenida da República no. 21-A, ☎ 353 05 22)*, the Câmara Municipal's official bookstore. Aficionados of Lisbon, do not miss out!

TOUR G: RESTAURADORES AND LIBERDADE

For inexpensive shopping, head to **Rua Barros Queiros** and **Rua Dom Duarte**. If you like rummaging about you'll have a terrific time. The selection and quality are on a par with the prices, however. Given the crowds, be sure to keep a watchful eye out for pick-pockets.

Groceries

Located in the Centro Commercial Libercil, the **Super Nobrescolha** *(Avenida da Liberdade no. 20)*, while not the most pleasant grocer's, offers a vast choice and the advantage of being open later than the others.

Azulejos

Be sure to stop by the marvellous **Viúva Lamego** boutique *(Mon to Fri 9am to 1pm and 3pm to 7pm, Sat 9am to 1pm; Largo do Intendente Pina Manique no. 25, ☎ 885 24 08)* while exploring the Graça district. In addition to a wide choice of *azulejos*, available in numerous styles and colours, you can also admire the storefront's extraordinary façade, a real work of art, also entirely covered in *azulejos*. Oriental characters and landscapes are depicted and, to the right of the balcony, an amusing little monkey can be seen. Founded in 1849, the establishment owes its reputation to the parent company, the Fábrica Cerâmica Viúva Lamego, set up in the Sintra region. The only small disappointment in the face of such refinement is the high prices. Count on spending between 42,400 and 46,400 ESC for a panel with 12 *azulejos*!

Bookstores and Stationer's

Ipsilon *(corner of Avenida da Liberdade no. 9 and Calçada da Glória, next to the Borges bank, facing the Restauradores metro)*. Wide choice of foreign magazines and newspapers.

Souvenirs

The **Mercearia Liberdade** *(until 9pm in summer; Avenida da Liberdade no. 207, near Rua Barata Salgueiro)* is a beautiful craft shop selling everything from *azulejos* and pottery to excellent port wine. Good selection, reasonable prices and friendly service.

TOUR H: SANTA CATARINA AND CAIS DO SODRÉ

Bookstores and Stationer's

Livraria Centro Cultural Brasileiro *(Largo do Dr. António de Sousa Macedo no. 5, ☎ 60 87 60)*. You guessed it, Brazilian literature holds a place of honour here, in lovely wood-panelled surroundings.

TOUR I: ESTRÊLA AND LAPA

Azulejos

Ratton *(Mon to Fri 10am to 1pm and 3pm to 7:30pm; Rua Academia das Ciêncas no. 2C, ☎ 346 09 48)*. *Azulejos* certainly, but not just any *azulejos*! Indeed, here, modernism complements an age-old art form, offering original patterns and new compositions. In addition to the works exhibited in this little gallery, visitors can consult a thick catalogue containing numerous creations. As artists cannot live on inspiration and fresh air alone, expect to pay the modest sum of 82,000 ESC per *azulejo*! Who says you can't put a price on art?

TOUR J: ALCÂNTARA, SANTO AMARO AND BELÉM

Decorative Items and Knick-knacks

Lovers of the sea and everything related to navigation should not miss out on visiting the **Museu de Marinha**'s boutique *(summer Tue to Sun 10am to 6pm, winter Tue to Sun 10am to 5pm; Praça do Império)*, which, though rather ill-matched in terms of decoration, offers lovely curios at very reasonable prices. Collectors of miniatures will find magnificent reproductions of Portuguese vessels such as the typical *moliceiras* from Aveiro, the *barcos rabelos* from the Douro Valley, the *fragatas* from the Tagus, and the famous *caravelas*, jewels of Portuguese navigation. Count on spending from 11,000 to 23,000 ESC.

TOUR L: ESTORIL TO CASCAIS

Shopping Centres

On par with the Amoreiras shopping centre in Lisbon as well as all of those in the great European capitals, the **Cascais Shopping** *(Alcabideche, 6.8 km from the centre of Cascais via the EN9)* has no less than 130 shops and seven cinemas – bring your credit card!

TOUR M: QUELUZ TO SINTRA

Azulejos

In the charming **Azul Cobalto** studio-boutique *(Calçada de São Pedro no. 38, São Pedro da Sintra)*, you can purchase *azulejos* with imaginative patterns and even, if you so desire, have your own made-to-order design reproduced. It's worth a look!

Decorative Items and Knick-knacks

In search of beautiful fabric or original curios? Stop by **Ikat Interiores** *(corner of Calçada de São Pedro and Rua Dr. Higínio de Sousa, São Pedro da Sintra)*, where a friendly woman will show you various little "marvels".

The magnificent artifacts exhibited at the **A Janela de São Pedro** boutique *(Mon to Sat; Calçada de São Pedro no. 32, São Pedro da Sintra, ☎ 924 43 97)* clearly attest to the proprietors' passion for Africa. Wood and stone knick-knacks, masks and fabrics, there is nothing commonplace here, particularly the sculptures, for their original forms and use of materials. Surely the most exceptional boutique in Sintra!

Bookstores and Stationer's

Walking into the little **Livraria** bookshop *(Wed to Sun 10am to 7:30pm; Volta do Duche no. 16, Sintra, ☎ 923 19 98)* is like entering an old library, with that peculiar bookish smell that seems to herald the discovery of precious documents or a rare tome. Great piles of books fill the shelves here, from the book on the history of the Sintra region to the obscure novel, forgotten by the general public. Those looking for the latest best-seller or simply a map of the region can rest assured, however, for the friendly staff here will help you find anything you're looking for – with a smile at no extra charge.

PRONUNCIATION GUIDE

Anyone with a smattering of Spanish or French should not have too much difficulty pronouncing Portuguese. This little pronunciation guide should help with some of the exceptions.

One of the major considerations in Portuguese is the use of the diphthong, which is two vowels pronounced as a single vowel sound. For example **toy** in English is an *o* with a weak *i* sound. In Portuguese *ai* is like fly, *au* is like bow; in other cases weak vowels combine and are occasionally pronounced nasally, for example **informação** which is pronounced "infourmasaong". Generally, however it is not easy to predict Portuguese diphthongs.

Consonants are pronounced as in English, except the following exceptions:

c	before *a*, *o*, *u*, is hard like *k* in king; *casa* is pronounced "kahza".
	before *i* and *e*, it is soft; *cebola* is pronounced "saybola"
ç	the use of the cedilla (ˌ) softens the *c*, like *s* in soft; *praça* is pronounced "prassa".
ch	is soft like *sh* in shout; *chamar* is pronounced "shamahr".
g	before *a*, *o*, *u* is hard like *g* in gut; *gata* is pronounced "gata"
	before *e* and *i*, it is soft like *s* in leisure; *giro* is pronounced "zheero".
h	is always silent; *hora* is pronounced "ora"
j	like *s* in leisure; *azulejo* is pronounced "azulezho"
lh	like *lli* in trillion; *olho* is pronounced "olliyoo"
n	when at the beginning or between vowels like *n* in not; *nove* is pronounced "novay"

with other consonants or in a plural ending, the preceding vowel becomes nasal and the *n* softens; *branco* is pronounced "brahngkoo".

nh	like *ni* in onion; *vinho* is pronounced "vinyoo"
q	like *k* in king; *querer* is pronounced "kerrayr"
r	rolled like in French
s	when at the beginning or after a consonant, like *s* in soft
	at the end of a word or before *c*, *f*, *p*, *q* and *t* like *sh* in shout; *país* is pronounced "pahyish" and *pescador* is pronounced "peshcador"
x	generally like *sh* in shout; *baixa* is pronounced "bighsha"
z	at the end of a word or before *c*, *f*, *p*, *q*, *s* and *t* like *sh* in shout; *feliz* is pronounced "fehleesh"
	elsewhere like *s* in leisure; *luz da* is pronounced "loozh dah"

Vowels are pronounced as in English, with the following exceptions:

a	like the second and third *a* in bazaar; *nado* is pronounced "nahdo"
e	when stressed and before a weak consonant, like *e* in get; *perto* is pronounced "pehrto"
	when stressed and before a strong consonant, like *a* in cake; *cabelo* is pronounced "kahbaylo"
	when unstressed like *e* in father; *pesado* is pronounced "pehzahdo"
é	like *e* get; *café* is pronounced cafeh

ê	like *a* in cake; *pêra* is pronounced "payrah"
i	when stressed, like *i* in rice; *riso* is pronounced "reezo"
	when unstressed like *i* in give; *final* is pronounced "finnahl"
u	like *oo* in soon; *número* is pronounced "noomerro"
	silent in *qu* and *gu* before *e* and *i*; *aqui* is pronounced "ahkee"

PORTUGUESE-ENGLISH GLOSSARY

GREETINGS

Good Morning	*bom dia*
How are you?	*como está?*
I am fine	*muito bem*
Good afternoon, good evening	*boa tarde*
Good night	*boa noite*
Goodbye (long term)	*adeus*
Goodbye (short term)	*até logo*
yes	*sim*
no	*não*
please	*por favor*
Thank you	*obrigado* (said by a man)
Thank you	*obrigada* (said by a woman)
Your welcome	*não tem de quê*
Excuse-me	*desculpe*
I am a tourist	*Sou turista*
I am from Canada	*Sou de Canadá*
I am from Belgium	*Sou de Belgia*
I am from Switzerland	*Sou de Suíça*
I am from the United States	*Sou de Estados Unidos*
I am from Australia	*Sou de Austrália*
I am from Italy	*Sou de Itália*
I am from Germany	*Sou de Alemanha*
I am from New Zealand	*Sou de Nova Zelândia*
I am from Greay Britain	*Sou de Grã-Bretanha*
I am sorry, I do not speak Portuguese	*Desculpe, não falo portuguese*

Do you speak English	*fala Inglês?*
Slower, please	*mais devagar, por favor*
What is your name?	*como se chama você?*
My name is...	*o meu nome é...*
husband/wife	*esposo/esposa*
brother/sister	*irmão/irmã*
friend (m/f)	*amigo/a*
child	*criança*
father	*pai*
mother	*mãe*
single (m/f)	*celibatário(a)*
married (m/f)	*casado(a)*
divorced (m/f)	*divorciado(a)*
widow	*viúva*
widower	*viúvo*

DIRECTIONS

How do I get to ...?	*Como se ir a...?*
Is there a tourist office here?	*há um serviço de informão turistica por aqui?*
There is no...	*não há...*
Where is ...?	*onde está... ?*
straight ahead	*sempre em frente*
to the right	*à direita*
to the left	*à esquerda*
next to	*ao lado de*
near the	*perto de*
here	*aqui*
there	*além*
in	*em*
outside	*fora*
far from	*longe de*
between	*entre, no meio de*
in front of	*diante, frente*
behind	*atrás*

MONEY

exchange	*câmbio*
money	*dinheiro*
dollars	*dólares*
I don't have any money	*não tenho dinheiro*
credit card	*carta de crédito*

Portuguese-English Glossary 285

traveller's cheque	*cheque de viagem*
the bill, please	*a conta, por favor*
receipt	*recibo*

SHOPPING

open (m/f)	*aberto(a)*
closed (m/f)	*cerrado(a)*
How much is this?	*quanto custa isto?*
I would like...	*queri...*
I need...	*me precisa...*
store	*uma loja*
market	*mercado*
salesperson (m/f)	*vendedor(a)*
customer (m/f)	*cliente(a)*
buy	*comprar*
sell	*vender*
batteries	*pilha*
blouse	*uma blus*
camera	*máquina fotográfica*
cosmetics and perfume	*cosméticos e perfumes*
cotton	*algodão*
crafts	*artesanato*
film	*filme*
gift	*presente*
gold	*ouro*
guidebook	*guia*
jacket	*um casaco*
jewellery	*joía*
leather	*cabedal*
magazines	*revistas*
map	*mapa*
newspaper	*jornal*
pair of jeans	*um par de jeans*
pants	*um par de calças*
precious stones	*piedras preciosas*
shoes	*uns sapatos*
skirt	*uma saia*
shirt	*uma camisa*
silver	*prata*
records, cassettes	*discos, casetas*
watch	*relógio*
wool	*lã*

MISCELLANEOUS

new	*novo*
old	*velho*
expensive	*caro*
inexpensive	*barato*
beautiful	*belo*
ugly	*feio*
big, tall	*grande*
small	*pequeno*
short	*curto*
large	*largo*
narrow	*estreito*
dark (colour)	*escuro*
bright (colour)	*claro*
fat	*gordo*
skinny, thin	*delgado*
a little	*poco*
a lot	*muito*
something	*algo*
nothing	*nada*
good	*bom*
bad	*mau*
more	*mais*
less	*menos*
do not touch	*não tocar*
quickly, fast	*rápido*
slowly	*lento*
hot	*quente*
cold	*frio*
I am ill	*estou doente (doenta)*
I am hungry	*tenho fome*
I am thirsty	*tenho sede*
What is this?	*que e isto?*
when	*quando*
where	*onde...?*

WEATHER

rain	*chuva*
sun	*sol*
it is hot	*está calor*
it is cold	*está frio*

Portuguese-English Glossary

TIME

What time is it?	*que horas são?*
It is ...	*É... São*
minute	*minuto*
hour	*hora*
day	*día*
week	*semana*
month	*mês*
year	*anho*
yesterday	*ontem*
today	*hoje*
tomorrow	*amanha*
morning	*de manhã*
afternoon, evening	*tarde*
night	*noite*
now	*agora*
never	*jamais /nunca*
Sunday	*domingo*
Monday	*segunda-feira*
Tuesday	*terça-feira*
Wednesday	*quarta-feira*
Thursday	*quinta-feira*
Friday	*sexta-feira*
Saturday	*sábado*
January	*janeiro*
February	*fevereiro*
March	*março*
April	*abril*
May	*maio*
June	*junho*
July	*julho*
August	*agosto*
September	*septembro*
October	*outubro*
November	*novembro*
December	*dezembro*

COMMUNICATIONS

air mail	*correios por avião*
collect call	*chamada pagada pelo destinatário*
envelope	*sobrescrito*
fax machine	*telecopia*
long-distance	*larga distância*

288 Portuguese-English Glossary

phone book	*uma lista telefónica*
post and telegram office	*correios, telégrafos*
post office	*estação dos correios*
rate	*tarifa*
stamps	*selos*
telegram	*telegrama*

ACTIVITIES
beach	*praia*
museum or gallery	*museu*
mountain	*serra*
swimming	*banhar-se* or *nadar*
walking	*passear*

TRANSPORTATION
airport	*aeroporto*
arrival	*chegada*
avenue	*avenida*
boat	*barco*
bus	*autocarro*
bus stop	*a paragem dos autocarros*
bicycle	*bicicleta*
cancel	*anular*
car	*auto*
corner	*esquina*
departure	*partida*
luggage	*bagagem*
neighbourhood	*bairro*
one-way (ticket)	*ida*
plane	*avião*
railroad crossing	*passagem de nivel*
return (ticket)	*ida e volta*
safe, no danger	*seguro*
schedule	*horário*
station	*estação*
street	*rua*
train	*comboio*
north	*norte*
south	*sul*
east	*este*
west	*oeste*

The Serra de Sintra's Castelo dos Mouros defies invasion still. (T.B.)

The Aqueduto das Águas Livres once served various Lisbon neighbourhoods. (Camâra Munici Lisboa)

The Moorish-style royal summer residence: the Palácio Nacional de Sintra. (T.B.)

DRIVING

caution	*cuidado*
gas station	*posto de gasolina*
gasoline	*gasolina*
do not enter	*proibido a entrada*
highway	*auto-estrada*
no passing	*prohibido ultrapassar*
no parking	*estacionamento prohibido*
pedestrians	*peão*
slow down	*reduzir a velocidade*
speed limit	*velocidad máxima*
stop	*alto, pare*
traffic light	*semáforo*
to rent	*alugar*

ACCOMMODATIONS

air conditioning	*ar condicionado*
accommodation	*alojamento*
bed	*cama*
breakfast	*pequeno almoço*
double (room)	*casal*
elevator	*elevador*
fan	*ventilador*
floor	*andar*
hot water	*água quente*
high season	*época alta*
lobby	*rés-do-chão*
low season	*época baixa*
manager, boss	*gerente, dono*
mid season	*época média*
pool	*piscina*
room	*quarto*
single (room)	*individual (de solteiro)*
toilet	*banho*
with bathroom	*com banho*

290 Portuguese-English Glossary

NUMBERS

0	*zero*
1	*um ou uma*
2	*dos, duas*
3	*três*
4	*quatro*
5	*cinco*
6	*seis*
7	*sete*
8	*oito*
9	*nove*
10	*dez*
11	*onze*
12	*doze*
13	*treze*
14	*catorze*
15	*quinze*
16	*dezasseis*
17	*dezassete*
18	*dezoito*
19	*dezanove*
20	*vinte*
21	*vinte e um*
22	*vinte e dois*
23	*vinte e três*
30	*trinta*
31	*trinta e um*
32	*treinta e dois*
40	*quarenta*
50	*cinquenta*
60	*sessenta*
70	*setenta*
80	*oitenta*
90	*noventa*
100	*cem*
101	*cento e um*
200	*duzentos*
300	*trezentos*
500	*quinhentos*
1 000	*mil*
10 000	*dez mil*
1 000 000	*um milhão*

INDEX

ABC	268
Accommodations	73, 185
A Toca do Pai Lopes	208
Albergaria Senhora do Monte	188
Albergaria Solaris	208
Alcântara	201
Alfama	188
Amazónia Hotéis	190
Amoreiras	190
As Janelas Verdes	200
Bairro Alto	189
Baixa	185
Belém	201
Cais do Sodré	199
Campismo Amistad	208
Campismo do Guincho / Orbitur	203
Campismo Municipal de Lisboa	201
Casa da Pérgola	203
Casa de Hóspedes Adelaide	205
Cascais	201
Castelo	188
Chiado	189
Clube de Campismo de Lisboa	208
East Lisbon	188
Estalagem Solar dos Mouros	205
Estoril	201
Estrêla	199
Graça	188
Holiday Inn Lisboa	193
Hotel Albatroz	203
Hotel Americano	187
Hotel Avenida Palace	198
Hotel Borges	189
Hotel Central	205
Hotel da Lapa	200
Hotel da Torre	201
Hotel do Guincho	203
Hotel Dom Carlos	192
Hotel Dom Manuel I	192
Hotel Excelsior	191
Hotel Fénix	192
Hotel Flamingo	191

Accommodations, cont'd.
- Hotel Inglaterra 202
- Hotel Internacional 187
- Hotel Jorge V 196
- Hotel Metrópole 188
- Hotel Miraparque 192
- Hotel Palácio de Seteais 206
- Hotel Palácio Estoril 202
- Hotel Presidente 196
- Hotel Rex 192
- Hotel Sofitel 199
- Hotel Veneza 197
- Hotel York House 199
- Lapa 199
- Liberdade 194
- Lisboa Plaza 198
- Marquês de Pombal 190
- Orion 197
- North Lisbon 190
- Parque Florestal de Monsanto 201
- Pátio do Saloio 206
- Pensão Aljubarrota 186
- Pensão Globo 189
- Pensão Imperial 194
- Pensão Londres 189
- Pensão Ninho das Águias 188
- Pensão Nossa Senharo do Rosario 195
- Pensão Pension Galicia 185
- Pensão Residencial 13 da Sorte 195
- Pensão Residencial Monumental 195
- Pensão Residencial Santa Catarina 199
- Pensão Residencial Setubalense 201
- Pensão Smart 201
- Pensão-Residencial Gerês 187
- Pensão-Residêncial Sintra 205
- Pousada da Juventude 204
- Pousada de Juventude 190
- Pousada de Juventude Catalazete 202
- Pousada de Palmela 210
- Pousada de São Filipe 209
- Pousada Dona Maria I 204
- Príncipe Real 189
- Queluz 204
- Quinta da Capela 207

Accommodations, cont'd.
- Quinta do Patrício 209
- Rato 190
- Residência Roma 196
- Residencial Avenida Alameda 191
- Residencial Avenida Parque 191
- Residencial Bocage 208
- Residencial Casa de São Mamede 189
- Residencial Dom Sancho I 196
- Residencial Florescente 195
- Residencial Monte da Lua 205
- Residencial Palma 202
- Residencial Restauradores 195
- Residencial Setubalense 208
- Residencial Vila Nova 191
- Residencial-Albergaria Insulana 187
- Restauradores 194
- Ritz 194
- Rossio 185
- Saldanha 190
- Santa Catarina 199
- Santo Amaro 201
- Setúbal and Surroundings 208
- Sheraton and Towers Lisboa 194
- Sintra 204
- Suíço Atlántico 196
- Suite Hotel Dom Rodrigo 193
- The Méridien 193
- Tívoli Jardim 198
- Tívoli Lisboa 199
- Tívoli Sintra 206

Agenda Cultural 267

Airport
- Portela de Sacavém 45, 48

Alcântara 133
- Accommodations 201
- Entertainment 262
- Restaurants 238
- Shopping 278

Alfama 97, 100
- Accommodations 188
- Entertainment 251
- Restaurants 219
- Shopping 271

Index

Almornos
    Accommodations ... 208
Amoreiras ... 116
    Accommodations ... 190
    Entertainment ... 258
    Restaurants ... 228
    Shopping ... 275
Aqueduto das Águas Livres (Parque Florestal de
    Monsanto) ... 143
Architecture ... 29
Armillary Sphere ... 95
Arts and Culture ... 29
Avenida da Liberdade (Restauradores and Liberdade) ... 124
Azulejos ... 32
Bairro Alto ... 107, 112
    Accommodations ... 189
    Entertainment ... 252
    Restaurants ... 220
    Shopping ... 272
Baixa ... 88, 92
    Accommodations ... 185
    Restaurants ... 216
    Shopping ... 269
Banking ... 72
Bars and Nightclubs
    ΛΚΛΔΣ ΠΥΚΦΣ (AKADE NYKOS) ... 260
    7 Mares ... 264
    A Capela ... 253
    A Lontra ... 260
    A Tasca-Tequila Bar ... 252
    A Ultima Ceia ... 260
    Adega do Ribatejo ... 252
    Alfama ... 252
    Agua no Bico ... 257
    Alcântara ... 262
    Alcântara-Mar ... 262
    Até Qu'Enfim ... 260
    Bairro Alto ... 252
    Bar 106 ... 256
    Bar Fonte da Pipa ... 265
    Bar Gráfico's ... 252
    Bar Iguana ... 266
    Bar Pintál ... 256
    Bar-Restaurante Bachus ... 256

Bars and Nightclubs, cont'd.
- Belém 262
- Bistrobar Opera Prima 266
- Blues Café 263
- Bricabar 256
- Café Central 260
- Café do Ponte 264
- Café Santos 259
- Café Suave 253
- Café Targus 254
- Café Webs 254
- Cafediário 254
- Cais da Princesa 265
- Cais do Sodré 258
- Cascais 265
- Castelo 252
- Céu de Lisboa 256
- Chiado 252
- Clube de Fado 251
- Conventual 266
- Danse Pub Alô Alô 265
- Disco Fabrica 266
- Discoteca Benzina 262
- Discoteca Rock Line 262
- Doca de Santo 264
- Dock's Club 263
- Estoril 265
- Estrêla 259
- Finalmente 257
- Foxtrot 259
- Frágil 255
- Fremitus 253
- Havana 264
- Hot Clube de Portugal 258
- Indochina 263
- Kapital 261
- Keops 255
- KGB 254
- Kings and Queens 263
- Kremlin 261
- Lapa 259
- Le Plateau 261
- Liberdade 258
- Memorial 257

Bars and Nightclubs, cont'd.
- Metalúrgica 260
- Mezcal 253
- Ó Gilín's Irish Pub 258
- Páginas Tantas 254
- Património Bar 265
- Pavilhão Chines 255
- Pé Sujo 252
- Pedro Quinto Bar-Restaurant 254
- Pérola 259
- Pillon II 258
- Portas Largas 253
- Queluz 265
- Restauradores 258
- Restaurante O Forcado 252
- Santa Catarina 258
- Santo Amaro 262
- Santo Amaro Café 264
- Satyros 257
- Senhor Vinho 259
- Setúbal and Surroundings 266
- Sintra 265
- Solar do Vinho do Porto 255
- Tattoo 257
- Taverna d'El Red 251
- Tertulia do Tejo 264
- Trumps 257
- WIP 259

Basílica da Estrêla (Estrêla and the Lapa) 132
Beaches 177
- Costa da Caparica 180
- Praia da Carcavelos 178
- Praia da Figueirinha 180
- Praia da Galé 179
- Praia do Guincho 179
- Praia do Portinho da Arrábida 180
- Tamariz 178

Belém 133, 136
- Accommodations 201
- Entertainment 262
- Restaurants 238
- Shopping 278

Biblioteca Camões (Santa Catarina and Cais do Sodré) . 127
Boat 60

Index

Boat Tours 47
Bus 51
Bus Tours 46
Cabo da Roca 160
    Finding Your Way Around 61
Caesar Park Penha Longa 183
Café Nicolas (Rossio and the Baixa) 88
Cais das Colunas (Rossio and the Baixa) 94
Cais do Sodré 127
    Accommodations 199
    Entertainment 258
    Restaurants 234
    Shopping 277
Calçada do Lavra (Restauradores and Liberdade) 126
Caldeirada (Fish Stew) 212
Câmara Municipal (Cascais) 147
Câmara Municipal (Palmela) 164
Câmara Municipal (Sintra) 156
Campo de Santa Clara (Graça and East Lisbon) 102
Campo dos Mártires da Patria (Restauradores and
    Liberdade) 126
Cancellation Insurance 63
Capela de São João Baptista (Chiado and the Bairro Alto) 114
Capuchos 159
Car 49
Car Rentals 51
Carris 46
Carvalho, Mario de 38
Carvalho, Ottelo Saraiva de 23
Casa do Alentejo (Restauradores and Liberdade) 124
Casa dos Bicos (Rossio and the Baixa) 95
Casa Visconde de Sacavém (Estrêla and the Lapa) 133
Cascais 147
    Accommodations 202
    Finding Your Way Around 60
    Restaurants 243
    Shopping 279
    Tourist Information 46
Castelo 97
    Accommodations 188
    Entertainment 251
    Restaurants 219
    Shopping 271
Castelo de São Filipe (Setúbal) 162

Index

Castelo de São Jorge (Castelo and the Alfama) 97
Castelo dos Mouros (Queluz to Sintra) 159
Centro Comercial Amoreiras (Rato and Amoreiras) 118
Centro Cultural de Belém (Alcântara, Santo Amaro and
    Belém) 140, 268
Centro de Arte Moderna (Marquês de Pombal, Saldanha
    and North Lisbon) 122
Chafariz del Rei (Castelo and the Alfama) 101
Chiado 107
    Accommodations 189
    Entertainment 252
    Restaurants 220
    Shopping 272
Cinema 38
Cinema São Jorge 268
Cinema Tivoli 268
Cinemateca Portuguesa 267
Climate 67
Clube de Campo de Portugal-Aroeira 183
Coliseu dos Recreios (Restauradores and Liberdade) 126, 268
Companies and Organizations Areas (EXPO 98) 175
Consulates 42
Convento da Madre de Deus (Graça and East Lisbon) . . 105
Convento dos Capuchos (Capuchos) 159
Costa da Caparica 180
    Restaurants 247
Credit Cards 73
Cruz Alta 181
Culture 29
Customs 42
Da Gama, Vasco 171
Diário de Notícias 267
East Lisbon 101
    Accommodations 188
    Restaurants 220
    Shopping 272
Economy 24
Electricity 81
Eléctrico de Tourismo 47
Elevador da Bica (Santa Catarina and Cais do Sodré) 55, 127
Elevador da Glória (Restauradores and Liberdade) . . 55, 123
Elevador da Lavra 55
Elevador de Santa Justa (Rossio and the Baixa) 55, 92
Elevadores 54

Index

Embassies	42
Emergencies	83
Entertainment	77, 251
Alcântara, Santo Amaro and Belém	262
Castelo and the Alfama	251
Chiado and the Bairro Alto	252
Cultural Activities	266
Estoril to Cascais	265
Estrêla and Lapa	259
Queluz to Sintra	265
Rato and Amoreiras	258
Restauradores and Liberdade	258
Santa Catarina and Cais do Sodré	258
Setúbal and Surroundings	266
Entrance Formalities	41
Espace Oikos (Rossio and the Baixa)	97
Estação do Rossio (Rossio and the Baixa)	91
Estalagem	76
Estoril	145
Accommodations	201
Entertainment	265
Finding Your Way Around	60
Restaurants	242
Tourist Information	45
Estoril Palácio Golf Club	182
Estrêla	130
Accommodations	199
Entertainment	259
Restaurants	235
Shopping	278
Estufa Fria e Quente (Marquês de Pombal, Saldanha and North Lisbon)	119
Exchange Rates	72
Exploring	85
Alcântara, Santo Amaro and Belém	133
Castelo and the Alfama	97
Chiado and the Bairro Alto	107
Estoril to Cascais	145
Estrêla and the Lapa	130
EXPO 98	165
Graça and East Lisbon	101
Marquês de Pombal, Saldanha and North Lisbon	118
Parque Florestal de Monsanto	143
Queluz to Sintra	149

Index

Exploring, cont'd.
    Rato and Amoreiras 116
    Restauradores and Liberdade 123
    Rossio and the Baixa 88
    Santa Catarina and Cais do Sodré 127
    Setúbal and Surroundings 160
EXPO 98 165
    Exploring 170
    Finding Your Way Around 168
    Independent World Commission on the Oceans .. 166
    Maris Project 166
    Practical Information 169
Fado
    Castelo and the Alfama 251
    Chiado and the Bairro Alto 252
    Estrêla and Lapa 259
First-Aid Kit 65
Flora 15
Flower Revolution 24
Galeria Nacional do Chiado (Chiado and the Bairro Alto) . 112
Garcia de Orta Gardens (EXPO 98) 175
Gay Life 78
Geography 14
Glossary 283
Golf 182
Graça 101
    Accommodations 188
    Restaurants 220
    Shopping 272
Grande Auditório Gulbenkian 268
Guided Tours 46
    Boat Tours 47
    Bus Tours 46
    Eléctrico de Tourismo 47
Gulbenkian, Calouste Sarkis 122
Health 64
    First-Aid Kit 65
    Sun 64
Health Insurance 64
Henry the Navigator 19
Hiking 181
History 16
    Lisbon 16
    Portugal 18

Index 301

Hitchhiking 52
Holidays 79
ICEP 42
Igreja da Graça (Graça and East Lisbon) 104
Igreja da Madre de Deus (Graça and East Lisbon) 106
Igreja de la Conceição Velha (Rossio and the Baixa) 95
Igreja de São Julião (Setúbal) 162
Igreja do Carmo (Chiado and the Bairro Alto) 107
Igreja e Mosteiro de São Vicente da Fora (Graça and
    East Lisbon) 102
Igreja Jésus (Setúbal) 161
Igreja Nossa Senhora da Assunção (Cascais) 147
Igreja Santa Maria (Alcântara, Santo Amaro and Belém) . 139
Igreja Santa Maria do Castelo (Palmela) 164
Igreja São Roque (Chiado and the Bairro Alto) 114
Igreja-Panteão de Santa Engrácia (Graça and East Lisbon) 102
Independent World Commission on the Oceans 166
Instituto Nacional de Estatística (Marquês de Pombal,
    Saldanha and North Lisbon) 123
Insurance 63
    Cancellation Insurance 63
    Health Insurance 64
    Life Insurance 63
    Theft Insurance 63
International Pavilions (EXPO 98) 174
Internet 71
Jardim Botânico (Chiado and Bairro Alto) 115
Jardim da Estrêla (Estrêla and the Lapa) 132
Jardim do Torel (Restauradores and Liberdade) 126
JL Jornal de Letras, Artes e Ideias 267
Knowledge of the Seas Pavilion (EXPO 98) 173
Language 81
Lapa 130, 132
    Accommodations 199
    Entertainment 259
    Restaurants 235
    Shopping 278
Largo Barão de Quintela (Santa Catarina and Cais do
    Sodré) 127
Largo das Portas do Sol (Castelo and the Alfama) 98
Largo do Carmo (Chiado and the Bairro Alto) 107
Largo do Chiado (Chiado and the Bairro Alto) 111
Largo do Rato (Rato and Amoreiras) 116

Index

- Liberdade 123
  - Accommodations 194
  - Entertainment 258
  - Restaurants 231
  - Shopping 276
- Life Insurance 63
- Lisboa Cartão 58
- Literature 37
- MadreDeus 40
- Mãe d'Água Reservoir (Rato and Amoreiras) 118
- Mail 69
- Manueline style 29
- Maria Vitória 268
- Maris Project 166
- Marquês de Pombal 118
  - Accommodations 190
  - Restaurants 229
  - Shopping 276
- Metro 56
- Miradouro de Monsanto (Parque Florestal de Monsanto) 145, 178
- Miradouro de Santa Catarina (Santa Catarina and Cais do Sodré) 128
- Miradouro de Santa Luzia (Castelo and the Alfama) 98
- Miradouro de São Pedro de Alcântara (Chiado and the Bairro Alto) 115
- Money 72
- Monserrate 157
  - Accommodations 207
- Mosteiro dos Jerónimos (Alcântara, Santo Amaro and Belém) 138
- Museu António (Rossio and the Baixa) 97
- Museu Arpad Szenes-Vieira da Silva (Rato and Amoreiras) 116
- Museu Arqueológico do Carmo (Chiado and the Bairro Alto) 107
- Museu Calouste Gulbenkian (Marquês de Pombal, Saldanha and North Lisbon) 120
- Museu da Água Manuel da Maia (Graça and East Lisbon) 104
- Museu da Cidade (Marquês de Pombal, Saldanha and North Lisbon) 122
- Museu da Marioneta (Graça and East Lisbon) 104
- Museu da Sociedade de Geografia de Lisboa (Restauradores and Liberdade) 126
- Museu de Arte Moderna (Sintra) 156

Index 303

Museu de Arte Popular (Alcântara, Santo Amaro and
    Belém) 141
Museu de Arte Sacra de São Roque (Chiado and the
    Bairro Alto) 114
Museu de Ciência (Chiado and the Bairro Alto) 116
Museu de Marinha (Alcântara, Santo Amaro and Belém) 140
Museu de Setúbal (Setúbal) 162
Museu do Palácio Nacional da Ajuda (Alcântara, Santo
    Amaro and Belém) 136
Museu Escola de Artes Decorativas (Castelo and the
    Alfama) 98
Museu Militar (Graça and East Lisbon) 101
Museu Nacional de Arqueologia (Alcântara, Santo
    Amaro and Belém) 139
Museu Nacional de Arte Antiga (Estrêla and the Lapa) .. 133
Museu Nacional de Etnologia (Alcântara, Santo Amaro
    and Belém) 142
Museu Nacional do Azulejo (Graça and East Lisbon) ... 105
Museu Nacional do Traje (Marquês de Pombal, Saldanha
    and North Lisbon) 123
Museu Nacional dos Coches (Alcântara, Santo Amaro
    and Belém) 136
Museu Núcleo Arqueológico (Rossio and the Baixa) 93
Museu Oceanográfico (Praia do Portinho da Arrábida) .. 164
Music 39
Nautical Exhibition (EXPO 98) 175
Nightclubs, see "Bars and Nightclubs"
North International Area (EXPO 98) 174
North Lisbon 118
    Accommodations 190
    Restaurants 229
    Shopping 276
Nossa Senhora de l'Encarnação (Chiado and the Bairro
    Alto) 111
Nossa Senhora do Loreto (Chiado and the Bairro Alto) .. 111
Oceanarium (EXPO 98) 172
Oeiras
    Accommodations 202
Oliveira, Manoel de 39
Outdoors 177
    Golf 182
    Hiking 181
    Parks and Beaches 177

Index

Packing 69
Padrão dos Descobrimentos (Alcântara, Santo Amaro
    and Belém) 141
Paginas de Lisboa 267
Painting 38
Palacete Ribeiro da Cunha (Chiado and the Bairro Alto) . 115
Palácio da Assembleia Nacional (Estrêla and the Lapa) . . 130
Palácio da Pena (Queluz to Sintra) 158
Palácio das Necessidades (Alcântara, Santo Amaro and
    Belém) 134
Palácio de Monserrate (Monserrate) 157
Palácio de Seteais (Seteais) 157
Palácio dos Valenças (Estrêla and the Lapa) 132
Palácio Foz (Restauradores and Liberdade) 123
Palácio Nacional (Sintra) 153
Palácio Nacional de Queluz (Queluz) 149
Palácio Valenças (Sintra) 156
Palácio-Museu Condes Castro Guimarães (Cascais) 147
Palmela 163
    Accommodations 210
    Finding Your Way Around 61
    Restaurants 249
Parking 53
Parks 177
    Parque da Pena 179
    Parque de Monserrate 179
    Parque Florestal de Monsanto 143
    Praia de Galapos 180
    Serra da Arrábida 182
Parque da Pena 179
Parque de Monserrate 179
Parque Eduardo VII (Marquês de Pombal, Saldanha and
    North Lisbon) 118
Parque Florestal de Monsanto 143
    Accommodations 201
    Restaurants 241
Parque Mayer 268
Parque Urbano dos Moinhos (Alcântara, Santo Amaro
    and Belém) 143
Passe Turístico 56
Pavilhão dos Desportos (Marquês de Pombal, Saldanha
    and North Lisbon) 119
Pavilion of the Future (EXPO 98) 174
Península de Tróia 163

Pensão 76
Pessõa, Fernando 37
Plane 47
Police 83
Politics 26
Ponte 25 de Abril (Alcântara, Santo Amaro and Belém) . 134
Population 27
Portão dos Lagos 181
Portela de Sacavém Airport 45, 48
Porto Covo (Estrêla and the Lapa) 132
Portrait 13
Portuguese National Pavilion (EXPO 98) 172
Posto de Turismo da Região de Setúbal (Setúbal) 162
Pousadas 74
Praça da Figueira (Rossio and the Baixa) 92
Praça das Amoreiras (Rato and Amoreiras) 116
Praça das Flores (Estrêla and the Lapa) 132
Praça de Bocage (Setúbal) 162
Praça de Touros (Marquês de Pombal, Saldanha and
    North Lisbon) 122
Praça do Comércio (Rossio and the Baixa) 93
Praça do Minicipio (Rossio and the Baixa) 94
Praça do Príncipa Real (Chiado and the Bairro Alto) . . . 115
Praça dos Restauradores (Restauradores and Liberdade) 123
Praça João da Câmara (Rossio and the Baixa) 91
Praça Largo Contador-Mor (Castelo and the Alfama) 98
Praça Luís de Camões (Chiado and the Bairro Alto) . . . 111
Praça Marquês de Pombal (Marquês de Pombal,
    Saldanha and North Lisbon) 119
Practical Information 41
Praia da Carcavelos 178
Praia da Figueirinha 180
Praia da Galé 179
Praia de Galapos 180
Praia do Guincho 179
    Accommodations 203
    Restaurants 244
Praia do Portinho da Arrábida 164, 180
Praia Grande
    Accommodations 208
Pronunciation 281
Public Transportation 53
Público 267

Index

Queluz 149
    Accommodations 204
    Entertainment 265
    Finding Your Way Around 61
    Restaurants 244
    Shopping 279
Rato 116
    Accommodations 190
    Entertainment 258
    Restaurants 228
    Shopping 275
Residencial 76
Restauradores 123
    Accommodations 194
    Entertainment 258
    Restaurants 231
    Shopping 276
Restaurants 76, 211
    A Brasileira 227
    A Commenda 239
    Abracadabra 216
    Adega das Caves 246
    Alfama 219
    Alcântara 238
    Alcântara Café 240
    Ali-a-Papa 222
    Amoreiras 228
    Antiga Confeitaria de Belém 240
    Atira-te ao Rio 247
    Bairro Alto 220
    Baixa 216
    Bar Cerca Moura 219
    Belém 238
    Bibikas 231
    Bistrobar Opera Prima 245
    Brasserie de L'Entrecôte 222
    Café Comm C 249
    Café de Paris 246
    Café Estadio Silva Seixas 228
    Café Nicola 218
    Café no Chiado 220
    Café O Paço do Principe 228
    Café Papasom 220
    Café Snack-Bar Pastelaria Zante 233

Restaurants, cont'd.
- Cafetaria do Museu da Marinha 241
- Cais da Ribeira 234
- Cais do Sodré 234
- California Dream 234
- Campesina 216
- Cantinha da Paz 234
- Casa Chimeza 218
- Casa da Comida 229
- Casa do Alentejo 231
- Casa do Leão 219
- Casa México 236
- Casa Nostra 226
- Cascais 242
- Castelo 219
- Cervejaria A Berlenga 217
- Cervejaria da Trindade 222
- Cervejaria O 10 248
- Charcuteria Francesa 221
- Chez Degroote 221
- Chiado 220
- Ciber-Chiado 228
- Confeitaria Marquês Pombal 233
- Confeitaria Nacional 218
- Consenso 224
- Costa do Castelo 219
- Cozinha Velha 245
- Doca do Santo 239
- Dom Sopas 217
- East Lisbon 220
- El Ultimo Tango 224
- Esplanada da Avenida-Café Lisboa 231
- Estoril 242
- Estrada Velha Bar 246
- Estrêla 235
- Four Season Grill 242
- Foxtrot 236
- Frej Contente 236
- Furusato 242
- Galeto 230
- Gambrinus 233
- Graça 220
- Grill 20 232
- Gringo's Café 235

Restaurants, cont'd.
- Guillaume Tell 226
- Hell's Kitchen 222
- Hotel do Guincho 244
- Hotel Palácio de Seteais 247
- Huá Li Tou 222
- Ideal de São Bento 234
- Já Sei! 239
- Lapa 235
- Liberdade 231
- Lucullus Restaurante 243
- Majong 222
- Marquês de Pombal 229
- Martinho da Arcada 218
- Massima Culpa 225
- Mercado Original 229
- Music Bar 243
- Nicola Gourmet 218
- North Lisbon 229
- O Antigo Ferrador 220
- O Capuchinho 221
- O Cardador 248
- O Farnel 216
- O Golfinho 243
- O Leão da Estrêla 235
- O Miradouro 235
- O Natraj 228
- O Pelourinho 246
- O Primeiro da Conceição Velha 216
- O Sol 221
- Os Doze 243
- Os Tibetanos 231
- Panorâmico de Monsanto 241
- Pão Pão Queijo Queijo 239
- Pap'Açorda 225
- Parque Florestal de Monsanto 241
- Pastelaria Apolo XI 235
- Pastelaria Flor da Sé 219
- Pastelaria São Roque 228
- Pastelaria Snack-Bar Veneza 233
- Pastelaria Versailles 230
- Pasteleria Parrisol 244
- Pátio do Saloio 247
- Pato Baton 225

Index

Restaurants, cont'd.
- Pedro das Arábias 223
- Picanha 235
- Pitada Daqui Pitada Dali 245
- Pizzeria Mama Rosa 223
- Poeta na Bicha 223
- Ponto Final 248
- Pousada de Palmela 249
- Pousada de São Filipe 248
- Pub Eduardo VII 230
- Queluz 244
- Rage Bar Pub 242
- Rato 228
- Restauradores 231
- Restaurante Adega do Teixeira 223
- Restaurante Arameiro 231
- Restaurante Assóporco 236
- Restaurante Bachus 226
- Restaurante Bizzaro 225
- Restaurante Cervejaria Lua Dourada 217
- Restaurante Conventual 237
- Restaurante de Rua em Rua 223
- Restaurante do Museu 220
- Restaurante Embaixada 238
- Restaurante Flor des Estrêla 236
- Restaurante Flor do Duque 221
- Restaurante Janela do Bairro 224
- Restaurante Monte Verde 241
- Restaurante Novo Bonsai 226
- Restaurante O Tacão Pequeno 225
- Restaurante Palácio del Rei 244
- Restaurante Porta Branca 226
- Restaurante Regional de Sintra 246
- Restaurante Serra da Estrêla 229
- Restaurante Solmar 232
- Restaurante Tagide 227
- Restaurante Tavares Rico 227
- Restaurante Tropical Brasil 243
- Restaurante Xi Hu 239
- Restaurante York House 238
- Restaurante Zutzu 238
- Retiro da Mina 244
- Rossio 216
- Saldanha 229

Restaurants, cont'd.
- Sancho ... 232
- Santa Catarina ... 234
- Santo Amaro ... 238
- Securas ... 224
- Setúbal and Surroundings ... 247
- Siesta Brava ... 237
- Sintra ... 244
- Solar dos Bicos ... 218
- Solar dos Presuntos ... 232
- Tacho Real ... 247
- Tapas-Bar El Gordo ... 224
- Tasca a Latina ... 246
- Tavares Self Service ... 227
- Umpuntocinco ... 238
- Xêlê Bananas ... 237
- Xico's Bar Restaurante ... 237
- Yin-Yan ... 217

Rio Grande ... 40
Rodrigues, Amália ... 39
Rossio ... 88
- Accommodations ... 185
- Restaurants ... 216
- Shopping ... 269

Rua das Portas de Santo Antão (Restauradores and Liberdade) ... 124
Rua São Bento (Estrêla and the Lapa) ... 130
Rua Viera-Portuense (Alcântara, Santo Amaro and Belém) ... 138
Safety ... 65
Salazar, Antonio de Oliveira ... 23
Saldanha ... 118
- Accommodations ... 190
- Restaurants ... 229
- Shopping ... 276

Santa Catarina ... 127
- Accommodations ... 199
- Entertainment ... 258
- Restaurants ... 234
- Shopping ... 277

Santa Cruz (Castelo and the Alfama) ... 97
Santo Amaro ... 133
- Accommodations ... 201
- Entertainment ... 262
- Restaurants ... 238

Santo Amaro, cont'd.
    Shopping 278
Sé Patriarcal (Rossio and the Baixa) 96
Sebastião I 20
Security 65
Serra da Arrábida 182
Sete 267
Seteais 157
    Accommodations 206
    Restaurants 247
Sétima Colina 128
Setúbal 160
    Accommodations 208
    Entertainment 266
    Finding Your Way Around 61
    Restaurants 248
    Tourist Information 46
Shopping 79, 269
Silva, Vieira da 38
Sintra 151
    Accommodations 204
    Entertainment 265
    Finding Your Way Around 61
    Restaurants 245
    Shopping 279
    Tourist Information 46
South International Area (EXPO 98) 174
Sports Clubs 80
Tabacaria Mónaco (Rossio and the Baixa) 88
Talha Dourada 31
Tamariz 178
Tãriq Ibn Ziyad 18
Taxi 58
Teatro Eden (Restauradores and Liberdade) 124
Teatro Nacional de São Carlos (Chiado and the Bairro
    Alto) 111, 268
Teatro Nacional Dona Maria II (Rossio and the Baixa) 90, 268
Telecommunications 70
Telephones 70
Tetvocal 40
Theft in Cars 66
Theft Insurance 63
Time Zone 81
Tipping 77

Torga, Miguel 38
Torre de Belém (Alcântara, Santo Amaro and Belém) ... 141
Torre de São Pedro (Castelo and the Alfama) 101
Tourist Information 45
Tourist Office 42
Train 52
Trams 54
Transtejo 47
Travellers' Cheques 73
Travessa da Laranjeira (Santa Catarina and Cais do Sodré)128
Travessa da Portuguesa (Santa Catarina and Cais do
   Sodré) 128
Treaty of Methuen 22
Treaty of Tordesillas 22
Treaty of Westminster 22
Urban Planning 33
Utopia Pavilion (EXPO 98) 174
Várzea de Sintra
   Accommodations 206
   Restaurants 247
Vasco de Gama 20
Water Gardens (EXPO 98) 175
Weights and Measures 82
Women Travellers 81

Travel Notes

Travel Notes

Other Ulysses Guides

Cycling in France
Cycling the picturesque back roads of France — everyone has dreamed of doing it, and now Ulysses makes it possible. Burgundy, the Loire Valley, the Vaucluse and other splendid regions are revealed thanks to numerous suggested tours. All of this is complemented by information on preparing your journey and the services available along the way.
Carole Saint-Laurent
212 pages, 20 maps
$22.95 CAN $16.95 US   £9.99
2-89464-008-0

Portugal, 2nd edition
A new edition of the most practical guide covering every region in Portugal. *Pousadas*, *quintas*, medieval chateaux, museums, festivals, Algarve beaches... it's all in there! The riches of Porto are also revealed as is Lisbon, host-city of the 1998 World Exposition.
Marc Rigole, Claude-Victor Langlois
384 pages, 32 maps
8 pages of colour photos
$24.95 CAN $17.95 US   £12.99
2-89464-080-3

Provence-Côte d'Azur, 2nd edition
Once again Ulysses offers both these magnificent French regions in one book. Monaco, Nice, Marseille and Avignon are just some of the legendary sites covered. Spend some time by the seaside, in the casinos or explore hillside villages on the Vaucluse plateau and in the Luberon.
Hans Jörg Mettler, Benoit Éthier, Howard Rombough
368 pages, 38 maps
8 pages of colour photos
$29.95 CAN $21.95 US   £14.99
2-89464-112-5

Affordable B&B in Québec 98-99
Four types of accommodations are described to help discover the intimate side of Québec: rooms in private homes with breakfast included, small country inns, farm-stays, and country houses which can be rented for longer stays. All the information for making reservations is included.
300 pages, 19 maps
Fédération des Agricotours
14 pages of colour photos
$12.95 CAN $9.95 US   £6.50
2-89464-096-X

Atlantic Canada, 2nd edition
This second edition sees the province of Newfoundland and Labrador added to the those of New Brunswick, Nova Scotia and Prince Edward Island. Picturesque fishing villages, the famous Cabot Trail, national parks, beaches and, of course, the brand new Confederation Bridge linking Prince Edward Island to the mainland, it's all in there!
Benoit Prieur
304 pages, 25 maps
8 pages of colour photos
$24.95 CAN $17.95 US   £12.99
2-89464-113-3

Calgary
Set between the Rocky Mountains and vast ranchlands and prairies, Calgary is one of the fastest growing cities in North America. This Ulysses Guide reveals the best of this dynamic Western city: museums, parks, gardens, Olympic installations and of course the famous Stampede, the "greatest show on earth"!
Jennifer McMorran
192 pages, 12 maps
$17.95 CAN $12.95 US   £8.99
2-89464-168-0

Canada
Finally a Ulysses Guide on this vast country. Every province and territory, right up to the Arctic Circle and beyond, has been covered with a fine-tooth comb in order to produce the most complete travel guide. The major cities like Vancouver, Toronto and Montreal, the smallest hamlets, exhilarating outdoor adventures from sea to sea!
Collective
544 pages, 100 maps
8 pages of colour photos
$29.95 CAN $21.95 US   £14.99
2-89464-159-12

Hiking in Québec, 2nd edition
The only hiking guide devoted exclusively to all regions of Québec! This guide presents descriptions of close to 100 hikes in every corner of Québec, classified according to their level of difficulty. Tables with distances and altitude changes for each hike are also included.
Yves Séguin
270 pages, 15 maps
$22.95 CAN $16.95 US   £11.50
2-89464-013-7

Montréal 98-99
Revised every year, this guide reveals more than 300 sights in this Québec metropolis along 20 walking, bicycling and driving tours. There are detailed maps for each tour, plans of the galleries of the Museum of Fine Arts and maps of the underground city. Hundreds of practical addresses for every budget.
François Rémillard et al.
416 pages, 26 maps
8 pages of colour photos
$19.95 CAN $14.95 US   £9.99
2-89464-111-7

Ontario, 2nd edition
This guide covers Canada's richest and most populous province thoroughly, with sections on Niagara Falls, the Thousand Islands, Ottawa, Toronto, and even Northern Ontario.
Pascale Couture
336 pages, 26 maps
$24.95 CAN $14.95 US   £11.50
2-89464-011-0

Ontario & Québec with Via
Travel the rails between Canada's two most populous provinces. Tour exciting and fascinating cities like Montréal, Québec City, Toronto and Ottawa and take a break in peaceful hamlets throughout the province. This guide is the perfect complement to your next train journey.
Collective
128 pages, 10 maps
$9.95 CAN $7.95 US   £5.99
2-89464-158-3

Ottawa
Here is the first complete practical and cultural guide on the Canadian capital. Visitors will be lead through the city's fine museums and across Parliament Hill, shown to the best tables and given the inside track on the festivals that liven the streets in the summer and the Rideau Canal in the winter.
Pascale Couture
192 pages, 12 maps
$17.95 CAN $12.95 US   £8.99
2-89464-170-2

Toronto
Discover another side of Canada's biggest metropolis, from the hustle of downtown Yonge Street to the picturesque shores of Lake Ontario, to the shops and theatres. Walking tours through its multicultural neighbourhoods and city streets; restaurants and bars for all tastes and budgets.
Jennifer McMorran, Alain Rondeau
260 pages, 16 maps
$18.95 CAN $13.95 US   £9.99
2-89464-015-3

Québec, 2nd edition
The long-awaited 2nd edition of the Bible on *la belle province* is here! Still more sights and thousands of practical addresses for every region. Travellers will also find an augmented outdoor activities section, more maps, brilliant colour photos and illustrations.
François Rémillard et al.
608 pages, 85 maps
32 pages of colour photos
$29.95 CAN $21.95 US   £14.99
2-921444-78-X

Western Canada, 2nd edition
A new edition for the only travel guide to cover both Alberta and British Columbia. The mighty Rocky Mountains, superb skiing resorts, national and provincial parks: they're all in here! And so is the western metropolis of Vancouver, the burgeoning city of Calgary and Victoria, for a spot of tea!
Collective
464 pages, 51 maps
8 pages of colour photos
$29.95 CAN $21.95 US   £14.99
2-89464-086-2

Vancouver, 2nd edition
Completely updated, revised and augmented, this new edition reveals the best of this young and vibrant metropolis. Coverage of its multi-ethnic neighbourhoods, magnificent parks and great restaurants is joined by a rich cultural perspective. Practical addresses for every budget and taste.
Collective
200 pages, 15 maps
$17.95 CAN $12.95 US   £8.99
2-89464-120-6

TRAVEL BETTER... TRAVEL THE NET

Visit our web site
to travel better...
to discover, to explore
and to enjoy more.

http://www.ulysse.ca

Travel better... enjoy more

CATALOGUE

TALK TO US

HISTORY

ORDER

DISTRIBUTORS

INTERNET TRAVEL

■ ULYSSES TRAVEL GUIDES

- ☐ Affordable B&Bs in Québec $12.95 CAN / $9.95 US
- ☐ Atlantic Canada ..... $24.95 CAN / $17.95 US
- ☐ Beaches of Maine ..... $12.95 CAN / $9.95 US
- ☐ Bahamas ..... $24.95 CAN / $17.95 US
- ☐ Calgary ..... $17.95 CAN / $12.95 US
- ☐ Canada ..... $29.95 CAN / $21.95 US
- ☐ Chicago ..... $19.95 CAN / $14.95 US
- ☐ Chile ..... $27.95 CAN / $17.95 US
- ☐ Costa Rica ..... $27.95 CAN / $19.95 US
- ☐ Cuba ..... $24.95 CAN / $17.95 US
- ☐ Dominican Republic ..... $24.95 CAN / $17.95 US
- ☐ Ecuador Galapagos Islands $24.95 CAN / $17.95 US
- ☐ El Salvador ..... $22.95 CAN / $14.95 US
- ☐ Guadeloupe ..... $24.95 CAN / $17.95 US
- ☐ Guatemala ..... $24.95 CAN / $17.95 US
- ☐ Honduras ..... $24.95 CAN / $17.95 US
- ☐ Jamaica ..... $24.95 CAN / $17.95 US
- ☐ Lisbon ..... $18.95 CAN / $13.95 US
- ☐ Louisiana ..... $29.95 CAN / $21.95 US
- ☐ Martinique ..... $24.95 CAN / $17.95 US
- ☐ Montréal ..... $19.95 CAN / $14.95 US
- ☐ New Orleans ..... $17.95 CAN / $12.95 US
- ☐ New York City ..... $19.95 CAN / $14.95 US
- ☐ Nicaragua ..... $24.95 CAN / $16.95 US
- ☐ Ontario ..... $24.95 CAN / $14.95 US
- ☐ Ottawa ..... $17.95 CAN / $12.95 US
- ☐ Panamá ..... $24.95 CAN / $16.95 US
- ☐ Portugal ..... $24.95 CAN / $16.95 US
- ☐ Provence - Côte d'Azur ..... $29.95 CAN / $21.95 US
- ☐ Québec ..... $29.95 CAN / $21.95 US
- ☐ Québec and Ontario with Via ..... $9.95 CAN / $7.95 US
- ☐ Toronto ..... $18.95 CAN / $13.95 US
- ☐ Vancouver ..... $17.95 CAN / $12.95 US
- ☐ Washington D.C. ..... $18.95 CAN / $13.95 US
- ☐ Western Canada ..... $29.95 CAN / $21.95 US

■ ULYSSES GREEN ESCAPES

- ☐ Cycling in France ..... $22.95 CAN / $16.95 US
- ☐ Hiking in the Northeastern United States ..... $19.95 CAN / $13.95 US
- ☐ Hiking in Québec ..... $19.95 CAN / $13.95 US

■ ULYSSES DUE SOUTH

- ☐ Acapulco ..... $14.95 CAN / $9.95 US
- ☐ Belize ..... $16.95 CAN / $12.95 US
- ☐ Cartagena (Colombia) ..... $12.95 CAN / $9.95 US
- ☐ Cancun Cozumel ..... $17.95 CAN / $12.95 US
- ☐ Puerto Vallarta ..... $14.95 CAN / $9.95 US
- ☐ St. Martin and St. Barts ..... $16.95 CAN / $12.95 US

■ ULYSSES TRAVEL JOURNAL

- ☐ Ulysses Travel Journal (Blue, Red, Green, Yellow, Sextant) ..... $9.95 CAN / $7.95 US

QUANTITY	TITLES	PRICE	TOTAL

NAME: _____

ADDRESS: _____

Payment: ☐ Money Order ☐ Visa ☐ MasterCard

Card Number: _____ Exp.: _____

Signature: _____

Sub-total	
Postage & Handling	$8.00*
Sub-total	
G.S.T. in Canada 7%	
TOTAL	

ULYSSES TRAVEL PUBLICATIONS
4176 St-Denis, Montréal, QC, H2W 2M5
(514) 843-9447 fax (514) 843-9448
www.ulysse.ca
*$15 for overseas orders

U.S. ORDERS: **GLOBE PEQUOT PRESS**
P.O. Box 833, 6 Business Park Road,
Old Saybrook, CT 06475-0833
1-800-243-0495 fax 1-800-820-2329
www.globe-pequot.com